# The Grand Duke's Portraitist
Cosimo III de' Medici and his "Chamber of Paintings" by Giusto Suttermans

# THE GRAND DUKE'S PORTRAITIST
## COSIMO III DE' MEDICI
### AND HIS "CHAMBER OF PAINTINGS"
### BY GIUSTO SUTTERMANS

Florence, Palazzo Pitti, Galleria Palatina, Sala Bianca
16 June – 22 October 2006

PROMOTERS
Ministero per i Beni e le Attività Culturali
Soprintendenza Speciale per il Polo Museale Fiorentino
Galleria Palatina
Firenze Musei
*with the contribution of*
Monte dei Paschi di Siena

EXHIBITION PROJECT
Lisa Goldenberg Stoppato

EXHIBITION CURATOR
Serena Padovani
*with the collaboration of*
Rosanna Morozzi

ADMINISTRATION DIRECTOR
Giovanni Lenza

EXHIBITION DESIGN AND SUPERVISION
Mauro Linari
*with*
Giuseppe Melani

SET-UP
Opera Laboratori Fiorentini

PRESS OFFICE
Camilla Speranza

PUBLIC RELATIONS OFFICE
Firenze Musei

PHOTO CREDITS
Sergio Garbari, Gabinetto Fotografico Polo Museale Fiorentino: cat. nos. 2, 5–10, 12, 16–18, 20, 21, 23
Paolo Giusti: cat. no. 22
Luca Lupi: cat. no. 14

RESTORATION (PAINTINGS)
Manola Bernini: cat. nos. 20–22
Mario Celesia, Laboratorio di Restauro Polo Museale Fiorentino: cat. no. 8
Loredana Gallo: cat. nos. 5–7, 10, 12, 14, 18, 23, 24

RESTORATION (FRAMES)
Giuseppe Montagna, Laboratorio di Restauro Polo Museale Fiorentino: cat. no. 8

This exhibition was made possible thanks to many colleagues: Marco Chiarini, Anna Evangelista, Marco Fiorilli, Elena Fumagalli, Edward Goldberg e i borsisti del Medici Archive Project, Karla Langedijk, Giovanni Lenza, Douglas Macrae Brown, Silvia Mascalchi, Silvia Meloni Trkulja, Antonio Natali, Xosé Antonio Neira Cruz, Danilo Pesci, Angela Rossi, Maria Sframeli, Francesca Simoncini, Demetrio Sorace, Eleonora Sorri, Paola Squellati Brizio, Marilena Tamassia, Patrizia Tarchi, Rita Toma, Patrizia Urbani.

Special thanks to the Director, Rosalia Manno Tolu, and the entire staff at the State Archive of Florence for their invaluable assistance.

Heartfelt thanks also to the staff at the Galleria Palatina who, as always, has given an essential contribution to this initiative, especially Donatella Boschi, Rita Cappelli, Maurizio Catolfi, Sonia Cecconi, Daniela Cresti, Tina Gelsomino.

ISBN 88-8347-328-0
© 2006 Ministero per i Beni e le Attività Culturali
Soprintendenza Speciale per il Polo Museale Fiorentino

A publication by
s i l l a b e  s.r.l.
Livorno
http://www.sillabe.it
e-mail: info@sillabe.it

*managing editor:* Maddalena Paola Winspeare
*graphic design:* Susanna Coseschi
*editing:* Giulia Bastianelli
*translation of the forewords:* Emily Ligniti

ABBREVIATIONS

| | |
|---|---|
| ASF = Archivio di Stato di Firenze (Florence, State Archive) | inv. = inventory |
| | mm = millimeters |
| | ms. = manuscript |
| BNCF = Biblioteca Nazionale di Firenze (Florence, National Library) | n.d.= no date |
| | no. = number (plural nos.) |
| | p. = page (plural pp.) |
| cm = centimeters | pl. = plate |
| d = right | r = recto |
| fasc. = fascicle | s = left |
| fig. = figure | v = verso |
| fol. = folio (plural fols.) | vol. = volume (plural vols.) |

Ministero per i Beni e le Attività Culturali
Soprintendenza Speciale per il Polo Museale Fiorentino

Galleria Palatina

# The Grand Duke's Portraitist
## Cosimo III de' Medici and his "Chamber of Paintings" by Giusto Suttermans

Lisa Goldenberg Stoppato

sillabe

*Giusto Suttermans was "rediscovered" in 1983, with a small exhibition Marco Chiarini and a group of collaborators dedicated to him in the "Sala delle Nicchie" of the Galleria Palatina. The event was held to celebrate the purchase, on the part of the Florentine galleries, of one of the three sketches for the enormous painting with* The Pledge of Allegiance of the Florentine Senate to Ferdinando II de'Medici, *executed by Suttermans and placed, in 1626, in the "Sala delle Nicchie" in the cambered space above the main door.*

*The lunette was not displayed, since it was in a poor state of preservation due to the many decades it had passed in the storage rooms of the Florentine galleries. Along with the sketch purchased from a private collection, forty paintings by Suttermans, enriched with a nucleus of his drawings, were also showcased. An "appendix", in the catalogue, rounded off this Flemish painter's Florentine œuvre, thereby giving a rather precise idea of the impressive consistency of his work for the Medici court.*

*Since then, Suttermans' personality was outlined in a thorough profile by Lisa Goldenberg Stoppato in the catalogue of the noteworthy 1986 exhibition on seventeenth-century Florentine art.* The Pledge of Allegiance, *which arrived at the Uffizi in 1733 and was placed by Lanzi, in 1782, in the "Sala della Niobe", returned here in 2002 after a rather difficult restoration.*

*Before arriving at the Uffizi, at the end of the seventeenth century that painting, exceptional for its importance and size, was moved by Cosimo III to the second floor of his palace, in the room that had once been the Hearing Hall of Cardinal Leopoldo, who had died a few years earlier. It was precisely here that Cosimo wished to pay special tribute to his court painter, dedicating an exhibition, with forty works, to him.*

*This initiative, so ahead of its time and so modern, has today been re-proposed in the "Sala Bianca" of Palazzo Pitti, which greatly resembles the seventeenth-century, second-floor hall that no longer exists, thanks to one of its former collaborators, Lisa Goldenberg Stoppato. She began studying Suttermans for her thesis and who contributed on this specific topic in the catalogue for the 2004 exhibition on Cosimo III's trip to Santiago de Compostela.*

*And so, in line with the tradition of the exhibitions at Pitti aimed at enhancing and spreading awareness and understanding of the palace's artists and treasures, the circle that was opened in 1983 regarding the figure of Giusto Suttermans comes to a close by re-proposing the exhibition of his paintings Grand Duke Cosimo III once dedicated to him.*

Serena Padovani
*Director of the Galleria Palatina*

*Lisa Goldenberg Stoppato is a scholar specialized in the history and iconography of the Medici family. Giusto Suttermans was, during the seventeenth century, the official portraitist of the Grand Dukes. He was held in such esteem that Grand Duke Cosimo III, in 1678, had an exhibition, consisting in about forty works, dedicated to him; this event was held, at the time, in a room on the second floor of Palazzo Pitti. Lisa Goldenberg Stoppato and the Director of the Galleria Palatina, Serena Padovani, re-propose, today, the exhibition that took place back then. But not in the location where it was originally held (as it no longer exists due to the various structural modifications carried out over the years), but in the Sala Bianca, the only space that can offer, at the same time, the ease of convenient public use and a regal, courtly setting. I shall not discuss here the style of a painter who knew how to give an image to the faces of the Medici "Ancien Régime" in complete compliance with the symbolic value of the age. This will be done by the editor of the catalogue, with her expertise and effectiveness, in the pages that follow.*

*As the Superintendent of Florentine museums, I am interested in emphasising something that is as simple as it is important. The Italian Ministry of "Beni Culturali" employs the greatest talents, fosters research on an international level and guarantees this city "great" prestige and image as no one else (not even Universities or publishing houses) is still capable of doing. We do not limit ourselves to keeping museums open and to "working", every year, nearly 5 million visitors, but we organize some of the most beautiful art exhibitions currently underway in Europe (*Giambologna *at the Bargello,* Lorenzo Monaco *at the Accademia, the* Manifattura Siriés *at Pitti), are responsible for impressive publications and encourage and finance specialized studies of absolute excellence, such as the one entrusted to the catalogue that this brief introduction presents.*

*All this is possible thanks to the professionalism and admirable dedication of the technical-scientific personnel working at our Superintendence. My staff and I sincerely wish to thank our friends and colleagues at Pitti (and more specifically, in this case, Serena Padovani, Stefano Casciu, Fausta Navarro, Rosanna Morozzi and Mauro Linari).*

Antonio Paolucci
*Soprintendente per il Polo Museale Fiorentino*

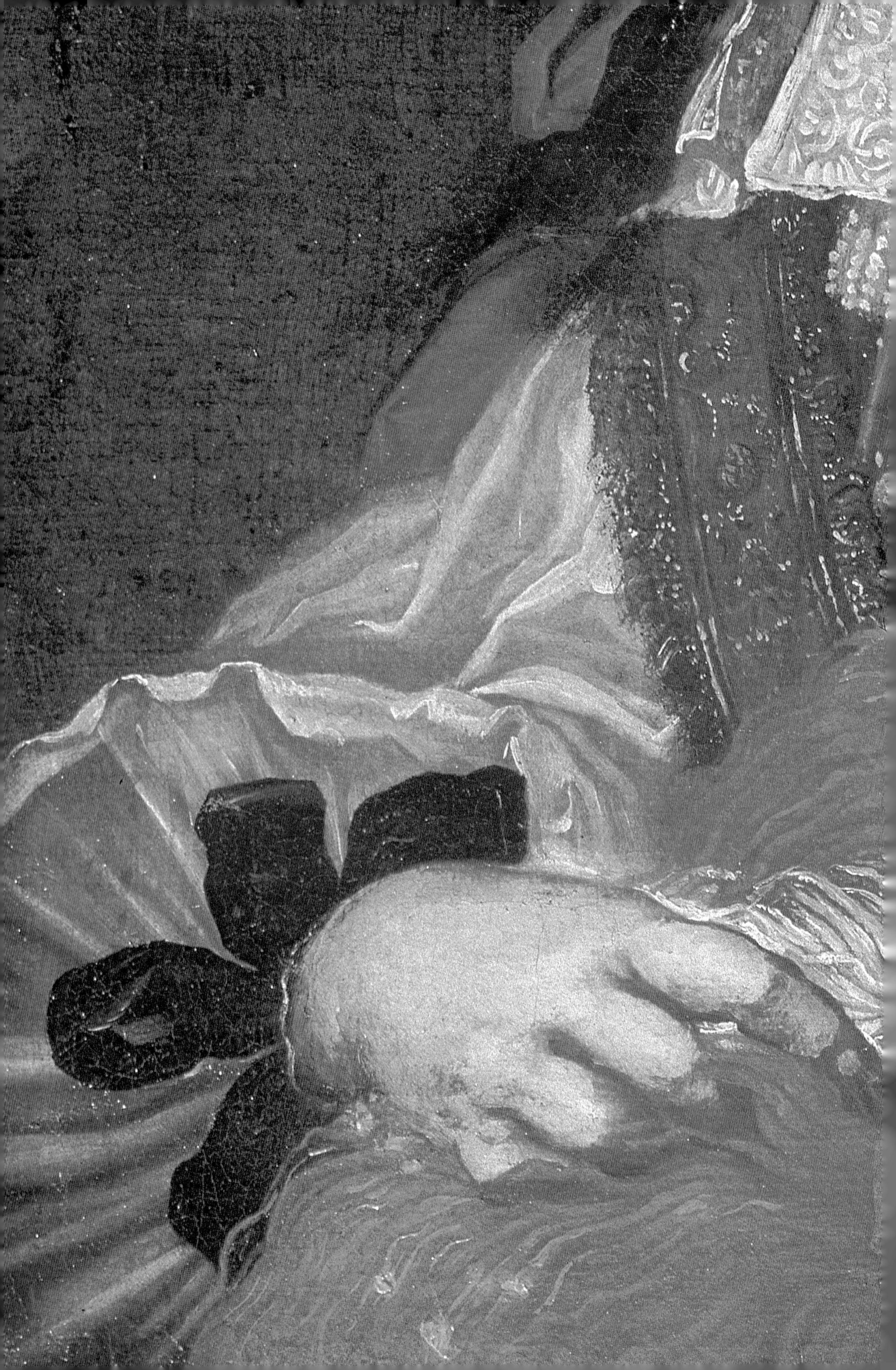

# Cosimo III de' Medici and the 1678 exhibition in honor of Giusto Suttermans

The first task awaiting the curator of a monographic exhibition is normally the careful choice of the works that best represent the artist's qualities. In this sense the exhibition that we are presenting is an exception to the rule. It is a faithful reconstruction of an exhibition which was organized more than three hundred years ago, in 1678, by Grand Duke Cosimo III de' Medici to honor his portraitist Giusto Suttermans (as he signed his name). For this reason the curator of this exhibition is obliged to respect the choices made more than three centuries ago. He is thus free from all responsibility for the choice of the paintings, except for the portrait of *Cosimo III* painted by Suttermans in 1658 (cat. no. 1) and the painter's *Self-portrait* (cat. no. 2), which have been added in order to present the protagonists of the exhibition to today's public. The curator's primary task is in this case a rather different and, perhaps, far more difficult one. He must attempt to draw a clear profile of the artist, comprehensible to the modern eye, through the filter of the personal tastes of the curator who organized the exhibition for the grand duke in 1678. Since the original curator was the eminent art historian Filippo Baldinucci and a significant number of the paintings he chose are still in Florence today, we believe that the undertaking is well worth the effort, especially because monographic exhibitions were quite rare in the 17th century. The exhibition has been recreated in Palazzo Pitti, the same building where it was organized in 1678, though not in the same room, which belonged to the apartment of Cardinal Leopoldo de' Medici on the second floor and has been irreparably altered in the meantime. Fortunately, the 'Sala Bianca' provides an analogous and entirely appropriate backdrop for the exhibition.

Grand Duke Cosimo III was born in Florence on 14 August 1642. Though he was the third of four children born to Grand Duke Ferdinando II de' Medici (1610–1670) and his wife Vittoria della Rovere (1622–1694), Cosimo was the first to survive early childhood.[1] Thus, unlike the previous Medici grand dukes who grew up in the company of a great number of brothers and sisters (his grandfather Cosimo II had eight siblings and his father Ferdinando seven), Cosimo III had a lonely childhood, since his younger brother Francesco Maria (1660–1710) was born eighteen years after him and raised with his children. Cosimo probably felt even more lonely when he succeeded his father on the grand ducal throne in May 1670, especially after 1675 when the last of his uncles Cardinal Leopoldo (1617–1675) died and his estranged wife Marguerite Louise d'Orléans (1645–1721) returned to France. He found himself alone with a grand duchy to rule and an immense patrimony of works of art collected by several generations of Medici patrons. He had in fact inherited not only the patrimony of the grand dukes of Tuscany, but also the collections of his uncle Leopoldo, a renowned connoisseur, and of his great-uncle Cardinal Carlo de' Medici who had died in 1666, a refined collector in his own right.[2] The exhibition in honor of Giusto Suttermans was conceived in 1678 by Cosimo III in this patrimonial and psychological context. Suttermans, portraitist to the Medici for almost sixty years, had served Cosimo's grandmother Archduchess Maria Magdalena von Habsburg, known in Italy as Maria Maddalena of Austria, from 1621 to 1631 and had worked for his father Ferdinando II from 1631 to 1670. The paintings exhibited in 1678 included portraits from all the phases of his career. Both deceased members of the Medici family, their courtiers and the youngest members of the family were portrayed. Thus, while paying homage to his portraitist, Cosimo was also celebrating his own family. An exhibition in honor of Suttermans, who was Flemish, is also perfectly consistent with the grand duke's tastes as a collector. Cosimo had in fact acquired a taste for Flemish and Dutch art during his travels through Northern Europe in 1667 and 1669. He had purchased many works for his collection both while traveling and afterwards with the help of agents and correspondents abroad. The exhibition in Suttermans' honor also reveals Cosimo's intention to continue the patronage accorded him by his deceased uncle Leopoldo, who had purchased and commissioned a great number of works painted by the portraitist. This desire to follow in Leopoldo's footsteps as a patron of the arts is also evident in his determination to complete, once again with the help of Filippo Baldinucci, the collection of self-portraits which his uncle had begun. The same desire to present himself as the successor to his ancestors' policies is apparent in an unpublished portrait of *Cosimo III de' Medici* (fig. 1) in Warsaw, which was painted by Volterrano in 1677,[3] a year before the exhibition in Suttermans' honor. In this portrait Cosimo is portrayed in grand ducal robes standing on the waterfront of Livorno, near the statue of his great-grandfather Ferdinando I de' Medici by Giovanni Bandini, which has four bronze Moorish slaves by Pietro Tacca on its' base. Ferdinando's head, which is facing left in Bandini's statue, is turned in the opposite direction in the painting, directly towards his great-grandson. Cosimo, who signed an edict freeing much trade in Livorno from customs in 1676, had himself portrayed as a successor to the policies of Ferdinando, the port's greatest benefactor.

The exhibition in honor of Suttermans was certainly not an isolated episode of artistic patronage. It must be interpreted within the general context of many initiatives taken by Cosimo in this period. For example, in the same decade he founded an academy for young Tuscan sculptors in Palazzo Madama in Rome and began the restoration of the main chapel of Santa Maria Maddalena de' Pazzi in Florence. In 1677 the grand duke decided to bring the family's collection of ancient Roman and Greek sculptures back to Florence from Villa Medici in Rome and, as a consequence, to complete the fresco decoration of the outer hallway of the Galleria degli Uffizi where he intended to place them.[4]

Who was Giusto Suttermans, the painter honored by Cosimo III de' Medici? We know a great deal about his life thanks to the biography published in 1681 by Filippo Baldinucci,[5] which is based on information supplied to him by the painter himself.[6] According to Baldinucci, Giusto, one of the thirteen children of Frans and Esther Suttermans, was born in Antwerp and was baptized there on 28 September 1597.[7] As Baldinucci indicated, his first training took place in his hometown under Willem de Vos who was the nephew of the well-known painter Martin de Vos.[8] "Jooys Soeterman" was registered in 1609 in the books of the Antwerp painter's guild, dedicated to Saint Luke, as the apprentice of "Gilliam de Vos".[9] According to Baldinucci, Giusto also took lessons from Otto van Veen[10] before leaving Antwerp to complete his education in Paris under the court portraitist Frans Pourbus the younger.[11] Baldinucci states that three and a half years later Suttermans left Paris with a group of Flemish tapestry workers that had been called to Tuscany by Cosimo II de' Medici and arrived in Florence a few months before the death of the grand duke, who died on 28 February 1621.[12] The tapestry workers he traveled with can be identified with Jacob Ebert van Hasselt and his assistants "Pietro" and "Adriano", who arrived at the Medici court from France at the beginning of October 1620 and were immediately put to work in the grand ducal tapestry works.[13] The presence of "Monsù Giusto", as he was called in Florence, is documented from 20 April 1621. On this date "Justo Citermans" was paid for a painting of *Saint Barbara* by the Confraternity of Saints Barbara and Quirinus in the Florentine church of the Santissima Annunziata.[14] Relations between Suttermans and the Medici court are documented for the first time on 1 October 1621, the date on a letter from Caterina de' Medici (1593–1629), the wife of Ferdinando Gonzaga, to Maria Maddalena of Austria, Cosimo II's widow.[15] In her letter Caterina mentions miniatures portraits sent from Florence, which Maria Maddalena clearly attributes to "Giusto" in the answer she sent to Caterina on 11 November of the same year.[16] Two years later Suttermans appears on a "Ruolo de' Provvisionati della Serenissima Arciduchessa", a list of Maria Maddalena's salaried staff which can be dated between February and April 1623.[17] According to this document, his salary was paid at the time "in roba", literally in goods. An unpublished payment order, signed by "Maria Magdalena Arciduchessa" (fig. 2) and her secretary Orazio della Rena, proves that from 1 August 1623 he received a monthly salary

Fig. 1 - Baldassarre Franceschini known as Volterrano, *Cosimo III de' Medici*, 1677. Zamek Królewski w Warszawie (Royal Castle of Warsaw)

of twenty scudi.[18] By 1627 Suttermans' salary had increased: Maria Maddalena mentions a monthly salary of twenty-five scudi, above and beyond the payment he received for his portraits, in the letter of recommendation she sent to the Grand Master of the Military Order of Saint John of Jerusalem on 10 July 1627.[19] After the death of Maria Maddalena in 1631 the painter was put on the rolls of her son Ferdinando II de' Medici and received a salary from him until 1649, when the Tuscan court was forced to suspend the salaries of many courtiers, musicians and artisans as an austerity measure.[20] Even without a monthly salary Suttermans continued to work on a commission basis for the Medici for the following three decades, both for single members of the family and for the grand ducal Guardaroba, or Wardrobe department which administrated the grand duke's apparel, jewels, furniture, works of art and other movable possessions. Some kind of regular retribution was later re-instated. On 15 June 1670, a few weeks after the death of Grand Duke Ferdinando II, Suttermans asked for formal confirmation of the monthly payment of five scudi and Cosimo III duly granted him "la medesima parte che ha fin' hora goduto", the same amount he had received until that time.[21]

During his long career Giusto Suttermans often left Florence to work at other European courts. Towards the end of 1621 he was sent to Mantua to portray Princess *Eleonora Gonzaga*, the bride of Emperor Ferdinand II von Habsburg,[22] and between November 1623 and October 1624 he sojourned in Vienna at the court of the same emperor.[23] In 1627 he visited Rome[24] where he painted lost portraits of *Pope Urban VIII* and other members of the Barberini court. Between the end of 1639 and 1640 he worked at the Farnese courts in Parma and Piacenza in the service of Margherita de' Medici, the wife of Duke Odoardo Farnese and also visited Milan.[25] In 1645 he went to Rome in the retinue of Cardinal Giovan Carlo de' Medici.[26] In the summer of 1649 Suttermans went to Modena to work for Francesco I d'Este;[27] he traveled from there to Finale Ligure and sojourned in Genoa[28] before returning to Modena in November. In February 1650 he went from Modena to Parma, and in March returned to Modena,[29] where he remained until July of the same year. In 1653 he visited the Este court once again and from there went to Ferrara to paint a portrait of the *Cardinal legate Alderano Cybo (1613–1700)* and possibly to Mantua as well.[30] Suttermans worked in Modena again in 1654 and in 1656. At the end of his 1656 sojourn in Modena,

Fig. 2 - Giusto Suttermans, *Maria Maddalena of Austria*, 1622. Brussels, Musée Royaux des Beaux Arts
Fig. 3 - Giusto Suttermans, *Galileo Galilei*, 1635. Florence, Galleria degli Uffizi

he visited Parma and Mantua and traveled to Innsbruck where he stayed until the following summer at the court of Anna de' Medici (1616–1676) and her husband Archduke Ferdinand Karl von Habsburg (1628-1662).[31] Suttermans made his last trip outside Tuscany in 1659 when he was called for the last time to Modena by Alfonso IV d'Este (1634–1662).[32]

According to Filippo Baldinucci, Monsù Giusto worked until he was quite old and in 1678, when he was almost eighty years old, painted an excellent portrait of *Francesco Maria de' Medici* (fig. 16).[33] He died three years later, on 23 or 24 April 1681 and was buried in the Florentine Church of San Felice in Piazza.[34]

Baldinucci mentions the exhibition organized by Cosimo III in Suttermans' honor. He indicates that the grand duke decided to reserve the audience room in the apartment of Cardinal Leopoldo de' Medici, on the second floor of Palazzo Pitti, solely for the painter's works and sent his portrait of *Galileo Galilei* (fig. 3)[35] to the Tribuna in the Uffizi, where it was exhibited with the Medici's most precious works of art:

> [. . .] Volendo la clemenza del serenissimo granduca Cosimo III mostrare a Giusto alcun nuovo segno di stima del suo valore e di gradimento di sua lunga e lodevole servitù, comandò, che nel real palazzo de' Pitti, il salone, che servì per l'udienza del serenissimo cardinale Leopoldo, si dedicasse tutto all'opere di Giusto: ed avendo fatto far raccolta d'una gran quantità di esse, fra altre che si trovavano in diverse stanze, volle in esso salone fossero collocate, per farne un'intera e grande galleria: concetto veramente nobilissimo, toltone il tanto rinomato ritratto di Galileo Galilei, del quale facemmo altra volta menzione, a cui fece dar luogo nella stanza della real galleria, chiamata la Tribuna; [. . .] e quivi si conservano i preziosi tesori di pittura e scultura, di che è ricca questa serenissima casa: e ciò, credo io, per far vedere agli occhi degli eruditi in un tempo stesso due stupendi miracoli della natura, nella persona di colui che quivi si rappresenta al vivo, e anche dell'arte nella pittura di Giusto. Dacché tal cosa ebbe suo effetto, visse monsù Giusto tre anni, [. . .] godendo il frutto delle sue fatiche nel possedimento d'un ben radicato amore verso di sé di tutta la serenissima casa [. . .].[36]

Since Baldinucci specifies that the exhibition was organized three years before the painter's death, we can date the exhibition to 1678.

This information is confirmed by an entry in a journal of the Medici Guardaroba. The journal entry lists six portraits by the painter sent to the keeper of Palazzo Pitti, Diacinto Maria Marmi, on 28 February 1678 expressly for the "stanza de' quadri di Giusto Sutterman", the chamber of the paintings by Giusto Suttermans, in Cardinal Leopoldo's apartment:

> Jesus Maria, a dì 28 febbraio 1678 [ab nativitate]
>
> A Diacindto Maria Marmi gl'appiè quadri, cavati di Guardaroba per metterli, nel suddetto appartamento [ch'era del serenissimo cardinale Leopoldo] nella stanza de' quadri di Giusto Sutterman:
>
> Un quadro in tela senza adornamento alto braccia 2 ¾, largo braccia 1 ⅞, dipintovi il serenissimo principe Ferdinando da fanciullo, con gonnellino bianco, e rosso, e berretta in mano di mano di Giusto _____ 472 n. 1
>
> Un quadro simile alto e largo simile dipintovi il serenissimo Francesco vestito da prete, con la sinistra posa sopra la testa d'un cane _____ n. 1
>
> Un quadro in tela alto braccia 2, largo braccia 1 ½ dipintovi il serenissimo principe Mattias armato mezza figura, con bastone in mano e ciarpa rossa, di mano di Giusto suddetto _472 n. 1
>
> Un quadro in tela alto braccia 1 ⅔, con l'ornamento dorato liscio dipintovi il ritratto del serenissimo principe don Lorenzo, con giubbone nero affettato di mano del suddetto _____ 357 n. 1
>
> Un quadro simile senza ornamento alto braccia 1 ¼ largo braccia 1 dipintovi il ritratto del figlio del Re Danimarcha armato con ciarpa turchina, e biancha di mano del suddetto _144 n. 1
>
> Da Giovanni Bianchi custode della Galleria:
>
> Un quadro in tela alto anzi dipintovi il ritratto del Imperatrice di casa Gonzagha con adornamento di noce intagliato in parte, e dorato alto braccia 1 ¾, largo braccia 1 ½ in circha, di mano di Giusto n. 1
>
> A Diacinto Maria Marmi, come sopra - Notata altra volta in questo a 271.[37]

Handwritten notes, probably written by Baldinucci himself, supply further information about the plans for the exhibition. These unpublished notes are bound in the volume of miscellaneous information entitled *Notizie di vite e opere di diversi pittori*, gathered by Anton Francesco Marmi and donated to the Biblioteca Nazionale di Firenze in 1731.[38] They list the paintings by Monsù Giusto available for exhibition and are accompanied by two sketches or plans for the placement of the paintings on the walls of a room (fig. 4). The notes list six portraits "in mano al Bernardi", consigned to one of the keepers of the Medici Guardaroba Niccolò Bernardi; nineteen portraits held by the keepers Marmi and Bernardi in Palazzo Pitti; six "Ritratti di Monsù Giusto interi", full-length portraits by Suttermans; five others of similar format that had been "ritrovati", or found elsewhere; and, last of all, three other portraits of the same format found in the "Guardarobba Generale". The lists include five of the paintings that were sent to Palazzo Pitti in 1678 expressly for the Suttermans room and twenty-one of the thirty paintings by him which, as we will soon see, are described together in the same room by an inventory

Fig. 4 - Filippo Baldinucci, *Ritratti in mano al Bernardi, Marmi e Bernardi a Pitti, Ritratti di Monsù Giusto interi, Ritrovati altri simili ritrovati, Guardarobba Generale altri simili*, n.d. [1678 ca.], in MARMI n.d. [by 1731], BNCF, ms. II.II.110, fol. 351v.

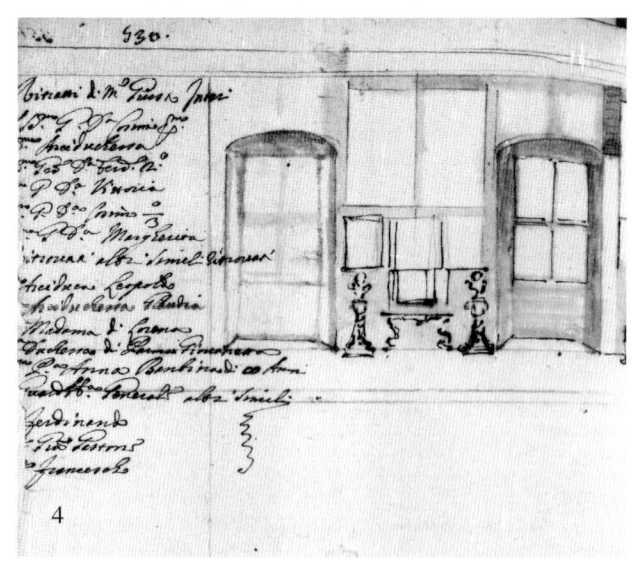

of the palace compiled in 1688. They also cite several other well-known works by Suttermans that apparently were not chosen for the exhibition, since they are not listed with the paintings described in the 1688 inventory: "1 Principe Francesco testa", a head of Prince Francesco, which can be identified with the portrait of *Francesco Maria de' Medici* (fig. 16) painted by Suttermans in 1678;[39] "Ritratti 3 insieme", 3 portraits together, possibly the portrait of *Ferdinando II de' Medici with his parents*;[40] a painting of " quochi", literally cooks, which can be identified with the Galleria Palatina's *Banquet of hunters and cooks*;[41] six full-length portraits of three Medici grand dukes and their wives seated in chairs that came from the collection of Cardinal Leopoldo de' Medici;[42] and last of all three full-length portraits of Grand Duchess *Christine of Lorraine*, known in Italy as Cristina di Lorena,[43] *Claudia de' Medici* and her husband *Leopold von Habsburg*.[44] The notes also list a handful of lost works: a portrait of "Cardinale di Ruceli", or *Cardinal de Richelieu*, attributed to "Giusto Surtmano" by a journal of the Guardaroba generale on 9 April 1639, when it was first sent to Palazzo Pitti;[45] a portrait of "Papa Lodovisio", *Pope Gregory XV*[46] attributed to "M. Giusto" by the 1663–1664 inventory of the same palace; a full-length portrait of Cosimo's third child "*Principe Gian Gastone*"; one of *Fabrizio Colloredo*;[47] and a portrait of the "*Nano di Crecqui*", the dwarf of the French envoy Charles, Sieur de Créqui and Duc de Lesdiguières.[48]

The inventory of Palazzo Pitti compiled at the beginning of 1688 supplies more precise information about the exhibition. It describes thirty paintings attributed to "Giusto Suttermanni", including four of the six portraits sent by the Guardaroba to Pitti in 1678, all hanging in one room on the second floor of the palace. In the same room there was also an un-attributed portrait of *Galileo Galilei* (cat. no. 14) and one of *Charles I Stuart with his wife Henriette Marie de Bourbon* (cat. no. 24), which was painted by the workshop of Antonie van Dyck and retouched by Suttermans in 1675. The inventory describes the room as "la terza stanza che segue con finestra e porta sul ballatoio", literally the third room with a window and a door on the balcony, and specifies that it belonged to the apartment next to the left-hand apartment. In the adjoining rooms there were two other works by Suttermans: the portrait of Giusto's first patron *Maria Maddalena of Austria as Saint Mary Magdalene* (fig. 5),[49] which was hanging in the second room of the same apartment, and the portrait of her daughter *Margherita de' Medici as Saint Margaret*,[50] hanging in the fourth room. According to the inventory, Suttermans' enormous canvas depicting *The Pledge of Allegiance of the Florentine Senate to Ferdinando II de' Medici* (1622–1625) was also exhibited on the same floor of the palace, in a large room with windows and a door overlooking the main courtyard.[51]

The paintings chosen for the exhibition in 1678 quite probably can be identified with the works by Suttermans described by the 1688 inventory in the same room on the second floor of Palazzo Pitti. Twenty-two of these paintings have been identified. All of them, with the exception of the portrait of *Mattias de' Medici* (cat. no. 19), belong to Florentine museums. Unfortunately twelve other portraits by Suttermans described by the 1688 inventory have since been lost. These paintings were probably removed from Palazzo Pitti during the reign of Pietro Leopoldo of Lorraine, who arrived in Florence in 1765, and reorganized the furnishings of the palace.[52] Short entries for the missing works, which include the description of each one from the 1688 inventory, have been published in an appendix to this catalogue in hopes that they can be tracked down in the future.

The exhibition includes works painted in all the phases of Giusto Suttermans' long career. Thus, examining them in chronological order, we can easily discern the evolution of his style of painting. The earliest works on exhibit are portraits of two daughters of Grand Duke Cosimo II and his wife Maria Maddalena of Austria, *Margherita* and *Anna de' Medici* (cat. nos. 3–4). These portraits were commissioned in October 1621 from "ms. Giusto fiamengo"[53] and completed by September of the following year.[54] They are good examples of Suttermans early manner of painting, which closely recalls the style of his master Frans Pourbus the younger. They present all of the characteristics of his early style: the careful definition of the details, the sharp, clear lighting and the tendency to model the hands, faces and skirts of his sitters after simple geometric shapes. The style of painting is substantially unchanged, though somewhat more self-possessed, in the portrait of their younger brother *Leopoldo de' Medici as a boy in canonicals* (cat. no. 8), which was painted a few years later. This canvas belonged to a set of full-length portraits of the five sons of Cosimo II and Maria Maddalena. These portraits were delivered to their mother on 8 April 1627[55] and are mentioned together by the Palazzo Pitti inventories compiled in 1638[56] and between 1663 and 1664.[57]

The first noticeable changes in Suttermans' style of painting appear in the next decade, after his visit to Rome in 1627 and the arrival at the Medici court in 1631 of the collection of Venetian paintings that belonged to the dukes of Urbino. This collection, which included the famous *Venus of Urbino* by Titian,[58] came to Florence as part of the dowry of Grand Duke Ferdinando II's bride Vittoria della Rovere. The free brushwork and the light palette Suttermans uses in his portrait of *Galileo Galilei* in the Uffizi (fig. 3), which dates from 1635,[59] can thus easily be explained as resulting from the influence of Venetian painting. Drawings by Monsù Giusto in the print and drawing room of the Uffizi bear mute witness to his admiration for the great Venetian painters of the 16th century. See for example, his sketch after Titian's *Worship of Venus*,[60] which he probably saw in the Ludovisi collection when he visited Rome in 1627, or his study of Sebastiano del Piombo's *Death of Adonis*, a painting which belonged to Leopoldo de' Medici in the 17th century.[61] We also know that Suttermans borrowed the Medici's portrait of *Pietro Aretino* by Titian for several years and kept it in his workshop at court.[62] His *Vestal Tuccia* (fig. 6),[63] painted sometime around 1634, is an unmistakable tribute to Titian.

One of the paintings exhibited in the Suttermans room in 1678 was painted precisely the same year, a portrait of two peasant women and a black servant of the Medici court whose names are indicated in the 1688 inventory of Palazzo Pitti: "Madonna Domenica dalle Cascine, la Maria di Pratolino e Piero moro". This painting, which is cited in the Palazzo Pitti inventories from 1638 to 1761, has since been lost. It is substituted in the exhibition by a second version of the painting that belongs to the Galleria degli Uffizi (cat. no. 13). This version comes from the collection of Cardinal Carlo de' Medici and is listed in the 1667 inventory of the possessions in his residence at the Casino mediceo. According to the inventory, the sitters were "Mona Domenica delle Cascine, la Ceccha di Pratolino e il Moro". After Carlo's death the painting entered the grand ducal collection and was later sent to the Medici Villa dell'Ambrogiana, one of Cosimo's favorite residences. Its presence in the villa is documented from 1732 to 1780, when it was moved to the Villa del Poggio Imperiale. Both paintings were mentioned on 30 September 1634 in a letter sent by Giovan Carlo de' Medici to his brother Mattias from Pratolino where the court had retired for the summer. In the letter Giovan Carlo describes the pastimes of the court at rest, including hunting and watching the painters Giovanni di San Giovanni and Giusto Suttermans at work. He expressly mentions portraits of local peasants painted by Giusto to entertain the court "nell'hore della quiete".[64] The recreational purpose of this painting explains its unconstrained, almost cursory brushwork. This alternative manner of painting, less formal than the style of his courtly portraits of the same period, appears once again in the Galleria Palatina's portrait of *Elia da Zia*, the pilot master of the grand ducal galley known as la Capitana (cat. no. 12).

One of the paintings sent to Palazzo Pitti in 1678 for the Suttermans room, the portrait of *Valdemar Kristian (1622–1656), prince of Denmark* (cat. no. 15), shows further stylistic evolution. This portrait was probably painted during the visit of young Prince Valdemar, a son of King Kristian IV of Denmark, who arrived in Florence in June 1638 and stayed in the city for the entire summer.[65] It is described on 17 September 1640 by an inventory of the Medici Guardaroba: "Un quadro in tela entrovi dipinto il figliuolo del Re d'Animarca con banda bianca e turchina, alto braccia 1 largo braccia ¾ incirca senza ornamento".[66] The portrait, which can be considered one of the painter's masterpieces, is painted in a grand manner with a palette of brilliant colors that seem to imitate the style of Pieter Paul Rubens. In 1638 Suttermans had in fact received the large canvas by Rubens depicting *The Consequences of War,* which he had ordered in Antwerp and now belongs to the Galleria Palatina.[67] He may also have been influenced by the frescoes that Pietro da Cortona, called to Florence in 1637, was painting for Ferdinando II de' Medici on the first floor of Palazzo Pitti at the time.

A year later, in the fall of 1639, Monsù Giusto went to serve the Farnese court in Parma and Piacenza and stayed on until half way through the following year. The works by Correggio that he had a chance to see during this trip certainly gave further impetus to the evolution of his painting style. During this period Suttermans painted portraits of the six children of Duke Odoardo Farnese and his wife Margherita de' Medici. Four of these portraits, which were sent to Florence in the spring of 1640, are mentioned in a letter sent from Piacenza by Margherita to her brother Ferdinando II on 24 May 1640:

[. . .] Se ne ritorna Giusto pittore a servire Vostra Altezza et ha tardato più di quello io havrei voluto, per causa della sua poca sanità, [. . .] Lui presenterà al Altezza Vostra i ritratti degl'altro quattro miei figlioli quali da hora offerisco a Vostra Altezza per que veri servitori et obbligati che sono et saranno molto più quando habbino più ingegno di conoscere le loro obbligazioni; [. . .].[68]

In short, Margherita informs Ferdinando that the painter Giusto is about to return to Florence bearing portraits of her four other children. Ferdinando II repeats the words "altri quattro", literally four other, on 16 June 1640 in his thank you letter.[69] It is thus clear that, in addition to the four portraits he brought to Florence by Suttermans in May 1640, the grand duke had already received portraits of Margherita's two other children. Three portraits of the young Farnese princes were identified in 1985 in the catalogue of the exhibition *I principi bambini* and are still in Palazzo Pitti. They portray *Ranuccio (1630–1694)*, *Maria Maddalena (1633–1714)* and *Alessandro Farnese (1635–1689)*[70] (figs. 7, 8, 9). Three more portraits of the set hang unrecognized in the offices of the Province of Siena, which are housed in Palazzo Reale, the residence of the grand dukes of Tuscany in the city. Like the portraits in Palazzo Pitti, the three Sienese portraits come from the Medici Villa del Poggio Imperiale that is just outside Porta Romana, one of the gates of Florence. All six portraits are listed together in the inventory of the villa compiled in 1692,[71] which describes in great detail not only the portraits, but also their frames. The three Sienese portraits still have the frames decorated with chains described by the inventory. The children portrayed have until this time been mistaken for Medici princes, but are clearly indicated in the Poggio Imperiale inventory as members of the Farnese family: "i suddetti quadri con adornamenti a catena, la maggior parte dicano esser principi di Casa Farnese". Thus the portraits in Siena can be properly identified with Margherita's three youngest children, *Orazio (1636-1656)*, *Maria Caterina (1637–1648)* and *Pietro (1639–1677) Farnese*[72] (figs. 10, 11, 12). The quality of the painting in these three portraits cannot compare to the fresh, masterly brushwork in the portraits of their siblings *Ranuccio* and *Maria Maddalena* in Palazzo Pitti. Most probably the Sienese portraits were painted with the help of a workshop hand who also collaborated with Suttermans in the portrait of *Alessandro Farnese*. Since this painting and the three Sienese portraits closely resemble each other, they may well be the four portraits mentioned in the letters cited above.

Since no paintings from the 1640's seem to have been exhibited in the Suttermans room in 1678, we are forced to leave Palazzo Pitti temporarily to find works from this period. Two excellent examples are the full-length portraits of members of the Pamphili family painted for Cardinal Carlo de' Medici during or shortly after the painter's visit to Rome in 1645. These paintings were mentioned in the 1667 inventory of the possessions of the cardinal in the Casino di San Marco.[73] After Carlo's death they entered the grand ducal collection and were deposited in the Guardaroba generale, which was located in Palazzo Vecchio.[74] One of the two paintings, the well-known portrait of *Camillo Pamphili (1622–1666) as cardinal* (fig. 13),[75] has always been attributed to Suttermans. It was sent to Palazzo Pitti for the apartment of Grand Prince Ferdinando in 1689[76] and is still exhibited in the palace today after a period in 'exile' at the Medici Villa di Poggio a Caiano from 1866 to 1911.[77] The second painting, a portrait of *Pope Innocent x* (fig. 14),[78] in the world Giovanni Battista Pamphili (1574–1655, pope from 1644), is practically unknown. Unlike the portrait of the pope's nephew *Camillo*, it was not attributed to Suttermans by the 1667 inventory of Carlo's collection. Perhaps for this reason when the portrait of *Camillo* was sent to Palazzo Pitti, the portrait of *Innocent x* was left behind in the Guardaroba and was later moved to a deposit of the Galleria degli Uffizi. Though the portrait of *Innocent x* was exhibited on the hallway that connects the Uffizi and Palazzo Pitti for a brief period between the end of the 19th century and of the beginning of the 20th century,[79] it was not taken into serious consideration until 2002.[80] Each detail of the portrait corresponds perfectly with the painting mentioned in the inventory of Cardinal Carlo de' Medici's collection, which describes the pope sitting next to a table with a bell on it:

Fig. 5 - Giusto Suttermans, *Maria Maddalena d'Austria in guise of Saint Mary Magdalene*. 1625 ca. Florence, Palazzo Pitti, Galleria Palatina
Fig. 6 - Giusto Suttermans, *Vestal Tuccia*, 1634 ca. Florence, Palazzo Pitti, Galleria Palatina

Uno quadro in tela alta braccia 3 ½, largo braccia 2 ⅛, entrovi il ritratto intero di Papa Innocenzio x$^{mo}$ a sedere con tavolino e campanello con adornamento d'albero tinto di nero e profilato d'oro.[81]

Though the inventory does not supply the name of the painter, his identity is clearly established by a letter sent by Belisario Guerrini, the secretary of the Medici embassy in Rome, to Cardinal Carlo on 23 April 1645. Belisario mentions portraits of the pope and his nephew Cardinal Pamphili that Suttermans was about to bring back to Florence, which can be identified with the portraits listed in Carlo's inventory:

[. . .] Giusto pittore nel ritorno suo a Fiorenza porterà i ritratti del Papa e del cardinale Panfilio e con quell'occasione Vostra Eminenza si farà servire dell'altezza e la larghezza del quadro nel modo che vorrà [. . .].[82]

Unfortunately the portrait of *Innocent x* is in poor repair. A great deal of pigment on the right side and on the lower half of the painting has been lost. The wax applied many years ago to stabilize the surface of the painting has swelled, causing further damage.[83] Thus it is quite difficult to judge the quality of the portrait and to analyze the manner of painting. For example, it is not easy to determine whether a workshop hand painted the hands and the clothing of the pope, since the painting surface in this area is severely damaged. Judging from the intact parts of the painting (the face, the back of the armchair and the bell on the table), it seems that Suttermans did at least part

Fig. 7 - Giusto Suttermans, *Ranuccio Farnese*, 1639–1640. Florence, Palazzo Pitti, storage
Fig. 8 - Giusto Suttermans, *Maria Maddalena Farnese*, 1639–1640. Florence, Palazzo Pitti, storage
Fig. 9 - Giusto Suttermans, *Alessandro Farnese*, 1640. Florence, Galleria Palatina

Fig. 10 - Giusto Suttermans and workshop, *Orazio Farnese*, 1640. Siena, Palazzo della Provincia
Fig. 11 - Giusto Suttermans and workshop, *Maria Caterina Farnese*, 1640. Siena, Palazzo della Provincia
Fig. 12 - Workshop of Giusto Suttermans, *Pietro Farnese*, 1640. Siena, Palazzo della Provincia

of the painting by himself. Final judgment will have to await the restoration of the work. This painting may well be a replica of the portrait that Suttermans painted for Innocent X, which is mentioned in a letter written on 25 June 1645:

> [. . .] Il signor Giusto pittore fu hieri dal Papa, che volse vedere tutti i ritratti fatti da lui de' suoi parenti, et hoggi vi ritorna per ritoccare un ritratto di Sua Santità che desidera che resti a Roma [. . .].[84]

From a stylistic point of view, the portraits of *Innocent X* and *Camillo Pamphili* commissioned by Carlo de' Medici are excellent examples of Monsù Giusto's painting in the 1640's. His brushwork of the period is slightly more somber than it was in the previous decade and his palette favors silver-toned highlights. The portrait of *Camillo* is clearly modeled after the portrait of *Cardinal Roberto Ubaldini* in the Los Angeles County Museum, which was painted in the 1620's by the renowned Bolognese painter Guido Reni. Suttermans probably had a chance to see Ubaldini's portrait during his 1645 visit to Rome.[85] The placement of the armchair, the position of the cardinal, who is turned three quarters to the left, and the view of landscape in the background clearly derive from the portrait by Reni. Suttermans shows, as on other occasions, more interest for a twenty-year-old masterpiece of portraiture than in the recent developments of the Roman art scene.

Only one of the portraits by Suttermans exhibited in 1678 was painted in the 1650's, the bust-length portrait of *Margherita de' Medici* (cat. no. 18), who was also portrayed as a child by the painter (cat. no. 3). The limited number of paintings from this period is not fortuitous. Rather, it actually reflects the limited amount of work commissioned by the Medici from him in this decade. As we mentioned above, due to the financial situation of the court, in 1649 Grand Duke Ferdinando II de' Medici decided to cut the monthly salary of a good number of his courtiers, including Suttermans' 'provvigione'.[86] A few years later, in 1654, the grand duke's Guardaroba also stipulated a strict price agreement with him.[87] Thus, it is not at all surprising that Giusto took frequent leave to work at other courts in this decade, for example at the courts in Modena, Parma and Innsbruck. This portrait of *Margherita de' Medici* was probably painted during one of Suttermans' visits to the Farnese courts in Parma and Piacenza. Since she is dressed

Fig. 13 - Giusto Suttermans, *Camillo Pamphili (1622–1666) as a cardinal*, 1645. Florence, Palazzo Pitti, Appartamenti reali

as a widow, we can date the portrait after 1646, when her husband Odoardo Farnese died. Archival sources prove that the painter went to Parma from Modena early in 1650[88] and traveled to the city once again in May 1656. The painting may well be one of the portraits mentioned by Margherita in a letter sent to her brother Leopoldo de' Medici from Parma on 16 September 1656, at the end of Suttermans' visit. In the letter the duchess informs Leopoldo that the painter had finally finished painting portraits of all the members of the family: "Finalmente Giusto ha finito i ritratti che sono stati molti, perché ci ha ritratto tutti più d'una volta".[89] The date 1656 would be quite appropriate both for Margherita's apparent age in the portrait and for the cut of her clothes. In this small painting it is not easy to perceive the changes that one notes starting from 1649 on in other paintings by Suttermans.

The trips Suttermans made in this period in fact had an impact on his painting style. When the painter visited Genoa in 1649 he had a chance to see a great number of portraits by Antonie van Dyck. During his sojourns in Modena he not only saw the renowned portrait of *Francesco I d'Este* by Diego Velázquez,[90] but also had a chance to meet the painters Guercino, Michele Colonna[91] and Pier Francesco Cittadini.[92] These contacts explain the evolution of his painting style, which is apparent in works he painted in this period, for example in the full-length portrait of *Grand Duchess Vittoria della Rovere (1622–1694)* (fig. 15).[93] This portrait is mentioned by the 1688 inventory of Palazzo Pitti, on the first floor of the palace, in the third room after the 'Salone delle Nicchie', which is now known as the 'Sala di Marte'.[94] Like the portrait of *Margherita* cited above, it came from the collection of Cardinal Leopoldo de' Medici.[95] The portrait of *Vittoria* has been identified with a portrait of the same grand duchess mentioned in a document from 1636, when she was fourteen years old,[96] but the identification must be reconsidered. In the first place, in this portrait she seems to be at least thirty years old, not fourteen. In the second place, the style of her dress dates from the 1650's, not from the 1630's. Thus the painting can more plausibly be identified with the portrait of the grand duchess painted for Leopoldo de' Medici and mentioned in a letter sent by Leopoldo to his brother Mattias on 8 May 1655. In the letter Leopoldo summons Suttermans to the Medici Villa di Poggio a Caiano to paint two small portraits for Grand Duke Ferdinando II, asking him to bring with him the very large, framed portrait of Vittoria he had painted for Leopoldo:

> [. . .] Mi commanda il serenissimo Gran Duca di dover far intendere a Vostra Altezza che ordini a Giusto pittore che lunedì mattina si trasferisca qua per far i ritratti e di Sua Altezza e della Serenissima in tele di grandezza di teste e con le mani. E li dica ancora, se si compiace per mia parte, che porti quella tela incorniciata per me con il ritratto della Serenissima Padrona, che è assai grande. [. . .][97]

To complete our chronological survey of Suttermans' artistic career we need look no farther than the room on the second floor of Palazzo Pitti. There, among the paintings chosen by Filippo Baldinucci for the 1678 exhibition, were three documented works painted between 1669 and 1670, when the artist was over seventy years old. These paintings portrayed Cosimo III's younger brother *Francesco Maria (1660–1710)* (cat. no. 20) and his two older children *Grand Prince Ferdinando (1663–1713)* and *Anna Maria Luisa (1667–1743) de' Medici* (cat. nos. 21, 22). In these portraits Suttermans' brushwork is so rapid and cursory that the dark underpainting shows through in many places. The style of painting is quite similar in the portrait of Cosimo's uncle *Mattias de' Medici (1613–1667)* formerly in the Crespi collection (cat. no. 19). This painting matches in every detail a portrait of Mattias described in a bill from the painter presented to the grand ducal Guardaroba generale in December 1668.[98] It was registered in the books of the Guardaroba two years later, on 30 December 1670,[99] and sent from there to Palazzo Pitti on 28 February 1678 for the Suttermans exhibition, along with the portraits of *Francesco Maria* and *Ferdinando* mentioned above.[100]

The portraits of *Mattias de' Medici* and his young nephews painted by the Fleming between 1668 and 1670 can be considered the last phase in the evolution of his painting. The works Suttermans painted during the following decade bear witness to his failing eyesight, which is mentioned in documents from 1668,[101] and to his waning creativity. A good example is the portrait of *Francesco Maria de' Medici* painted

Fig. 14 - Giusto Suttermans, *Pope Innocent X* (Giovanni Battista Pamphili), 1645. Florence, Galleria degli Uffizi, storage

in 1678 (fig. 16), which we mentioned above, among the paintings listed in Baldinucci's notes. Most of the portraits by Suttermans from this period were in fact painted with substantial assistance from his workshop. For example, the full-length version of the portrait of *Francesco Maria* (fig. 16) in Parma's Galleria Nazionale[102] was quite probably painted almost entirely by a brilliant workshop hand.

This portrait brings us to the question of Giusto Suttermans' workshop. Assistants were an essential support for any professional portraitist of the 17th century. Portraitists of the time were under constant pressure from their noble patrons to produce portraits and replicas of their works. Copies were sent to other courts as symbols of a ruler's sovereignty and to present the heirs to the throne who would guarantee the dynasty's continuity. Portraits were also commissioned to offer prospective brides to bridegrooms at the beginning of marriage negotiations or as gifts to relatives who lived far away. For a ruler the gift of his own portrait had significant diplomatic overtones: portraits were sent to decorate the homes and offices of his ambassadors abroad and given as gifts to faithful courtiers and correspondents to thank them for their services. Portraits were also exchanged by rulers anxious to exhibition images of their illustrious relations. A good example is the Galleria Palatina's double portrait of the King of England *Charles I Stuart with his wife Henriette Marie de Bourbon*, the son-in-law and daughter of Maria de' Medici (cat. no. 24). This portrait, painted by a follower of Antonie van Dyck and retouched by Giusto Suttermans in 1675, was exhibited with the works of the Medici's painter in 1678. It was probably sent to the Medici court from the England to reciprocate for two lost, half-length portraits of *Grand Duke Ferdinando II de' Medici* and his wife *Vittoria della Rovere* by Giusto, which were requested on 12 February 1638[103] and sent to England in 1639.[104]

The role of a workshop hand in the atelier of a portrait painter is clearly illustrated in a letter sent from Paris by Marquis Matteo Botti on 6 July 1611. In the letter Botti, who had been asked to order portraits of young King Louis XIII and his sister Élisabeth de Bourbon for the Dowager Grand Duchess of Tuscany Christine of Lorraine, advises her to have them painted by no other than Frans Pourbus the younger, whom he refers to as the Flemish painter. Botti also asks explicitly whether he should have them painted by Pourbus himself at the price of 100 scudi per painting or for half that price, painted by a workshop hand and retouched by Pourbus, who also would paint the sitter's heads and hands:

> [. . .] Quanto alle pitture, dovendo servir per la Galleria [. . .] d'altra mano che del pittor fiammingo non gli manderei [. . .] e però sarà ben sapere ancora se i vestiti si debbon fare di man sua e ben finiti che sarebbon così così cosa rara, ma costarebbono ^interi^ intorno a 100 scudi l'uno. Per 50 si harebbono con i vestiti di mano di un suo lavorante, che sarebbon ragionevoli, et harebbono le teste e le mani di man sua e tutta la persona disegnata e ritocca da lui [. . .].[105]

Suttermans, who learned the portrait trade from Pourbus, organized his workshop in more or less the same way. In the price agreement he stipulated with the Medici Guardaroba on 27 August 1654, the price for copies retouched by the master painter was exactly half the price of autograph portraits, provided that the Guardaroba supplied the canvas already stretched and primed: "Copie che si faccino fare da essi Ritratti e ritocche da lui, proprio la metà de' sopraddetti prezzi [. . .] con patto di darli telai, tele mesticate [. . .]".[106] The same distinction between the price for a copy and for an original, which Monsù Giusto describes as a "prima fatica", a first effort, appears in a letter sent to Cardinal Carlo de' Medici on 6 October 1658.[107]

17th-century sources supply the names of some of Suttermans' workshop hands: first and foremost they mention his brother Jan, who is cited on 13 January 1623 [modern style] in a journal of the Medici Guardaroba, as the author of a portrait of *Ferdinando II de' Medici*.[108] Later the same year Jan accompanied Giusto to Vienna, where he settled.[109] Archival sources also mention another brother, Frans Suttermans, who worked with Giusto towards the end of the same decade. Frans' presence in Florence is documented from 1627 until 1629, when he returned to Antwerp. According to Baldinucci, once in Antwerp, Frans entered the entourage of Van Dyck and became an imitator of his style.[110] Frans Suttermans may in fact be the author of one of the paintings exhibited in 1678, the Galleria Palatina's *Madonna* (cat. no. 23), which is a copy after a canvas painted by Antonie van Dyck. A third workshop hand is mentioned in an accounting book of the Accademia del Disegno: on 14 October 1648 canvases were supplied to Giusto and to his apprentice Carlo Bossi for two portraits of the academy's patron Leopoldo de' Medici.[111] Ten years earlier, on 10 January 1638 [modern style], Bossi had received a payment of five scudi from Grand Duchess Vittoria della Rovere for two miniature portraits.[112] In the 1650's Suttermans' was assisted by Jan van Ghelder, the son of his sister Clara, especially when he worked at the Este court in Modena where his nephew was granted a long-term court appointment.[113]

The monographic exhibition organized in 1678 to honor Giusto Suttermans was quite an unusual event for the times. In 17th-century Italy exhibitions were usually short-term events, organized primarily for religious occasions and for patron saints' days. As a rule, they presented works by different artists and from different periods and were chosen on the basis of the generosity of the collectors who loaned them for the event. The exhibitions organized periodically starting in 1674 by the members of the Florentine Accademia del Disegno in their chapel and in the adjoining courtyard of the Convent of the Santissima Annunziata were of this nature.[114] The same can be said for the exhibitions organized in San Salvatore in Lauro in Rome by Cardinal Decio Azzolini and Giuseppe Ghezzi.[115] According to Francis Haskell, even in Antwerp, where memorial celebrations for Pieter Paul Rubens were held for every fiftieth anniversary of his death, the paintings exhibited were not his own works; and in Nürnberg, the third centenary of the death of Albrecht Dürer was celebrated without an exhibition of paintings or engravings by the artist[116]. Art historians in fact consider the monographic exhibition a rather recent invention. Georg Friedrich Koch, for example, indicates the "one-man shows" organized in London towards the end of the 1700's by Nathaniel Hone, Thomas Gainsborough and John Copley as the first of their kind.[117] Haskell considers the exhibition of one hundred forty-three paintings by Joshua Reynolds, which opened on 10 May 1813, the oldest prototype of the modern monographic exhibition.[118]

The exhibition organized in Suttermans' honor thus can be considered an early precedent for the present day monographic exposition even if we must acknowledge the difference between an exhibition organized expressly for the public at large and one held in a room in a palace reserved for the use of the court and its guests. The honor granted by the grand duke to his portraitist was in any case exceptional. As Filippo Baldinucci aptly noted, this gesture of esteem was a "concetto veramente nobilissimo", a truly noble conception.

Fig. 15 - Giusto Suttermans, *Grand Duchess Vittoria della Rovere*, 1655. Poggio a Caiano (Florence), Medici Villa

Fig. 16 - Giusto Suttermans, *Francesco Maria de' Medici*, 1678. Florence, Gallerie fiorentine, storage
Fig. 17 - Follower of Giusto Suttermans, *Francesco Maria de' Medici*, 1678 ca. Parma, Galleria Nazionale

[1] Their first-born son Cosimo was born on 20 December 1639 and died late the following day. An unnamed daughter was born and died on 31 May 1641.

[2] Cosimo would later inherit both the famous Della Rovere collection, which his mother Vittoria had left in *fideicommissum* to his younger brother Francesco Maria de' Medici (who died in 1710), and the collection of his son grand prince Ferdinando (who died in 1713).

[3] Zamek Królewski w Warszawie (Royal Castle of Warsaw), inv. no. ZKW 100, oil on canvas, cm 196 × 122. This painting was given to the castle in 1981 by Andrzej Ciechanowiecki of the Heim Gallery, London. It can be identified with a portrait of Cosimo III that was registered in the books of the Medici Guardaroba in 1677 and sent to the Villa del Poggio Imperiale in 1780. A copy of this portrait in Palazzo Medici Riccardi in Florence (Gallerie Fiorentine, inv. 1890, no. 3195), comes from the Florentine hospital of Santa Maria Nuova. See GOLDENBERG STOPPATO 2005.

[4] For further information about the patronage of Cosimo III see RUDOLPH 1973, pp. 213–228; J. Southorn, in TURNER 1996, vol. 21, pp. 29–30; C. Acidini Luchinat, in *Il viaggio a Compostela 2004*, pp. 57–69.

[5] BALDINUCCI 1681–1728, ed. 1845–1847, vol. IV, 1846, pp. 473–511.

[6] According to Anton Francesco Marmi, Baldinucci wrote his biography based on information dictated to him by Suttermans, "[. . .] sopra le notizie fattegli dare nella maggior parte dalla viva voce dello stesso Giusto [. . .]" (see MARMI, n.d. [by 1731], fol. 286).

[7] BALDINUCCI 1681–1728, ed. 1845–1847, IV, 1846, p. 476.

[8] Ibid., p. 477.

[9] See ROMBOUT–VAN LERIUS 1872, p. 457.

[10] BALDINUCCI 1681–1728, ed. 1845–1847, IV, 1846, p. 617.

[11] Ibid., p. 477.

[12] Ibid., p. 477–478.

[13] See the letter from Vincenzo Giugni, the head of the Medici Guardaroba, to Guasparri Papini, head of the Medici tapestry works, October 1620, in *Ricordi dell'Arazzeria A*, 1598–1624, Archivio di Stato di Florence (from now on ASF), Guardaroba medicea 213, fol. 67r, published by GOLDENBERG STOPPATO 1990–1991, p. 122. On 7 October 1620 the Medici tapestry works paid the new Flemish tapestry worker 20 scudi to cover the cost of housing: "a Jacopo Ebert fiammingo nuovo arazziere [. . .] scudi venti di moneta [. . .] a conto di pigione di casa". See the manuscripts Debitori e Creditori dell'Arazzeria, 1598–1624, ASF, Guardaroba medicea 212, fol. 191s; Entrata e Uscita dell'Arazzeria, 1619–1621, ASF, Guardaroba medicea 376, fol. 14s.

[14] On the same day, the 20 April 1621, Theodor Rombouts was paid for a painting depicting *Saint Quirinus* (see Quaderuccio della compagnia dei Santi Barbara e Quirino, 1620–1627, ASF, Compagnie religiose soppresse 206, fasc. 13, fol. 99, published by PADOA RIZZO 1987, p. 16). The payment was registered in the confraternity's accounting book on the 30th of the same month (see Uscite della compagnia dei Santi Barbara e Quirino, 1589–1653, ASF, Compagnie religiose soppresse 206, fasc. 14, fol. 107, published by BATTISTINI 1930, p. 191). The depiction of *Saint Barbara* and its 'pendant' appear without attributions in all the confraternity's inventories until 1764 (see the inventories compiled in 1667, between the 17th and 18th centuries, in 1745 and 1764, ASF, Compagnie religiose soppresse 203, insert D, unpaginated, called to my attention by Maria Cecilia Fabbri and published by PADOA RIZZO 1987, p. 17). The paintings were probably sold off or given away when the confraternity was abolished in 1785.

[15] Letter from Caterina de' Medici, duchess of Mantua, to Maria Maddalena of Austria, grand duchess of Tuscany, Porto, 1 October 1621, ASF, Mediceo del Principato 5958, fol. 388. See the letter written the following day as well (ASF, Mediceo del Principato 5958, fol. 389).

[16] Letter from Maria Maddalena of Austria, grand duchess of Tuscany, to Caterina de' Medici, duchess of Mantua, Florence, 11 November 1621, Mantua, Archivio Gonzaga, busta 1097, transcribed by GIANNANTONI 1937, p. 12.

[17] ASF, Miscellanea Medicea 18, insert 2, fol. 71.

[18] Grassina (Florence), Alberto Bruschi collection, sepia ink on white paper, mm 267 × 200: "Domenico Montaguto, Pagherete a Giusto Suttermans pittore di Sua Altezza ogni mese scudi venti da cominciarsi al primo di agosto, per continuare finché non s'ordini in contrario, et tutto a nostro conto. Maria Magdalena Arciduchessa Horazio della Rena 31 luglio 1623."

[19] Letter from Maria Maddalena of Austria, grand duchess of Tuscany, to Antonio di Paula, grand master of the military order of Saint John of Jerusalem, 10 July 1627, ASF, Mediceo del Principato 6102, unpaginated; for a second version of the letter, see ASF, Mediceo del Principato 120, fols. 223–223 bis, published by BALDINUCCI 1681–1728, ed. 1845–1847, IV, 1846, pp. 487–489; BOTTARI–TICOZZI 1822–1825, III, 1822, pp. 523–525.

[20] In Rescritti e mandati della Segreteria, 1645–1650, ASF, Mediceo del Principato 1840, fols. 70–72, published by KIRKENDALE 1993, pp. 39–40. According to Kirkendale (p. 637, no. 335) his monthly salary was 20 scudi. For further information about the relations between Giusto Suttermans and the Medici court, see GOLDENBERG STOPPATO 2003, pp. 31–42.

[21] See Rescritti della Segreteria 1666–1688, ASF, Mediceo del Principato 1843, fol. 64r.

[22] The decision to send the painter to Mantua was announced both in the letter written by Maria Maddalena on the 11 November 1621 quoted in note 16 and in the one written the same day by Christine of Lorraine, the widow of grand duke Ferdinando I, to her daughter Caterina de' Medici, duchess of Mantua, from Florence (Mantua, Archivio Gonzaga, busta 1097, transcribed by GIANNANTONI 1937, p. 12). Suttermans' presence at the Gonzaga court is documented from the 11 December 1621. On that date he is mentioned already at work in Mantua in a letter written by Caterina de' Medici (see ASF, Mediceo del Principato 5958, fol. 417, mentioned by PIERACCINI 1924–1925, II, 1925, pp. 439, 448, note 13).

[23] Giusto Suttermans arrival in Vienna with his brother Jan "fin cinque giorni sono", literally five days ago, was mentioned in a letter addressed to Medici secretary Curzio Picchena by the Medici's ambassador at the emperor's court, Giovanni Altoviti on 11 November 1623 (ASF, Mediceo del Principato 4374a, fol. 214). Giusto most probably returned to Florence after the 1 October 1624, when Emperor Ferdinand II ennobled him and his brothers (Vienna, Adelsarchiv, published by HAJDECKI 1905, pp. 6–7).

[24] See BALDINUCCI 1681–1728, ed. 1845–1847, IV, 1846, pp. 483–489. A letter from Giusto Suttermans in Rome to Medici secretary Dimurgo Lambardi in Florence, written on 2 February 1627 [modern style] and published by CRINÒ (1955, pp. 217–218, note 1), can be non longer be found in the volume she cited (ASF, Mediceo del Principato 1449). Suttermans' stay a Rome probably lasted at least until 12 June 1627 when Pope Urban VIII signed a bull recommending the painter to the grand master of the military order of Saint John of Jerusalem (see ASF, Diplomatico, Cavalieri di Malta, 12 June 1627, transcribed both by BALDINUCCI 1681–1728, ed. 1845–1847, IV, 1846, pp. 485–487; and by GRÜNZWEIG 1919–1932, p. 535).

[25] See BALDINUCCI, 1681–1728, ed. 1845–1847, IV, 1846, pp. 496–498. Thanks to the draft of a letter sent by Medici secretary Andrea Cioli to the Tuscan ambassador in England Amerigo Salvetti, we know that by 15 October 1639 Suttermans had gone to serve "la Signora Duchessa di Parma", the Duchess of Parma Margherita de' Medici (see ASF, Mediceo del Principato 4208, unpaginated, cited by CRINÒ 1955, pp. 218–219). Suttermans returned to Florence by 16 June 1640 when Ferdinando II de' Medici thanked his sister Margherita for the four portraits of her children that the painter had brought back with him (ASF, Mediceo del Principato 144, fol. 173). See notes 69–72.

[26] See BALDINUCCI 1681–1728, ed. 1845–1847, IV, 1846, p. 498. For further information about Suttermans visit to Rome in 1645, see L. Goldenberg Stoppato (catalogue entry for the portrait of *Carlo de' Medici*, Milan, Museo Poldi Pezzoli), in *Fiamminghi e Olandesi* 2002, pp. 100–101.

[27] For information about Suttermans' sojourns in Modena between 1649 and 1650, in 1653, 1654, 1656 and 1659, see VENTURI 1882, pp. 212–216, 249, 266–267. Further documentation has been published by CRINÒ 1955, pp. 220–225.

[28] See BALDINUCCI 1681–1728, ed. 1845–1847, IV, 1846, p. 499. Documentation for the visit to Liguria, where Suttermans was sent in August 1649 to portray Maria Anna von Habsburg, the bride of Philip IV of Spain, has been published by CRINÒ 1955, pp. 220–221; GOLDENBERG STOPPATO 1997, p. 61.

[29] Margherita de' Medici announced that Suttermans had arrived, "è arrivato Giusto", in a letter addressed to her brother Giovan Carlo de' Medici from Piacenza on 3 February 1650 modern style (ASF, Mediceo del Principato 5315, fol. 659). In a second letter written on 25 March 1650 she mentioned that "Giusto pittore" had just left for Modena (ASF, Mediceo del Principato 5369, fol. 271, cited by PIERACCINI 1924–1925, II, 1925, p. 542, notes 4 and 25).

[30] See BALDINUCCI 1681–1728, ed. 1845–1847, IV, 1846, p. 499. In a letter sent from Modena on 28 August 1653 "Giusto Suttermano", who had just returned from Ferrara, promised Duke Carlo II Gonzaga that he would soon come to Mantua to serve him (see BERTOLOTTI 1885, pp. 67–68).

[31] See BALDINUCCI 1681–1728, ed. 1845–1847, IV, 1846, p. 500. Two letters written by Suttermans while he was in Innsbruck on 29 October and 24 December 1656, ASF, Mediceo del Principato 1479, fols. 1687, 1733, published by CRINÒ 1955, pp. 226–228.

[32] See VENTURI 1882, pp. 267–268.

[33] *Francesco Maria de' Medici*, Florence, Gallerie fiorentine, inv. 1890, no. 2852, oil on canvas, cm 72.5 × 54; BALDINUCCI 1681–1728, ed. 1845–1847, IV, 1846, p. 508.

[34] Filippo BALDINUCCI claims that the painter died on 23 April 1681 (see BALDINUCCI 1681–1728, ed. 1845–1847, IV, 1846, p. 510). The same death date appears at the beginning of the post mortem inventory of Suttermans' possessions (ASF, Pupilli del Principato 2722, fols. 296r). The official death date registered both in the books of the magistrates della Grascia (Morti della Grascia 1669–1694, ASF, Ufficiali poi Magistrato della Grascia 196, unpaginated) and in the death register of Florentine guild of Medici e Speziali (Morti 1671–1690, ASF, Medici e speziali 260, fol. 150v) is the 24 April of the same year.

[35] *Galileo Galilei*, Florence, Galleria degli Uffizi, inv. 1890, no. 745, oil on canvas, cm 66 × 56, this portrait was painted during the summer of 1635 and was sent a few months later to Elia Diodati in France. Twenty years later, in 1656, it was sent back to Florence by Diodati as a gift to Ferdinando II de' Medici (see the catalogue entry by L. Goldenberg Stoppato, in *I Della Rovere* 2004, pp. 496–498, no. XVI.7).

[36] BALDINUCCI 1681–1728, ed. 1845–1847, IV, 1846, pp. 508–509.

[37] Quaderno della Guardaroba generale, 1674–1680, ASF, Guardaroba medicea 799, fols. 271v and 276v, cited by K. Langedijk, in BOREA 1977, p. 141, note 3; LANGEDIJK 1981–1987, II, 1983, pp. 829 (sub no. 39/24), 932 (sub no. 45/8), 1127 (sub no. 79/10a), 1310 (sub no. 92/13).

[38] BALDINUCCI n.d. [1678 ca.], BNCF, ms. II.II.110, fols. 350–352, cited by CHIARINI 1977a, p. 41, note 1.

[39] *Francesco Maria de' Medici*, Florence, Gallerie fiorentine, inv. 1890, no. 2852, oil on canvas, cm 72.5 × 54. The young sitter was identified in the 1910 catalogue of the Uffizi as "Giustz M." (PIERACCINI 1910, p. 252, no. 870). He was identified correctly by Carlo GAMBA (1927, p. 97) who noted that the sitter closely resembled Francesco Maria as he appears in the full-length portrait on exhibit (see cat. no. 20). The painting is in fact indicated as a portrait of Francesco Maria in the inventory of Palazzo Pitti compiled in 1761 (ASF, Guardaroba medicea appendice 94, fol. 616v). It probably is the portrait of Francesco Maria painted by Suttermans when the painter was almost eighty-two years old and mentioned by Filippo Baldinucci (see L. Goldenberg Stoppato, in TURNER 1996, p. 42). According to Baldinucci the grand dukes of Tuscany, impressed that Suttermans was still able to paint at this age, had him write his name, the date and his age on the painting: "l'anno 1678, essendo egli di presso agli ottantadue anni, fece, di volontà de' serenissimi, il bel ritratto del serenissimo principe Francesco di Toscana, con tanta bravura, che vollero quelle altezze, che a perpetua memoria egli vi scrivesse il suo nome, l'anno e l'età" (BALDINUCCI 1681–1728, ed. 1845–1845, IV, 1846, p. 508). A full-length replica of this portrait belongs to the Galleria Nazionale in Parma (inv. no. 1021).

[40] *Ferdinando II de' Medici with his parents Cosimo II and Maria Maddalena of Austria*, Florence, Gallerie fiorentine, inv. 1890, no. 2402, oil on canvas, cm 179 × 145. This painting is mentioned without an attribution by the Medici Guardaroba inventories from 1640 to 1680 (see the inventory compiled in 1640, ASF, Guardaroba medicea 571 and 572, fol. 5r; the inventory for the period 1640–1666, ASF, Guardaroba medicea 585, fols. 32s-d; for the period 1666–1680, ASF, Guardaroba medicea 741, fol. 141s). It was attributed to Suttermans for the first time by Pierre Bautier (1912b, p. 19, no. 1092). The attribution has been accepted (see for a full list of bibliography C. Caneva, in *I Volti del Potere* 2002, pp. 75–78, no. 20) in all the following studies with the exception of the dissertation by MAX GÖZ (1928, p. 16, no. 1092). It is in truth a 'pastiche' of single figures copied by an unknown Florentine painter from original portraits by Suttermans, possibly by a workshop hand. The figure of *Maria Maddalena* is copied from the portrait by Suttermans that belongs to the set hanging along the outer hall way of Uffizi (inv. 1890, no. 2246, see *Sustermans* 1983, p. 21, no. 1). The figure of *Cosimo II* is a version of the oval bust in the Corsini collection (see LANGEDIJK 1981–1987, I, 1981, p. 544, no. 28/33) and the figure of *Ferdinando II* is copied from the portrait in Sestri Levante (Galleria Rizzi, inv. no. 3762, see *Repertory Liguria* 1998, p. 227, no. 363).

[41] *Banquet of Hunters and Cooks*, Florence, Galleria Palatina, inv. 1912, no. 137, oil on canvas, cm 149 × 202. The painting was confiscated by Napoleon's commissaries and sent to Paris in 1799 (Nota di quadri spediti a Parigi, 1 July 1799, Archivio Storico delle Gallerie fiorentine, shelf no. XL, 1816, no. 48). All of the 19th-century catalogues of the Galleria Palatina attributed this painting to the Tuscan painter Giovanni Mannozzi da San Giovanni. It was reattributed to Giusto Suttermans by Odoardo Giglioli (1917, pp. 52–53). It is in fact listed as his work in the inventories of Palazzo Pitti from 1638 to 1688 (see the 1638 inventories, ASF, Guardaroba medicea 525, fol. 57r; ASF, Guardaroba medicea 535, fol. 81s and ASF, Guardaroba medicea 530, fol. 166s; the inventory compiled between 1663 and 1664, ASF, Guardaroba medicea 725, fol. 54r; and the inventory compiled in 1688, ASF, Guardaroba medicea 932, fol. 59). It was exhibited as a work of Suttermans at the exhibition organized in 1681 by the Accademici del Disegno, the members of the artists' guild of Florence (*Quadri alla festa di S. Luca* 1681, BNCF, ms. II.II.10, fol. 133v, cited by MELONI TRKULJA 1976, pp. 579, 585, note 6). It appears without an attribution in the 18th-century inventories of Palazzo Pitti, both in the one compiled between 1716 and 1723 (Biblioteca degli Uffizi, ms. 79, fol. 103) and in 1761 (ASF, Guardaroba medicea appendice 94, fol. 534r). See for further bibliography S. Casciu, in CHIARINI–PADOVANI 2003, II, pp. 412–413, no. 679).

[42] The set included five canvases painted for Cardinal Leopoldo de' Medici in the late 1650's and the early 1660's: portraits of the Grand Dukes *Cosimo II*, *Ferdinando II* and *Cosimo III de' Medici*, and the Grand Duchesses *Vittoria della Rovere* and *Marguerite Louise d'Orléans* (inv. 1890, no. 2411, inv. Poggio a Caiano, nos. 134, 132 and 131, inv. 1890, no. 2724). It also included a portrait of *Maria Maddalena of Austria* painted by Suttermans in the 1620's and loaned to Leopoldo by the Guardaroba (inv. Poggio a Caiano, no. 133). The portraits are listed together in the cardinal's audience room on the second floor of Palazzo Pitti by the inventory of his collection compiled after his death in 1675 (ASF, Guardaroba medicea 826, fols. 80r-v). They were already in this room when Diacinto Maria Marmi wrote his *Norma per il Guardarobba di Palazzo Pitti* (n.d. [1662–1667], BNCF, ms. II, I. 284, fol. 195, quoted by BAROCCHI–GAETA BERTELÀ 2005, pp. 123–124). Like the rest of Leopoldo's possessions, these painting were left to his nephew Cosimo III. They were registered in the books of Cosimo's Guardaroba on 27 February 1677 modern style (see Quaderno della Guardaroba generale, 1674–1680, ASF, Guardaroba medicea 799, fol. 196r–197r) and entrusted to the keeper of Palazzo Pitti on 30 August 1680, (see Quaderno della Guardaroba generale, 1679–1685, ASF, Guardaroba medicea 870, fols. 66v–67v). These portraits were subsequently transferred to the first floor of the palace, where they are listed by the inventories compiled in 1688 (ASF, Guardaroba medicea 932, fol. 53v), between 1716 and 1723 (Florence, Biblioteca degli Uffizi, ms. 79, fols. 6–7) and in 1761 (ASF, Guardaroba medicea appendice 94, fol. 484v). In 1866 the portraits of *Maria Maddalena*, *Ferdinando II*, *Vittoria della Rovere*, and *Cosimo III*, were sent to the Medici Villa di Poggio a Caiano along with other full-length portraits by Suttermans (see S. Padovani, in *Gli Appartamenti Reali* 1993, pp. 216–217, no. I, 1–4; pp. 237–240, nos. IV, 1–10). They were brought back to Florence in 1911 for the exhibition on portraiture organized in Palazzo Vecchio (see *Mostra del Ritratto* 1911, pp. 224–226, nos. 19–32) and after the exhibition closed, they were returned to Palazzo Pitti, where they were divided between the Royal Apartments and the Museo degli Argenti. While other portraits by Suttermans from this set still hang in the 'Salotto Celeste' of the Royal Apartments, three of the portraits commissioned by Leopoldo de' Medici and the portrait of *Maria Maddalena of Austria* have recently been sent back to the Villa di Poggio a Caiano.

[43] *Christine of Lorraine (1565–1636), widow of Ferdinando I de' Medici* (Palazzo Pitti, Appartamenti reali, inv. Poggio a Caiano, no. 146, oil on canvas, cm 210 × 117). This portrait can be dated for stylistic reasons to the early 1620's. It is mentioned for the first time on 15 April 1638 when it was sent from the Guardaroba generale to Palazzo Pitti (see Debitori e Creditori [di oggetti] della Guardaroba generale 1637–1640, 13 April 1638, ASF, Guardaroba medicea 515, fol. 49s; Giornale della Guardaroba di Palazzo Pitti, 1637–1662, 15 April 1638, ASF, Guardaroba medicea 494, fol. 7d; Entrata e Uscita di Palazzo Pitti, 1638–1648, ASF, Guardaroba medicea 530, fol. 287s). It is listed in all the following inventories of the palace (Inventario di Palazzo Pitti, 1663–1664, ASF, Guardaroba medicea 725, fol. 104r; Inventario di Palazzo Pitti, 1688, ASF, Guardaroba medicea 932, fol. 50v; Inventario di Palazzo Pitti 1716–1723, Biblioteca degli Uffizi, ms. 79, fols. 2–3; Inventario di Palazzo Pitti, 1761, ASF, Guardaroba medicea appendice 94, fol. 484r). In 1866 it was sent with other Medici portraits of similar format to the Medici Villa di Poggio a Caiano (for information about the set see S. Padovani, in *Gli Appartamenti Reali* 1993, pp. 237–238, no. IV.1, fig. 1; S. Casciu, in CHIARINI–PADOVANI 2003, II, pp. 434–435, no. 717).

[44] It is not easy to identify these paintings since the Florentine museums own two full-length portraits both of *Claudia de' Medici* (1604–1648), and of her second husband *Leopold von Habsburg* (1586–1632). In the first portrait of Claudia, of better quality than the other one, she is wearing a pink dress (inv. 1890, no. 2267, oil on canvas, cm 204 × 116). Both the ruff she is wearing and the style of painting suggest a date in the early 1620's, presumably around the date of her marriage to Federigo Ubaldo della Rovere, which was celebrated on the 29 April 1621. The second portrait, painted with the help of Suttermans' workshop, shows Claudia in a black dress with a lace edged, raised collar that dates from the second half of the same decade (Palazzo Pitti, Appartamenti reali, inv. Poggio a Caiano, no. 142, oil on canvas, cm 201 × 117). It probably was painted in 1626 when Claudia married for the second time. The same can be said for the excellent quality, knee-length portrait of Claudia in black (Florence, Palazzo Pitti, Appartamenti reali, inv. 1890, no. 752, oil on canvas, cm 113 × 86). The first full-length portrait of *Archduke Leopold von Habsburg*, Claudia's second husband, is of rather good quality (Palazzo Pitti, Appartamenti reali, inv. Poggio a Caiano, no. 145, oil on canvas, cm 207 × 119). The second one is a workshop copy (inv. 1890, no. 2264, oil on canvas, cm 206 × 112). One of them is probably the portrait of Archduke Leopold that was sent to Florence by Suttermans in 1624 with a set of Habsburg portraits (see cat. no. 5). The first 17th-century inventories of Palazzo Pitti mention full-length portraits of Claudia de' Medici and Leopold von Habsburg in the summer apartment of Grand Duchess Vittoria della Rovere on the ground floor of the palace (see Inventario di Palazzo Pitti, 1638, ASF, Guardaroba medicea 525, fol. 3r; Inventario di Palazzo Pitti, 1638, ASF, Guardaroba medicea 725, fol. 2v). These portraits probably can be identified with the full-length portraits of a "Principessa della Serenissima Casa" and of the "Arciduca d'Austria", which the late 17th-century and 18th-century

inventories list with other full-length Medici portraits in the first room on the left in the apartment of Grand Prince Ferdinando (see Inventario di Palazzo Pitti, 1688, ASF, Guardaroba medicea 932, fol. 50v; Inventario di Palazzo Pitti, 1716–1723, Biblioteca degli Uffizi, ms. 79, fol. 2; Inventario di Palazzo Pitti, 1761, ASF, Guardaroba medicea appendice 94, fol. 484v). In 1866 these portraits of Claudia and Leopold were sent, along with the rest of the series of full-length portraits to the Medici Villa di Poggio a Caiano (see S. Padovani, in *Gli Appartamenti Reali* 1993, pp. 237–240; the portraits of Claudia and Leopold are reproduced by S. Casciu, in CHIARINI–PADOVANI 2003, vol. II, pp. 434–435, nos. 715–716). Two other full-length portraits of the Archdukes Claudia and Leopold belonged to Cardinal Carlo de' Medici. They are described in the inventory of Cardinal Carlo's collection (see ASF, Guardaroba medicea 758, fol. 16v) and after his death when they entered the grand ducal collection (see ASF, Guardaroba medicea 741, fol. 378s).

[45] *Cardinal Armand-Jean Du Plessis de Richelieu (1585–1642, cardinal from 1622)* or his brother *Cardinal Alphonse-Louis (1582–1653, cardinal from 1629)*, oil on canvas, braccia 1 ½ × 1 ⅓ =cm 87 × 77 circa. According to a book of debtors and creditors for objects belonging to the Medici Guardaroba generale, this lost portrait was sent from the Guardaroba to Palazzo Pitti on 9 April 1639 (see ASF, Guardaroba medicea 515, fol. 97s): "Un quadro in tela con adornamento tutto dorato alto braccia 1 ½ e largo braccia 1 ⅓, dentrovi dipinto il Cardinale di Roccelli di mano di Giusto Surtmano --n.° 1". The same painting is mentioned in a list of daily expenses of Grand Duke Ferdinando II de' Medici for the month of April 1639: "Al signor Cavaliere Gondi per il ritratto del Cardinale di Ricelliu scudi 11 lire 3" (see Spese della Camera del Granduca, 1638–1639, ASF, Camera del Granduca 20b, fol. 36v). This portrait of "Cardinale Ruscellui" is listed without an attribution in the inventory of Palazzo Pitti compiled between 1663 and 1664 (ASF, Guardaroba medicea 725, fol. 59r). Thanks to Cesare Tinghi's court diary we know that Richelieu, "segretario di Stato del Re di Francia", visited the Medici court in June 1633 (TINGHI 1623–1644, ASF, Miscellanea medicea 11, fol. 294). Suttermans would have had the chance to portray him at that time.

[46] *Pope Gregory XV* (Alessandro Ludovisi, Bologna 1554–Rome 1623, pope from 1621), oil on canvas, braccia 1 ½ × 1 ⅓ =cm 87 × 77 circa. The lost portrait is listed without an attribution in the inventory of Palazzo Pitti compiled in 1638 (ASF, Guardaroba medicea 525, fol. 38r) and as a work of "M. Giusto" in the following inventory that was compiled between 1663 and 1664 (ASF, Guardaroba medicea 725, fol. 58v). It might well be the portrait of the same pope mentioned in the 1625 inventory of the Archduchess of Austria and Grand Duchess of Tuscany Maria Maddalena von Habsburg: "Un quadro in tela d'altezza un braccio dipintovi Papa Gregorio XV [. . .]" (Inventario di Maria Maddalena of Austria, 1625, ASF, Guardaroba medicea 423, fol. 61s).

[47] *Fabrizio Colloredo (1576–1645)*, oil on canvas, oval, braccia 1 ½ × 1 ⅓ = cm 87 × 77 circa. This lost portrait is mentioned without the name of the painter in the inventory of Palazzo Pitti compiled between 1663 and 1664 (ASF, Guardaroba medicea 725, fol. 55v): "Un Quadro in tela entrovi dipinto il ritratto del Generale Colloreto, vestito di nero, in mezzo aovato senza adornamento alto braccia 1 ½ e largo 1 ⅓ in circa n.°1". Fabrizio Colloredo was a trusted courtier of Grand Dukes Ferdinando I, Cosimo II and Ferdinando II de' Medici. He carried out several diplomatic missions for the Medici and was one of the three council members named to oversee the regency for young Grand Duke Ferdinando II. He governed Siena for the Medici from 1622 to 1627 and was later named chief Major-domo of the Medici court (see M. R. Pardi Malanima, in *Dizionario Biografico degli Italiani* 1960– [. . .], vol. 27, 1982, pp. 78–80). He was portrayed in the fresco *The Commanders of the Knights of Saint Stephen received by Grand Duke Cosimo II after the capture of Bona*, painted by Baldassare Franceschini, known as Volterrano, in the courtyard of the Medici Villa della Petraia (see WINNER 1963, pp. 244–245, 246, fig. 26).

[48] *Créqui's Dwarf*, oil on canvas, braccia 2 ⅛ × 1 ⅔=cm 124 × 77 circa. The portrait of this dwarf, the "Nano del Duca di Crichi", is listed without an attribution in the 1638 inventory of Palazzo Pitti (ASF, Guardaroba medicea 525, fol. 38v) and in the inventory of the palace compiled between 1663 and 1664 (ASF, Guardaroba medicea 725, fol. 54v). According to Irving Lavin, who published a marble bust of the same dwarf sculpted by François Duquesnoy (Rome, Prince Urbano Barberini collection), he came to Italy in the retinue of Charles, Sieur de Créqui and Duc de Lesdiguières, the ambassador sent by King Louis XIII of France to Rome in June 1633 (see LAVIN 1970, pp. 132–134, figs. 1, 2, 3). The so-called dwarf (he was actually a midget) was used by the Duke of Créqui to present messages and gifts and evidently aroused the interest of the Grand Dukes of Tuscany. Suttermans would have had a chance to portray him during Créqui's visit to Florence in 1634. According to Cesare Tinghi the duke visited Florence and was hosted by Ferdinando II in Palazzo Pitti from 15th to 26th July 1634 (see TINGHI 1623–1644, ASF, Miscellanea medicea 11, fol. 310v).

[49] *Maria Maddalena of Austria as Saint Mary Magdalene*, Florence, Palazzo Pitti, Galleria Palatina, inv. 1890, no. 563, oil on canvas, cm 168 × 90. See LANGEDIJK 1981–1987, I, 1981, p. 184, II, 1983, pp. 1288 (no. 90/28), 1289 (fig. 90/28), 1511 (no. 110/79); C. Pizzorusso, in *La Maddalena tra sacro e profano* 1986, pp. 235–236, no. 99; S. Casciu, in CHIARINI–PADOVANI 2003, II, p. 421, no. 694. This painting is cited in the inventories of Palazzo Pitti compiled or begun in 1638 (ASF, Guardaroba medicea 525, fol. 40v; Guardaroba medicea 535, fol. 54s; Guardaroba medicea 530, fol. 136s), between 1663 and 1664 (ASF, Guardaroba medicea 725, fol. 59r), between 1716 and 1723 (Florence, Biblioteca degli Uffizi, ms. 79, fol. 90) and in 1761 (ASF, Guardaroba medicea appendice 94, fol. 531v).

[50] *Margherita de' Medici as Saint Margaret*, Florence, Palazzo Pitti, deposit, inv. 1890, no. 4357, oil on canvas, cm 187 × 115. See LANGEDIJK 1981–1987, I, 1981, p. 193, II, 1983, pp. 1224–1225, no. 83/9, fig. 83/9; L. Goldenberg Stoppato, in *Il Seicento fiorentino* 1986, p. 321, sub no. 1.165. This portrait of Margherita was painted before 31 May 1630 when a copy by Giovanni Lionardo Henner (later sent to Spain) was delivered to the Medici Guardaroba (see Inventario della Guardaroba generale, 1624–1638, ASF, Guardaroba medicea 435, fol. 269s).

[51] *The Pledge of Allegiance of the Florentine Senate to Ferdinando II de' Medici*, Florence, Galleria degli Uffizi, inv. 1890, no. 721, oil on canvas, cm 397 × 626 (see L. Goldenberg Stoppato, in CANEVA–VERVAT 2002, pp. 11–27). Filippo Baldinucci mentions that this painting was moved to the hall on the second floor which was used as audience room by Cardinal Leopoldo de' Medici" (BALDINUCCI 1681–1728, ed. 1845–1847, IV, 1846, p. 481).

[52] Ten of the missing portraits were still in Palazzo Pitti in 1761 when a new inventory of the furnishings was compiled (see Inventario di Palazzo Pitti, 1761, ASF, Guardaroba medicea appendice 94). For information about the changes made in the palace during Pietro Leopoldo's reign see CHIARINI 1977b, pp. 215–216; PINTO 1977, p. 220.

[53] Letter from Domenico Montaguto, Medici court secretary, to Vincenzo Giugni, chief keeper of the Guardaroba, Palazzo Pitti, 4 October 1621, in *Affari diversi della Guardaroba*, ASF, Guardaroba medicea 391, insert 3, fol. 285.

[54] There are two payment orders, both for 55 scudi, for the portraits of princesses Margherita and Anna de' Medici in a volume of documentation of the Depositeria generale, the grand ducal treasury department. They bear the date 10 September 1622 (see *Recapiti della Depositeria*, 1621–1622, ASF, Depositeria Generale, Parte Antica 1010, unpaginated, no. 328). On the 15 of the same month secretary Montaguto sent back to keeper Bernardo Migliorati the fabric used as a model for the princesses' dresses in the portraits: "Remandoli il drappo scarnatino con fiori d'oro et argento servito per dipingere li vesti d'eccellentissime signore principesse" (see ASF, Guardaroba medicea 391, insert 9, fol. 846).

[55] See Inventario della Guardaroba generale, 1624–1638, ASF, Guardaroba medicea 435, fols. 170s-d, quoted by LANGEDIJK 1981–1987, II, 1983, p. 779, no. 38/31a), who thought that the archduchess mentioned in the document was Claudia de' Medici, the wife of Archduke Leopold von Habsburg.

[56] See Inventario di Palazzo Pitti, 1638, ASF, Guardaroba medicea 525, fol. 62v; Inventario della Guardaroba di Palazzo Pitti, 1638, ASF, Guardaroba medicea 535, fol. 90s; Entrata e Uscita di Palazzo Pitti, 1638–1648, ASF, Guardaroba medicea 530, fol. 166s. These inventories mention the portraits of Cosimo's sons in a room of Leopoldo de' Medici's apartment on the second floor.

[57] Inventario di Palazzo Pitti, 1663–1664, ASF, Guardaroba medicea 725, fol. 41r. This inventory cites the portraits on the first floor in Cardinal Carlo de' Medici's apartment, in a room on the left with two large windows overlooking the square. The portraits of *Ferdinando II*, *Mattias* and *Francesco de' Medici* from this set are listed by the 1688 inventory of Palazzo Pitti once again on the first floor, in the first room on the left, with windows over looking the square, a room used at the time as antechamber to the apartment of Grand Prince Ferdinando. In the same room there were also full-length portraits of their grandmother *Christine of Lorraine*, their aunt and uncle *Claudia de' Medici* and *Leopold von Habsburg*, their brother *Giovan Carlo de' Medici* and their sister *Margherita de' Medici* which were sent to the Medici Villa di Poggio a Caiano in 1866 and now hang in the royal apartments of Palazzo Pitti (inv. Poggio a Caiano, nos. 146, 142, 145, 143 and 139): "Otto quadri in tela alti braccia 3 soldi 8, larghi braccia 2 per ciascheduno, in uno dipintovi Madama di Lorena, in uno il Gran Duca Ferdinando Secondo, in uno una Principessa della Serenissima Casa, in uno l'Arciduca d'Austria, in uno il Principe Giovan Carlo, in uno il Principe Mattia in abito di prete, in uno una Principessa della Serenissima Casa, e nell'altro il Principe Giovan Francesco che morì in Germania; con adornamenti intagliati e tutti dorati n. 8" (Inventario di Palazzo Pitti, 1688, ASF, Guardaroba medicea 932, fol. 50v).

[58] Titian, *Venus of Urbino*, Florence, Galleria degli Uffizi, inv. 1890, no. 1437, see *Gli Uffizi* 1979, ed. 1980, p. 549, no. P1725.

[59] See note 35.

[60] Florence, Gabinetto Disegni e Stampe degli Uffizi, inv. no.14341F, black chalk on white paper, mm 184 × 131, see L. Goldenberg Stoppato in *Sustermans* 1983, p. 85, no. 55.

[61] Florence, Gabinetto Disegni e Stampe degli Uffizi, inv. no. 681Pv, black chalk, pen with sepia ink and bistre on white paper, mm 240 × 166, see L. Goldenberg Stoppato, in *Sustermans* 1983, p. 84, no. 54.

[62] Titian, *Portrait of Pietro Aretino*, Florence, Palazzo Pitti, Galleria Palatina, inv. 1912, no. 54, see S. Casciu, in CHIARINI–PADOVANI 2003, II, pp. 452–453, no. 745).

[63] *Vestal Tuccia*, Florence, Palazzo Pitti, Galleria Palatina, inv. 1912, no. 116, oil on canvas, cm 101 × 80, see the catalogue entry by C. Pizzorusso, in *Sustermans* 1983, p. 42, no. 21; S. Casciu, in CHIARINI–PADOVANI 2003, I, p. 270, pl. 211, II, p. 411, no. 677. This canvas is mentioned in the 1688 Palazzo Pitti inventory on the first floor, in the seventh room with a window overlooking the square (see Inventario di Palazzo Pitti, 1688, ASF, Guardaroba medicea 932, fol. 68r).

[64] ASF, Mediceo del Principato 5392, fol. 252, called to my attention by Silvia Mascalchi.

[65] Valdemar Kristian of Denmark arrived in Florence in June 1638 and stayed in the city for the whole summer. He was hosted in the house on Via della Scala, the residence of Prince Giovan Carlo de' Medici (see TINGHI 1623–1644, ASF, Miscellanea medicea 11, fol. 361v).

[66] Inventario della Guardaroba generale 1640, ASF, Guardaroba medicea 572, fol. 6v.

[67] Pieter Paul Rubens, *The Consequences of War*, Florence, Palazzo Pitti, inv. 1912, no. 86, oil on canvas, cm 206 × 345, see BODART 1977, pp. 226–230.

[68] Letter from Margherita de' Medici, duchess of Parma, to Ferdinando II de' Medici, grand duke of Tuscany, Piacenza, 24 May 1640, ASF, Mediceo del Principato 2870, unpaginated, called to the attention of S. Meloni Trkulja (see *I principi bambini* 1985, p. 52) by the present author.

[69] Letter of Ferdinando II de' Medici, grand duke of Tuscany, to Margherita de' Medici, duchess di Parma, 16 June 1640, ASF, Mediceo del Principato 144, fol. 173, called to the attention of S. Meloni Trkulja (see *I principi bambini* 1985, p. 52) by the present author.

[70] *Ranuccio Farnese (1630–1694)*, Florence, Palazzo Pitti, deposit, inv. 1890, no. 2200, oil on canvas, cm 78 × 62; *Maria Maddalena Farnese (1633–1714)*, Florence, Palazzo Pitti, deposit, inv. 1890, no. 2208, oil on canvas, cm 78 × 61; *Alessandro Farnese (1635–1689)*, Florence, Galleria Palatina, inv. 1890, no. 2203, oil on canvas, cm 79 × 64. See S. Meloni Trkulja, in *I principi bambini* 1985, p. 52; L. Goldenberg Stoppato, in *Il Seicento fiorentino* 1986, *Biografie*, p. 168; L. Goldenberg Stoppato, in TURNER 1996, p. 41; S. Casciu, in CHIARINI–PADOVANI 2003, II, pp. 424–425, no. 701.

[71] Inventario della Villa del Poggio Imperiale (property of Vittoria della Rovere), 1692, ASF, Guardaroba 995, fol. 153d, nos. 655, 657, fol. 157d, no. 665. After describing the portraits which were hanging in the small room next to the chapel in the grand duchess' apartment, the inventory specifies that the paintings in frames decorated with chains were princes of the Farnese family: "i suddetti quadri con adornamenti a catena, la maggior parte dicano esser principi di Casa Farnese".

[72] Siena, Palazzo della Provincia: *Orazio Farnese (1636–1656)*, oil on canvas, cm 78 × 65; *Maria Caterina Farnese (1637–1648)*, oil on canvas, cm 77 × 66; and *Pietro Farnese (1639–1677)*, oil on canvas, cm 78 × 65.5. These portraits were published without an attribution by M. Ciampolini (in *Il Palazzo della Provincia a Siena* 1990, pp. 192, 208, notes 19, 20, figs. 5.4, 5.5, 5.6), who identifies the sitters as Cosimo III's three children, Ferdinando, Anna Maria Luisa and Gian Gastone. As Ciampolini pointed out these paintings came to the Sienese palace on the 10 March 1800 (see the appendix to the Inventario del Palazzo di Siena, 1798, ASF, Imperiale e Reale Corte 5028, fol. 288).

[73] See Inventario di Carlo de' Medici, 1667, ASF, Guardaroba medicea 758, fols. 8r (no. 153) and 26v (no. 461).

[74] After Carlo de' Medici's death the two portraits were registered in the books of the grand ducal Guardaroba on 30 June 1667, along with the rest of the cardinal's collection (see both the Quaderno della Guardaroba generale, 1666–1674, ASF, Guardaroba medicea 750, fols. 62v and 74r and the Inventario della Guardaroba generale, 1666–1680, ASF, Guardaroba medicea 741, fols. 374s and 384s).

[75] *Camillo Pamphili (1622–1666) as cardinal*, Florence, Palazzo Pitti, Appartamenti reali, inv. Poggio a Caiano, no. 135, oil on canvas, cm 205 × 122. See *Mostra del Ritratto* 1911, p. 226, no. 31; BAUTIER 1912a, p. 10; BAUTIER 1912b, pp. 64, 113, 128, pl. XX; ZIMMERMANN 1912, p. 61; BAUTIER 1926–1929, p. 322; GAMBA 1927, pp. 97–98, pl. XVIII; GÖZ 1928, p. 42; SINGER 1937–1938, IV, 1938, p. 6, no. 27177; HEINZ 1963, p. 158; LEVI PISETZKY 1966, pl. 217; BODART 1970, I, p. 191; L. Goldenberg Stoppato, in *Sustermans* 1983, pp. 68, 72, sub no. 42; S. Meloni Trkulja in *Sustermans* 1983, p. 110, no. LVI; L. Goldenberg Stoppato, in *Il Seicento fiorentino* 1986, *Disegno*, p. 300, sub no. 2.263, *Biografie*, p. 168; L. Goldenberg Stoppato, in *La pittura in Italia. Il Seicento* 1988, ed. 1989, II, p. 895; S. Padovani, in *Gli Appartamenti Reali* 1993, p. 240, no. IV, 10; CAPITELLI 1996, pp. 57 (fig.), 69, note 71; L. Goldenberg Stoppato, in TURNER 1996, vol. 30, p. 41; G. Capitelli, in *Le virtù e i piaceri in Villa* 1998, pp. 99, 256–257, no. D3; CHIARINI–PADOVANI 1999, p. 163; L. Goldenberg Stoppato, in *Fiamminghi e Olandesi* 2002, p. 101, no. 51; S. Casciu, in CHIARINI–PADOVANI 2003, II, p. 429, no. 709.

[76] According to a journal of the Medici Guardaroba (Quaderno della Guardaroba generale, 1685–1696, ASF, Guardaroba medicea 904, fol. 207r), on 26 August 1689 the portrait of *Camillo Pamphili* was sent to the chambers of Grand Prince Ferdinando in Palazzo Pitti along with the full-length portraits of *Cardinal Carlo*, *Mattias* and *Francesco de' Medici* (Florence, Palazzo Pitti, Appartamenti Reali, inv. Poggio a Caiano, nos. 141, 144 and 137, reproduced by S. Padovani, in *Gli Appartamenti Reali* 1993, pp. 239–239, nos. IV.7,8–IV.9; S. Casciu, in CHIARINI–PADOVANI 2003, vol. II, pp. 433, no. 714, 430–431, no. 711a-b). The Pamphili portrait is listed in the inventory of the palace compiled between 1716 and 1723 (Florence, Biblioteca degli Uffizi, ms. 79, fol. 3).

[77] For information about the so-called Poggio a Caiano set by Suttermans, see note 96.

[78] *Innocent X*, Florence, Galleria degli Uffizi, deposit, inv. 1890, no. 2648, oil on canvas, cm 195.5 × 120, photo. Soprintendenza 136554. The curator's files list the following locations: Galleria degli Uffizi, Hallway, Passage G.; Hallway Pitti 10/09/1949; Palazzo Pitti, Magazzino Occhi, 18/09/1972; Uffizi, ex Archivio di Stato deposit 8/11/1990. On the back of the canvas, which is original, there are the following numbers: 6607, 686, 3363, 76 (in red), 762, 6, 36, 96 (crossed out), 631. On the 19th-century stretcher there are the following numbers: 132, 194/121.

[79] This portrait is listed without an attribution in the catalogue of the Uffizi published in 1910 (see PIERACCINI 1910, p. 246, no. 162).

[80] See L. Goldenberg Stoppato, in *Fiamminghi e Olandesi* 2002, p. 101, sub no. 5.

[81] Inventario di Carlo de' Medici, 1667, ASF, Guardaroba medicea 758, fol. 8r, no. 153.

[82] Letter from Belisario Guerrini to Cardinal Carlo de' Medici, Rome, 23 April 1645, ASF, Mediceo del Principato 5275, fol. 407, called to my attention by Elena Fumagalli and quoted by L. Goldenberg Stoppato, in *Fiamminghi e Olandesi* 2002, p. 101, sub no. 5. It was also published by Giovanni Capitelli (in *Le virtù e i piaceri in Villa* 1998, p. 103, note 22, and p. 256), who thought that the portraits mentioned in the letters might have been drawings to be used by Suttermans to paint the portraits of *Innocent X* and *Camillo Pamphili* in Florence for Carlo. Since Suttermans rarely used drawings in his work, the letter more plausibly refers to canvases painted for Carlo. The other portrait still to be made which Guerrini mentions was probably a replica of one of them. We know, for example, that in 1645 a portrait of the pope by Giusto, "un ritratto del Papa di mano di Giusto", was requested for Monsignor Ottoboni and that the request was repeated in April of the following year (see the letter from Gabriello Riccardi, Medici ambassador in Rome, to Giovanni Battista Gondi, Medici court secretary, 21 April 1646, ASF, Mediceo del Principato 3374, unpaginated).

[83] The painting was probably restored towards the end of the 19th century when it was hung on the hallway which connects the Uffizi to Palazzo Pitti. At the same time the original canvas was restretched over a new stretcher. The frame seems to date from the same period.

[84] Letter from Fabrizio Permattei to Cardinal Giovan Carlo de' Medici, Rome, 25 June 1645, ASF, Mediceo del Principato, 5309, fol. 164r, called to my attention by Silvia Mascalchi. It probably can be identified with a portrait which is mentioned in 1652, along with a portrait of Camillo Pamphili by Suttermans, in an inventory of Camillo's possessions: "ritratto di Nostro Signore Innocentio X che sta sedendo, con un memoriale in mano, alto palmi cinque e largo palmi 4, mano di Giusto fiammengo" (see the "Nota di guardarobba" of prince Camillo Pamphili, 1652, transcribed by CAPITELLI 1996, pp. 71, 72). Pierre Bautier (1912B, p. 63) mentions a portrait of *Innocent X* attributed to Suttermans (oil on canvas, cm 44 × 34), in 1885 in the sales catalogue of a Roman collection (Palazzo Accoramboni, piazza Rusticucci, 18).

[85] Guido Reni, *Cardinal Roberto Ubaldini*, Los Angeles, County Museum, inv. no. M83.109, see *Baroque Portraiture* 1984–1985, pp. 144–145, no. 51.

[86] Copy of a note sent by Desiderio Montemagni, Medici court secretary, to Marquis Vincenzo Salviati, 3 October 1649, in Rescritti e mandati della Segreteria, 1645–1650, ASF, Mediceo del Principato 1840, fols. 70–72, quoted by KIRKENDALE 1993, pp. 39–40.

[87] *Prezzi Accordati con il signor Giusto Suttermano pittore per i Lavori che occorreranno farsi*, 27 August 1654, ASF, Guardaroba medicea 669bis, fol. 727.

[88] See note 29.

[89] Letter from Margherita de' Medici to Leopoldo de' Medici, 16 September

1656, ASF, Mediceo del Principato 5503, fol. 276, published by PIERACCINI 1924–1925, II, 1925, pp. 530, 542, notes 4, 26. The portrait could also have been painted during Margherita's visit to Florence in 1655, see PIERACCINI 1924–1925, II, 1925, pp. 535, 543, note 44.

[90] Diego Velázquez, *Francesco I d'Este*, Modena, Galleria Estense, inv. no. 472, oil on canvas, cm 108 × 89.5, painted in 1638, see S. Salort Pons, in *Velázquez* 2001, pp. 204–205.

[91] In a letter written on 12 November 1649 in Modena, Tommaso Guidoni informed Medici secretary Giovanni Battista Gondi they were expecting three painters at court the following day "Guercino, Colonna e Giusto. Si discorrerà di molto della pittura et della caccia, et così ce l'andremo passando." (see ASF, Mediceo del Principato 1484, fol. 975, published by CRINÒ 1955, p. 222).

[92] Pier Francesco Cittadini, who collaborated with Jean Boulanger for the Este palace frescoes starting in 1650, painted the flowers in Suttermans' portrait of *Isabella d'Este as Flora* now in the collection of the Cassa di Risparmio di Prato (see L. Goldenberg Stoppato, in PAOLUCCI–LAPI BALLERINI 2004, pp. 93–96, no. 30.

[93] *Vittoria della Rovere (1622–1694)*, Poggio a Caiano (Florence), Medici villa, inv. Poggio a Caiano, no. 131, oil on canvas, cm 205 × 145. BALDINUCCI 1681–1728, ed. 1845–1847, IV, 1846, p. 504; WURZBACH 1906–1910, II, 1910, p. 676; *Mostra del Ritratto* 1911, p. 224, no. 22; BAUTIER 1912b, pp. 27, 113, 128, pl. VII; BAUTIER 1912d, p. 6; BAUTIER 1912e, p. 155; HOOGEWERFF 1915, pp. 9, 11, pl. 7; FRIZZONI 1919, p. 7; PIERACCINI 1924–1925, II, 1925, pl. LXXX; fig. LXXXVI; BAUTIER 1926–1929, p. 317; GAMBA 1927, p. 92, pl. XIV; GÖZ 1928, pp. 23, 24, 35; HENDY 1931, p. 349; SINGER 1937–1938, V, 1938, p. 57, no. 37204; J. Lavalleye, in THIEME–BECKER 1907–1950, XXXII, 1938, p. 324; *Mostra Medicea* 1939, p. 57, no. 16; BAUTIER 1940, no. 1, p. 36, fig. II; GAMULIN 1961, p. 26; GAMULIN 1964, p. 106; ROSSI NISSIM 1968, p. 128, fig.; LANGEDIJK 1981–1987, II, 1983, pp. 1484–1485, no. 110/22; S. Meloni Trkulja, in *Suttermans* 1983, p. 106, no. XLV; DAMIAN 1990, p. 129, sub no. 74; M. Chiarini, in *Gli Appartamenti Reali* 1993, p. 152, fig. 3; S. Padovani, in *Gli Appartamenti Reali* 1993, pp. 216–217, no. I, 2; L. Goldenberg Stoppato, in TURNER 1996, p. 42; M. Chiarini, in CHIARINI–PADOVANI 2003, I, p. 19, fig. 5. There is a half-length version of this portrait, which was originally octagonal, in Chambéry (Musée des Beaux-Arts, inv. no. M980, oil on canvas, cm 81 × 65, reproduced by DAMIAN 1990, p. 129, no. 74).

[94] According to the 1688 inventory of Palazzo Pitti it was exhibited with six other full length Medici portraits (see ASF, Guardaroba medicea 932, fol. 53v). For the series see note 42.

[95] The portrait of *Vittoria della Rovere* is mentioned in the first inventory of Leopoldo de' Medici's collection (Inventario di Leopoldo de' Medici, n.d. [1663–1671?], Florence, Biblioteca Riccardiana, ms. Riccardi 2443, fols. 119–120) and is described in great detail in the one compiled in 1675, after he died (ASF, Guardaroba medicea 826, fol. 80v, no. 419). A journal of the Guardaroba generale documents the painting's entrance in the grand ducal collections on the 27 February 1677 modern style (Quaderno della Guardaroba generale 1674–1680, ASF, Guardaroba medicea 799, fol. 196v, no. 419). Another journal mentions that it was entrusted to the keeper of Palazzo Pitti on 30 August 1680 (Quaderno della Guardaroba generale 1679–1685, ASF, Guardaroba medicea 870, fol. 67r). The portrait is listed not only in the 1688 inventory, but also in the one compiled between 1716 and 1723 (Inventario di Palazzo Pitti, 1716–1723, Florence, Biblioteca degli Uffizi, ms. 79, fol. 6).

[96] The bill mentions twenty-five scudi owed to Suttermans for a full-length portrait of the grand duchess painted from life: "A dì 3 di settembre 1636, la Serenissima Granduchessa deve dare a me Giusto Suttermano scudi ventecinque quali sono per la valuta di un ritratto intero in tela halta tutta sua haltezza, ritratto al naturale della Serenissima sopradetta [. . .]" (see Conti di Vittoria della Rovere, 1632–1638, ASF, Guardaroba medicea 955, fol. 752, cited by LANGEDIJK 1981–1987, II, 1983, pp. 1484–1485, no. 110/22).

[97] Letter from Leopoldo de' Medici to Mattias de' Medici, Poggio a Caiano, 8 May 1655, ASF, Mediceo del Principato 5393, fol. 587, cited by PIERACCINI 1924–1925, II, 1925, p. 502, note 67.

[98] Bill from Giusto Suttermans, ASF, Guardaroba medicea 768, fol. 518

[99] See Quaderno della Guardaroba Generale 1666–1674, I, ASF, Guardaroba medicea 750, fol. 198r; Inventario della Guardaroba generale 1666–1680, ASF, Guardaroba medicea 741, fols. 472s.

[100] See Quaderno della Guardaroba generale 1674–1680, ASF, Guardaroba medicea 799, fol. 276v, which is transcribed in the essay.

[101] A letter from Cosimo III de' Medici to Pio Enea degli Obizzi written on 29 May 1668 mentions the painter's severe eye ailment, "grave pregiudizio nelli occhi" (see ASF, Mediceo del Principato 3939, unpaginated, called to my attention by Silvia Papucci).

[102] *Francesco Maria de' Medici*, Parma, Galleria Nazionale, inv. no. 1021, oil on canvas, cm 191 × 131. See PIGORINI 1887, p. 51, no. 1021; RICCI 1896, p. 207, no. 1021; BAUTIER 1912b, pp. 84–85, 129, pl. XXVI; BAUTIER 1926–1929, p. 319; GAMBA 1927, pp. 89, 97; GÖZ 1928, pp. 40–41; J. Lavalleye in THIEME–BECKER 1907–1950, vol. XXXII, 1938, p. 324; QUINTAVALLE 1939, pp. 216–217; QUINTAVALLE 1948, p. 138, no. 261; LANGEDIJK 1981–1987, II, 1983, p. 936, no. 45/23; L. Goldenberg Stoppato, in *Il Seicento fiorentino* 1986, *Biografie*, p. 169; DE MAERE–WABBES 1994, I, p. 381; M. Pietrogiovanna, in LIMENTANI VIRDIS 1997, p. 297, fig. 27; M. Giusto, in FORNARI SCHIANCHI 1999, pp. 15–16, no. 447. The sitter was formerly identified as don Pedro Porto Carrero of the Latera branch of the Farnese family, who died quite old in 1662. The identification is not compatible with the cut of the clothing in the portrait, which dates it to the 1670's. The painting is in fact mentioned as a portrait of Francesco Maria in the inventory, compiled in 1693, of the possessions of his cousin Maria Maddalena Farnese, a daughter of Margherita de' Medici (see the transcription in BERTINI 1987, p. 279).

[103] See the letter from Andrea Salvetti, Medici ambassador to England, to Medici secretary Andrea Cioli, London, 12 February 1637 [ab Incarnatione=1638 modern style], see ASF, Mediceo del Principato 4199, unpaginated, published by CRINÒ 1961, p. 187.

[104] See the unpublished letter from Andrea Salvetti, Medici ambassador in England, to Medici secretary Andrea Cioli, from London, 15 July 1639, ASF, Mediceo del Principato 4200, unpaginated. Thanks to this letter we know that the portraits of *Ferdinando II* and *Vittoria della Rovere* sent to England in 1639 were half-length portraits and to Salvetti's great dismay, they were presented to the King by Henry Meilmey. Salvetti had requested a full-length portrait with both figures on the same canvas, "interi a capo a piè, et ambi due in un medesimo quadro", and insisted that the Medici should still send him the type of portrait that he had originally requested, so that he could present it to the king. He also requested another portrait for his own home. He repeated his request in vain in many other letters (see CRINÒ 1961, pp. 189–190), but as of the 28 February 1642 modern style, it had not been fulfilled (see the letter from Amerigo Salvetti to Medici secretary Giovan Battista Gondi, ASF, Mediceo del Principato 4201, unpaginated). Crinò suggested that the portrait requested by Salvetti might be the double portrait of *Ferdinando II de' Medici and Vittoria della Rovere* in the National Gallery of London (inv. no. 89, oil on canvas, cm 161 × 147, LANGEDIJK 1981–1987, II, 1983, pp. 787–788, no. 38/39, fig. 38/39). The National Gallery painting cannot possibly be Salvetti's portrait, since hitherto unpublished documentation dates it to 1666.

[105] Letter from Matteo Botti to Christine of Lorraine, Paris, 6 July 1611, ASF, Mediceo del Principato 4871, unpaginated, published by ROSSI 1889, p. 406. In the letter Botti refers to portraits of *Louis XIII* and *Élisabeth de Bourbon*, which he sent to Grand Duchess Christine (Florence, Palazzo Pitti, inv. 1890, nos. 2405 and 2399, oil on canvas, cm 185 × 100, see L. Goldenberg Stoppato, in *I gioielli dei Medici* 2003, pp. 126–127, no. 62).

[106] *Prezzi Accordati con il signor Giusto Suttermano pittore per i Lavori che occorreranno farsi*, 27 August 1654, ASF, Guardaroba medicea 669bis, fol. 727.

[107] Letter from Averardo Ximenes to Carlo de' Medici, 6 October 1658, ASF, Mediceo del Principato 5242, fol. 241, cited by PIERACCINI 1924–1925, II, 1925, pp. 405, 409, note 181 and called to my attention by Elena Fumagalli. See the transcription under cat. no. 1.

[108] Inventario della Guardaroba medicea, 1618–1624, ASF, Guardaroba medicea 373, fols. 323s, 344d, quoted by LANGEDIJK 1981–1987, vol. II, 1983, p. 774, no. 38/21.

[109] For Jan Suttermans, see BALDINUCCI 1681–1728, ed. 1845–1847, vol. IV, 1846, p. 476.

[110] BALDINUCCI 1681–1728, ed. 1845–1847, vol. IV, 1846, p. 476. The documents are transcribed in cat. no. 21.

[111] See Entrata e Uscita H dell'Accademia, 1641–1650, ASF, Accademia del Disegno 106, fol. 24r.

[112] Conti di Vittoria della Rovere, 1632–1638, ASF, Guardaroba medicea 955, fol. 1048, no. 447.

[113] In a letter published by Adolfo VENTURI (1882, p. 249, doc. I) Jan van Ghelder not only mentions copies he made of portraits by "signor Giusto", but also claims that he painted the clothing in several portraits by his uncle. For further information on Van Ghelder, see RIGHI 1979, pp. 141–158.

[114] See BORRONI SALVADORI 1974, pp. 1–58; BORRONI SALVADORI 1975, pp. 393–402; MELONI TRKULJA 1976, pp. 579–585.

[115] See HASKELL 2000, pp. 8–12.

[116] See HASKELL 2001, pp. 49, 52.

[117] See KOCH 1967, pp. 215–216.

Catalogue

**1** *Cosimo III de' Medici (1642–1723) as grand prince*
1658
oil on canvas, cm 72 × 58
Florence, Galleria Palatina, inv. 1890, no. 2875

The sitter in this portrait, unidentified in Pieraccini's catalogue of the Galleria degli Uffizi (see the 1910 edition), was recognized for the first time in 1912 by Pierre Bautier in his monograph on Suttermans. Bautier suggested that this portrait of Cosimo was painted towards the end of the 1660's, around the time of his trips in Northern Italy and in Northern Europe (1667–1669) and it is generally dated to the same decade even in more recent studies. Documents published by the present author in 2004 prove that the portrait was actually painted in 1658.

Every detail of this painting matches the description of a portrait of Grand Prince Cosimo painted by Monsù Giusto in 1658 and cited in a long list of unpaid works commissioned by Grand Duchess Vittoria della Rovere (Copia di partite insolute del conto di Giusto Suttermans con Vittoria della Rovere, 1671, in Conti della Guardaroba generale, 1669–1671, ASF, Guardaroba medicea 785ter, insert 6, bill no. 335, fols. 525, 528). According to the bill, on 30 September 1658 Suttermans delivered a half-length portrait of the grand prince to 'Her Most Serene Highness', which was then sent to France. In the portrait Cosimo was holding his hat in one hand and playing with the red and white feathers on it with his other hand:

> E più a dì 30 settembre 1658, fatto e consegnato a Sua Altezza Serenissima in propria mano, un ritratto del Serenissimo Gran Principe da mezzo in su, vestito con le mani, che una tiene il cappello e l'altra scherzando tra le penne del cappello, di color di fuoco e bianche, e fu mandato in Francia, consegnato per mano, al signore cavaliere Cerchi -- scudi 25

The painting on exhibit can be identified with a second version of the same portrait, which was painted by Suttermans in the fall of 1658 for Cardinal Carlo de' Medici (1596–1666). This version of the portrait is mentioned in two letters sent to the cardinal by Averardo Ximenes in October of the same year and published by Gaetano Pieraccini in 1925. In the first letter, sent on 6 October, Ximenes informs the cardinal that Giusto Suttermans asked for 10 "doble" as payment for a portrait of Grand Prince Cosimo. When Ximenes objected that he had only asked for 7 "doble" for the portrait of Lorenzo de' Medici already painted for the cardinal, the painter pointed out the difference between a copy like the portrait of don Lorenzo and an original work:

> Giusto pittore hieri fu a trovarmi, domandando se Vostra Altezza Reverendissima haveva dato ordine alcuno per la sua sodisfatione del ritratto del serenissimo Gran Principe. Io non potei dirli cosa alcuna, né trovai ordine per il suo intento in Guardaroba; o al signor Poltri. Mi stimolò di passarne uffizio con Vostra Altezza, a cui se ho da rappresentare il prezzo che ne chiese dirò, che fu di doble dieci. Et, per suggerire quello che fu pagato il ritratto del serenissimo signor principe don Lorenzo di gloriosa memoria, dirò all'Altezza Vostra che furno doble sette, ma il medesimo Giusto replica che questo fosse copia d'originale et esser quello del serenissimo Gran Principe, di prima fatica. Si compiaccia Vostra Altezza d'ordinare il suo intento. [. . .]

In the second letter, sent on 11 October 1658, Ximenes promised to find out the price paid by Grand Duchess Vittoria for her portrait of the grand prince, thus establishing a clear link between the two versions of the painting:

> Obedirassi al comandamento di Vostra Altezza Reverendissima in sapere il prezzo del ritratto di mano di Giusto del serenissimo Principe fatto per la serenissima Gran Duchessa Padrona, per sodisfarlo di quello che ha havuto Vostra Altezza. [. . .]

We know that the price paid to the painter was twenty scudi, since a payment for this amount to "Giusto Sutterman" was registered on 12 November 1658 in a book of Carlo de' Medici's debtors and creditors (called to my attention by Elena Fumagalli). The portrait is listed in the inventory of Cardinal Carlo's collection compiled in 1667, as a part of a set of seven Medici portraits:

> Sette Quadri in tela a olio alti braccia 1 ½, larghi 1 ¼, entrovi in ciascheduno un ritratto, cioè Gran Duca [Ferdinando II], Gran Principe [Cosimo], don Lorenzo, Giovan Carlo, Mattias, Leopoldo e don Francesco, tutti con adornamenti d'albero liscio e tutto dorato n.° 7, scudi 140.-.-

The set of paintings, including this portrait, was left by Cardinal Carlo with the rest of his possessions to his grand-nephew Cosimo. The entire collection was ceded by Cosimo for an equivalent amount of money to the Guardaroba and on 30 June 1667 the portraits were registered in the books of the Guardaroba generale. The portrait of Grand Prince Cosimo was later sent to the Medici Villa di Pratolino where, as Karla Langedijk pointed out in 1981, it is mentioned by the 1748 inventory. The inventory describes a portrait of Cosimo as grand prince wearing a doublet with split sleeves and holding a hat with red feathers on it:

> Un quadro in tela alto braccia 1 ¼, largo soldi 19, dipintovi mezza figura ritratto del gran duca Cosimo quando era principe in abito alla spagnola, con maniche aperte e collare di trina, tiene sotto il braccio sinistro il cappello con penne scarnatine, e adornamento di tutto intaglio straforato e tutto dorato - n. 1

By 1761 the portrait had been brought back to Florence and placed on the second floor of Palazzo Pitti. It is described in great detail by the inventory of the palace compiled that same year with three other portraits of the same format:

> Quattro Detti simili alti braccia 1 soldi 6, larghi braccia 1 soldi 2 per ciascheduno dipintovi mezze figure in uno [. . .], e nell'altro il Gran Duca Cosimo Terzo da giovane vestito alla spagnola, con collare di trine, maniche aperte, e capello in mano con penne bianche, e rosse con adornamenti intagliati, straforati, e tutti dorati segnati n.° 948.

According to Marco Chiarini, the portrait of Grand Prince Cosimo was sent to the Galleria degli Uffizi in 1826 and was later sent back to Palazzo Pitti where it was exhibited in the Appartamenti reali. In 1928 it was transferred to the Galleria Palatina where it still can be seen today.

*Archival sources*
Letters from Averardo Ximenes to Cardinal Carlo de' Medici, 6, 11 October 1658, ASF, Mediceo del Principato 5242, fols. 241, 242; Debitori e creditori di Carlo de' Medici, 1651–1663, 12 November 1658, ASF, Scrittoio delle Regie Possessioni 4173, fols. 49s-d, 504d; Inventario di Carlo de' Medici, 1667, ASF, Guardaroba medicea 758, fol. 3v; Quaderno della Guardaroba generale, 1666–1674, I, 30 June 1667, ASF, Guardaroba medicea 750, fol. 58v; Inventario della Guardaroba generale, 1666–1680, 30 June 1667, ASF, Guardaroba medicea 741, fol. 357s; Inventario della Villa di Pratolino, 1748, ASF, Guardaroba medicea appendice 84, fol. 212; Inventario di Palazzo Pitti, 1761, ASF, Guardaroba medicea appendice 94, fol. 626r

*Bibliography*
PIERACCINI 1910, p. 117, no. 893; BAUTIER 1912b, pp. 93,126; GÖZ 1928, p. 31; JAHN RUSCONI 1937, p. 293, no. 2875; J. Lavalleye, in THIEME–BECKER 1907–1950, vol. XXXII, 1938, p. 324; PIERACCINI 1924–1925, vol. II, 1925, pp. 405, 409, note 181; TARCHIANI 1939, p. 25; CIPRIANI 1966, p. 122, no. 2875; CAMERANI 1968, pl. facing p. 152; *Artisti alla Corte Granducale* 1969, p. 53, no. 76, fig.; M. Chiarini, in *Gli Uffizi* 1979, ed. 1980, p. 535, no. P1669; LANGEDIJK 1981–1987, vol. I, 1981, p. 605, no. 29/35; K. Langedijk, in *Sustermans* 1983, p. 31, no. 1; *Palazzo Pitti* 1988, p. 74; GODI and MINGARDI, 1994, p. 43, sub no. 33; M. C. Masdea, in *Opere d'arte della famiglia Medici* 1997, pp. 89–90, no. 19, p. 142, pl. 19; M. Chiarini, in CHIARINI–PADOVANI, 2003, vol. I, p. 29, fig. 13; S. Casciu, in CHIARINI–PADOVANI 2003, vol. II, p. 427, no. 705

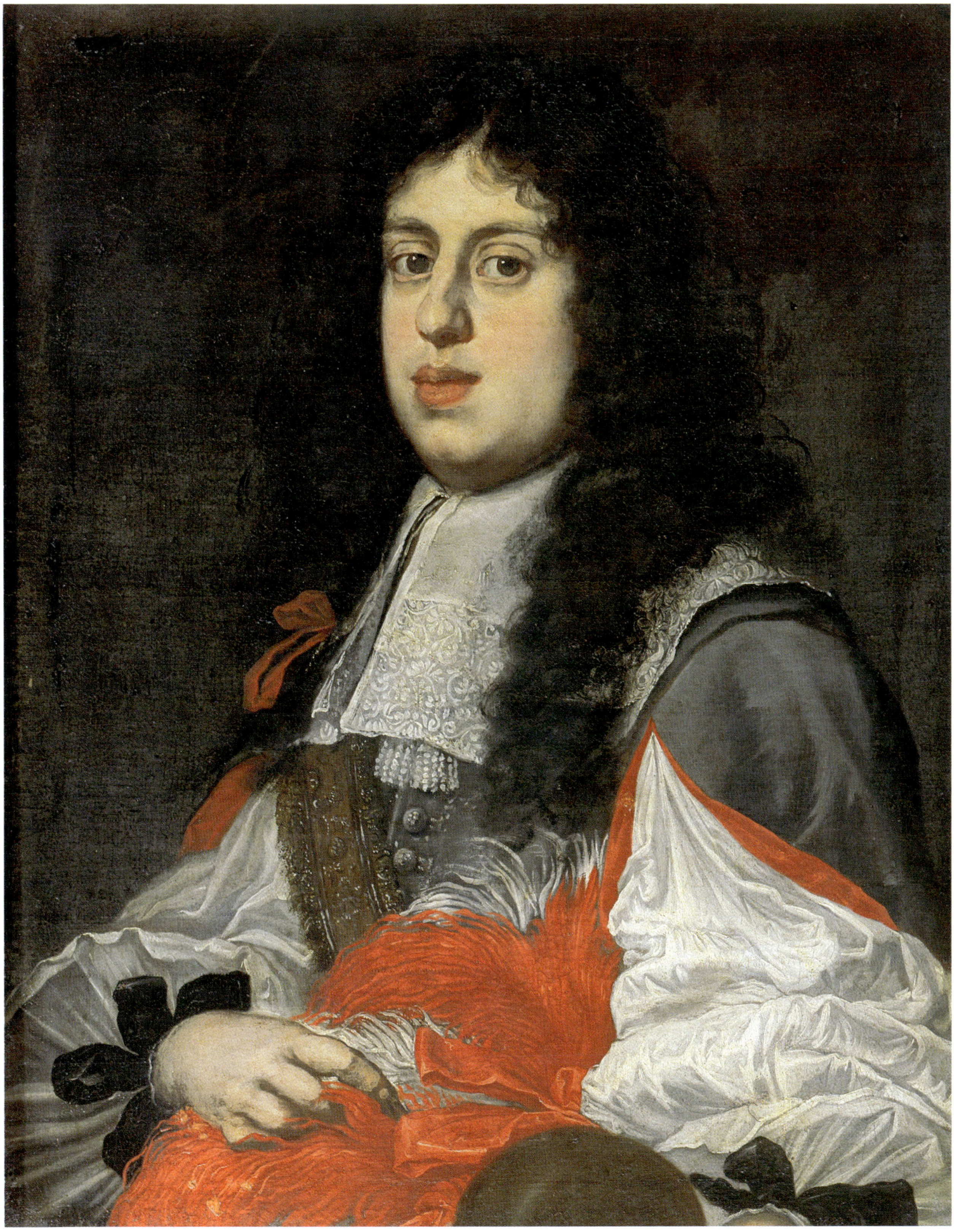

**2** *Giusto Suttermans (1597–1681)*
1655–1660 ca.
Florence, Galleria degli Uffizi, inv. 1890, no. 1646
oil on canvas, cm 79 × 63

In this half-length self-portrait Suttermans has portrayed himself turned three quarters to the left with his hand slightly raised, looking directly towards the observer. He is wearing a black doublet with split sleeves, a white shirt and a large, square white collar. He has dark curly hair and whiskers. Though he has aged, there is an apparent resemblance to the painter's youthful *Self-portrait in miniature* (Florence, Galleria degli Uffizi, inv. 1890, no. 9014, oil on copper, cm 4.5 × 3.4), and to the self-portrait in his *Pledge of Allegiance of the Florentine Senate to Ferdinando II de' Medici* (Florence, Galleria degli Uffizi, inv. 1890, no. 721, oil on canvas, cm 397 × 626, see L. Goldenberg Stoppato, in CANEVA–VERVAT 2002, pp. 11–27). One can also easily recognize the same features in the portrait of Suttermans engraved by Antonie van Dyck for his *Iconografia* (see *Sustermans* 1983, p. 11; LANGEDIJK 1992, fig. 64a). Another octagonal self-portrait, mentioned by the 1761 inventory of Palazzo Pitti, is now missing (ASF, Guardaroba medicea appendice 94, fol. 793r).

The *Self-portrait* we are exhibiting can be dated between 1655 and 1660 for the apparent age of the painter and for the cut of his clothes. The large, square collar is quite similar to the one worn by *Cosimo III de' Medici* in the 1658 portrait we are exhibiting (see cat. no. 1). The style of painting also dates the portrait to the same period. It is quite close to the brushwork in the full-length portrait of *Vittoria della Rovere* with a flower in her hand, which was painted by Suttermans in 1655 (Poggio a Caiano (Florence), Medici Villa, inv. Poggio a Caiano 1912, no. 131, oil on canvas, cm 205 × 145, see essay fig. 15).

The painter's urbane attitude in this *Self-portrait* is quite striking. Filippo Baldinucci claims that Suttermans was indeed graced with a noble disposition, endowed with a genteel appearance and the manners of a gentleman (BALDINUCCI 1681–1728, ed. 1845–1847, IV, 1846, p. 478):

> [. . .] Ora è da sapersi in questo luogo, che il Sustermans, siccome era stato dotato d'animo nobile, d'acuto ingegno, d'innocenti maniere, e di straordinaria abilità per ogni qualunque cosa virtuosa, così ancora avea sortito d'avere un vago aspetto, e presenza signorile, col quale, e coll'avvenenza che scorgeva in ogni suo gesto, accompagnava le proprie azioni tanto graziosamente, che era cosa maravigliosa [. . .].

Contemporary documents prove that Baldinucci's praise was not mere rhetoric. When Maria Maddalena of Austria, recommended him to the Grand Master of the Military Order of Saint John of Jerusalem on 18 August 1627, she praised him not only for his artistic merits, but also for the urbanity of his dress and behavior: "egli [. . .] merita questo honore per la nascita sua, et per essere ornato di virtuose qualità, col vestire, et praticare sempre nobilmente" (ASF, Mediceo del principato 120, fols. 223–223bis, published by BALDINUCCI 1681–1728, ed. 1845–1847, IV, 1846, pp. 487–489). This attitude did not pass unobserved in Florentine society which, unlike contemporary Flemish society, considered artists mere artisans and accorded them very low social status. The comments made by Marquis Paolo del Bufalo in a letter he sent to Cardinal Carlo de' Medici on 17 March 1637 [ab Incarnatione=1638 modern style] are an excellent example. The marquis, who had returned repeatedly to the painter's workshop to claim miniature portraits for Cardinal Carlo, complained that Suttermans had responded with a hauteur more appropriate to a knight than to an artist: "Et insomma sta con una grandezza straordinaria, più da cavaliere che da artista" (ASF, Mediceo del principato 5215, fol. 106, called to my attention by Elena Fumagalli).

The *Self-portrait* comes from the large collection of self-portraits that belonged to Cardinal Leopoldo de' Medici, which form the main core of the present day collection of self-portraits in the Galleria degli Uffizi. Suttermans' *Self-portrait* or "Ritratto di Giusto" is mentioned in the list of "Ritratti di pittori fatti di lor' propria mano", in the first inventory of Leopoldo's collection, which dates from the 1660's. It is also described by the inventory compiled after Leopoldo's death in 1675, in the "Stanza de' Pittori", the painters' room:

> Un Quadro simile in tela dipintovi il Ritratto di Giusto Sutterman di sua mano, con barba rasa, e basette arriciate, collare alla moderna, con ferraiolo inbracciato, e con la mano destra si tiene il ferraiolo, di mezz'età, con ornamento simile [intagliato, dorato, straforato]

According to a journal of the Guardaroba generale, this painting entered Cosimo III's collection with all of Leopoldo's possessions on 27 February 1676 [ab Incarnatione=1677 modern style]. Another Guardaroba journal documents the official consignment of the painting to the keeper of Palazzo Pitti on 30 August 1680. The *Self-portrait* is also mentioned by Filippo Baldinucci in a manuscript list of portraits of painters which he compiled for Grand Duke Cosimo III in February 1681, the *Nota di tutti ritratti de' Pittori che sono nel museo di Sua Altezza Serenissima*. A year later, exactly on 28 October 1682, the painting was sent to the Guardaroba generale and from there on to the Galleria degli Uffizi. It is in fact listed in all the inventories of the Uffizi from 1704 to 1890. We also know, thanks to a document cited by Karla Langedijk in 1992, that the canvas with the portrait of "M.r Giusto Subterman" was re-stretched, lined and touched up by Fedele Acciai in 1827. In this document Acciai asks for a reimbursement of 92 paoli for the new stretcher, the fabric used to line the painting and the pigments, paintbrushes and varnish used to retouch it.

Fig. 1 - Giusto Suttermans, *Self-portrait in miniature*. Florence, Galleria degli Uffizi, inv. 1890, no. 9014

*Archival sources*
Inventario di Leopoldo de' Medici, n.d. [1663–1671?], Firenze, Biblioteca Riccardiana, ms. Riccardi 2443, fol. 141; Inventario di Leopoldo de' Medici, 1675, ASF, Guardaroba medicea 826, fol. 69r, no. 230; Quaderno della Guardaroba generale 1674–1680, 27 febbraio 1676 [ab Incarnatione=1677 modern style], ASF, Guardaroba medicea 799, fol. 180r-v, no. 230; Quaderno della Guardaroba generale 1679–1685, 30 August 1680 and 28 October 1682, ASF, Guardaroba medicea 870, fol. 53v and 162r; BALDINUCCI 1681, ASF, Miscellanea medicea 368, fol. 420r; Inventario degli Uffizi 1704–1714, Biblioteca degli Uffizi, ms. 82, fol. 190, no. 1655; Inventario degli Uffizi 1753, Biblioteca degli Uffizi, ms. 95, unpaginated,

VII room, no. 3152; Inventario degli Uffizi 1769, Biblioteca degli Uffizi, ms. 98, fol. 539, no. 3260; Inventario degli Uffizi 1784, Biblioteca degli Uffizi, ms. 113, fol. 268, no. 564/21; Inventario degli Uffizi 1825, Biblioteca degli Uffizi, ms. 173, vol. III, tome III, pp. 34–35, no. 1508; Bill of Fedele Acciai, n.d. [1827?], Archivio storico delle Gallerie fiorentine, shelf no. LI/II, 1827, insert 50, fol. 60; Inventario degli Uffizi 1881, Soprintendenza speciale per il Polo Museale Fiorentino, Ufficio ricerche, vol. IV, Esposti, no. 1801; K. Langedijk, OA catalogue entry no. 09/00099598, 1977, Florence, Ufficio catalogo della Soprintendenza; D. Bodart, OA catalogue entry no. 09/00029601, 1979, Florence, Ufficio catalogo della Soprintendenza

*Bibliography*
MOÜCKE, 1752–1762, vol. II, 1754, pl. facing p. 293; NAGLER 1835–1852, vol. XVII, 1848, pp. 6–7; GUALANDI 1844–1856, vol. III, 1856, p. 256, no. 433; MICHIELS 1881, p. 134–135; MICHIELS 1882, p. 200; WAUTERS n.d. [1883?], p. 356; MÜLLER–SINGER 1894–1901, vol. IV, 1901, p. 368; *Bryan's Dictionary* 1904–1905, vol. V, 1905, p. 145; PIERACCINI 1910, p. 36, no. 218; WURZBACH 1906–1910, vol. II, 1910, p. 676, no. 2; BAUTIER 1912b, pp. 54, 126; BAUTIER 1926–1929, p. 324; SINGER 1937–1938, vol. IV, p. 329, no. 34976; J. Lavalleye, in THIEME–BECKER 1907–1950, vol. XXXII, 1938, p. 323; QUINTAVALLE 1939, p. 217, sub no. 1021; DENTLER 1974, fig. 209; PRINZ 1971, p. 233, doc. 216; *Rubens e la Pittura Fiamminga* 1977, pp. 270 (no. 117), 271 (fig.); MELONI TRKULJA 1978, p. 84, fig. 78; M. Chiarini, in *Gli Uffizi* 1979, pp. 532 (sub no. P1659), 1013 (no. A917); *Al servizio del granduca* 1980, p. 26, no. IV, 6; M. Chiarini, in *Sustermans* 1983, p. 63, no. 38; L. Borsatti, in *Fiamminghi* 1990, p. 38; LANGEDIJK 1992, pp. 183–184; L. Goldenberg Stoppato, in CANEVA–VERVAT 2002, pp. 23, 27, note 100, fig. 2

**3** *Margherita de' Medici (1612–1679) as a child*
1621–1622
Florence, Galleria degli Uffizi, inv. 1890, no. 3579
oil on canvas, cm 185 × 127

**4** *Anna de' Medici (1616–1676) as a child*
1621–1622
Florence, Galleria degli Uffizi, inv. 1890, no. 3763
oil on canvas, cm 183 × 124

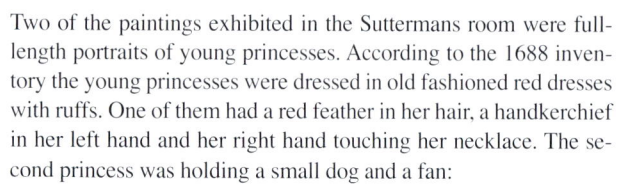

Two of the paintings exhibited in the Suttermans room were full-length portraits of young princesses. According to the 1688 inventory the young princesses were dressed in old fashioned red dresses with ruffs. One of them had a red feather in her hair, a handkerchief in her left hand and her right hand touching her necklace. The second princess was holding a small dog and a fan:

> Due quadri in tela alti braccia 2 soldi 16 in circa, larghi braccia 1 soldi 18, dipintovi di mano di Giusto Suttermanni due Principesse figure intere vestite di rosso all'antica, che una con pezzuola nella mano sinistra e con la destra si regge la collana che li pende dal collo, con penna rossa in testa, e l'altra con canino nel braccio sinistro, e con la mano destra tiene un ventaglio, con collare a lattughe, et adornamenti intagliati et tutti dorati n. 2

The details of the description make it easy for us to recognize the paintings, which both now belong to the Galleria degli Uffizi. They are portraits of *Margherita* and *Anna de' Medici*, the younger daughters of Grand Duke Cosimo II de' Medici and his wife Maria Maddalena of Austria. These portraits also appear in the census of works by Monsù Giusto compiled by Filippo Baldinucci while he was preparing the exhibition in 1678. He lists them among the full-length portraits by the painter "ritrovati", that he had found, mentioning Anna by name as the "Serenissima Principessa Anna banbina di 8 anni" and Margherita by the title she acquired by marriage, as the "Duchessa di Parma giovanetta". Margherita was born on 31 May 1612 and named after Queen Margarete (1584–1611) of Spain, her deceased maternal aunt. She married the Duke of Parma Odoardo Farnese in 1628. Anna, born on 21 July 1616, married her first cousin Archduke Ferdinand Karl von Habsburg, the governor of the Tyrolean region, in 1646.

These canvases belong to a group of portraits of the grand duke's eight children, five sons and three daughters, which were commissioned by their mother Maria Maddalena in the fall of 1621.

The portraits are mentioned in a letter written on 4 October 1621 by court secretary Domenico Montaguto. In the letter Montaguto forwarded to Vincenzo Giugni, the head keeper of the Guardaroba, Maria Maddalena's order for eight stretchers measuring three braccia by two braccia "per depingervi tutti gli eccellentissimi figlioli di Sua Altezza Serenissima da ms. Giusto fiamengo", so that the Fleming Giusto could paint the portraits of all the children of 'Her Most Serene Highness'. On 9 November of the same year Montaguto asked another keeper of the Guardaroba, Bernardo Migliorati, for "mezza oncia d'azzurro oltramarino et una oncia di cenere del medesimo per il pittore che depinge tutti gli figlioli de Sua Altezza Serenissima", half an once of azurite and an once of azurite powder for the painter who is painting portraits all the children of 'Her Most Serene Highness'. Suttermans was forced to interrupt his work on these portraits towards the end of November 1621, when he was sent to Mantua to portray Eleonora Gonzaga, the bride of Emperor Ferdinand II. He was free to work on them only after he returned to Florence on 4 January 1622.

Thanks to the inscriptions on the back of the three other surviving paintings from the set, the portraits of *Giovan Carlo*, *Francesco* and *Leopoldo de' Medici* (Galleria degli Uffizi, inv. 1890, nos. 3649, 4296 and 3660), we know that they were painted between February and March 1622. Suttermans was paid for them in August of the same year (see *Recapiti di Cassa della Depositeria Generale*, 1621–1622, ASF, Depositeria Generale, Parte Antica 1010, unpaginated, payment no. 304, bill no. 404, called to my attention by Anna Evangelista).

The portraits of *Margherita* and *Anna* were completed by 10 September 1622, the date which appears on two identical payment orders, one signed by Ferdinando II de' Medici and one signed by his mother Maria Maddalena of Austria, both called to my attention by Anna Evangelista. They order payments of thirty scudi for the portrait of Margherita and twenty-five scudi for the portrait of Anna:

> Alessandro Caccini nostro Depositario Generale, paghi in virtù di questo nostro ordine a Giusto Susermano Pittore della Casa Serenissima scudi cinquantacinque di moneta, che trenta sono per il ritratto della Principessa Margherita, et venticinque per il ritratto della Principessa Anna, che gli saranno fatti buoni nel saldo de' suoi conti
> Maria Magdalena tutrice

The painter's receipt for a total of fifty-five scudi appears at the bottom of the page. Suttermans specifies that the receipt was written for him by Domenico Montaguto, since his own knowledge of the Italian language was not adequate:

> Io Giusto Sutermano Pittore ho ricevuto dal sudetto signore Depositario Generale gli sudetti scudi cinquanta cinque, et per non sapere io scrivere Italiano ho fatto fare la presente a Domenico Montaguto questo dì 10 settembre 1622

The portraits of Margherita and Anna are mentioned once again a few days later, on 15 September 1622, in a letter sent by secretary Montaguto to Bernardo Migliorati. In the letter Montaguto sends back to Migliorati the fabric used by the painter as a model for the dresses of the 'most excellent princesses', specifying that the fabric was red with gold and silver flowers on it:

> Remandoli il drappo scarnatino con fiori d'oro et argento servito per dipingere li vesti d'eccellentissime signore principesse, pregandolo di farmelo scancellare. [...]

The portraits of the five boys were sent to the Villa del Poggio Imperiale, the suburban residence of their mother Maria Maddalena of Austria. They are mentioned in the inventories of the villa compiled in 1624, between 1654 and 1655 and in 1691. This last inventory described them in great detail (see ASF, Guardaroba medicea 479, fol. 27s; Guardaroba medicea 657, fol. 30; Guardaroba medicea 991, fols. 87v–88v). They probably were sent to the villa in July 1622 when a list of expenses of Ferdinando II de' Medici's Camera mentions one lira spent for "la portatura de' cinque quadri retratti gli serenissimi figlioli di Sua Altezza Serenissima", the transportation of the five portraits of the most serene sons of 'Her Most Serene Highness' (see *Ordini per il Serenissimo Gran Duca, l'Anno 1622*, ASF, Camera del Granduca 3b, fol. 19v). The portraits of princesses Margherita and Anna were instead sent to Palazzo Pitti. They are mentioned in the inventories of the palace starting in 1638, when they were exhibited in a room of Leopoldo de' Medici's apartment. The 1663–1664 inventory of the palace describes these paintings in the first room on the left of the apartment of the "principino", either Cosimo III's young brother Francesco Maria or his son Grand Prince Ferdinando. The portraits of the princesses are also cited in the inventories of Palazzo Pitti which were compiled between 1716 and 1723 and in 1761.

Fig. 1 - Giusto Suttermans, *Giovan Carlo de' Medici (1611–1663) as a child*, 1622. Florence, Galleria degli Uffizi, inv. 1890, no. 3649
Fig. 2 - Giusto Suttermans, *Francesco de' Medici (1614–1634) as a child*, 1622. Florence, Galleria degli Uffizi, inv. 1890, no. 4296
Fig. 3 - Giusto Suttermans, *Leopoldo de' Medici (1617–1675) as a child*, 1622. Florence, Galleria degli Uffizi, inv. 1890, no. 3660

cat. no **3**

*Archival sources*
Letter from Domenico Montaguto, Medici secretary, to Vincenzo Giugni, head of the Guardaroba, Palazzo Pitti, 4 October 1621, ASF, Guardaroba medicea 391, insert 3, fol. 285; Letter from Domenico Montaguto, Medici secretary, to Bernardo Migliorati, keeper of the Guardaroba, Palazzo di Baroncelli, 9 November 1621, ASF, Guardaroba medicea 391, insert 4, fol. 398; Payment order and receipt, 10 September 1622, in *Recapiti di Cassa della Depositeria Generale*, 1621–1622, ASF, Depositeria Generale, Parte Antica 1010, unpaginated, no. 328; Letter from Domenico Montaguto, Medici secretary, to Bernardo Migliorati, keeper of the Guardaroba, Palazzo Pitti, 15 September 1622, ASF, Guardaroba medicea 391, insert 9, fol. 846; Inventario di Palazzo Pitti, 1638, ASF, Guardaroba medicea 525, fol. 62v; Inventario della Guardaroba di Palazzo Pitti, 1638, ASF, Guardaroba medicea 535, fol. 90s; Entrata e Uscita di Palazzo Pitti, 1638–1648, ASF, Guardaroba medicea 530, fol. 166s; Inventario di Palazzo Pitti, 1663–1664, ASF, Guardaroba medicea 725, fol. 82v; Baldinucci n.d. [1678 ca.], BNCF, ms. II.II.110, fol. 351v; Inventario di Palazzo Pitti, 1688, ASF, Guardaroba medicea 932, fol. 129r; Inventario di Palazzo Pitti, 1716–1723, Biblioteca degli Uffizi, ms. 79, fol. 105; Inventario di Palazzo Pitti, 1761, ASF, Guardaroba medicea appendice 94, fol. 537v

*Bibliography*
Bautier 1911a, pp. 90, 91, fig. II; *Mostra del Ritratto* 1911, p. 211, no. 11; Bautier 1912b, pp. 38, 128; Bautier 1926–1929, p. 318; Gamba 1927, p. 93, pl. XIII; Göz 1928, pp. 30, 34; Singer 1937–1938, III, 1938, p. 195; J. Lavalleye, in Thieme–Becker 1907–1950, vol. XXXII, 1938, p. 324; Drei 1954, pl. XXVIII; Levi Pisetsky 1966, pl. 182; Langedijk 1981–1987, I, 1981, p. 181, II, 1983, pp. 1224–1225, no. 83/8; S. Meloni Trkulja, in *Sustermans* 1983, p. 103, no. XXXVI; S. Meloni Trkulja and G. Butazzi, in *I principi bambini* 1985, p. 55 , no. 21; L. Goldenberg Stoppato, in *Il Seicento fiorentino* 1986, *Biografie*, p. 168; Danesi Squarzina 1990, pp. 89, 94, note 9; L. Goldenberg Stoppato, in Turner 1996, p. 40; *Power & Glory* 2001, pp. 31, 64–65; *I Volti del Potere* 2002, pp. 82–83, no. 22; L. Goldenberg Stoppato, in *I gioielli dei Medici* 2003, pp. 150–151, sub no. 80; L. Goldenberg Stoppato, in *Il viaggio a Compostela* 2004, pp. 75, 89–90 (notes 36–38), 101, no. 1

cat. no **4**

*Archival sources*
Letter from Domenico Montaguto, Medici secretary, to Vincenzo Giugni, head of the Guardaroba, Palazzo Pitti, 4 October 1621, ASF, Guardaroba medicea 391, insert 3, fol. 285; Letter from Domenico Montaguto, Medici secretary, to Bernardo Migliorati, keeper of the Guardaroba, Palazzo di Baroncelli, 9 November 1621, ASF, Guardaroba medicea 391, insert 4, fol. 398; Payment order and receipt, 10 September 1622, in *Recapiti di Cassa della Depositeria Generale*, 1621–1622, ASF, Depositeria Generale, Parte Antica 1010, unpaginated, no. 328; Letter from Domenico Montaguto, Medici secretary, to Bernardo Migliorati, keeper of the Guardaroba, Palazzo Pitti, 15 September 1622, ASF, Guardaroba medicea 391, insert 9, fol. 846; Inventario di Palazzo Pitti, 1638, ASF, Guardaroba medicea 525, fol. 62v; Inventario della Guardaroba di Palazzo Pitti, 1638, ASF, Guardaroba medicea 535, fol. 90s; Entrata e Uscita di Palazzo Pitti, 1638–1648, ASF, Guardaroba medicea 530, fol. 166s; Inventario di Palazzo Pitti, 1663–1664, ASF, Guardaroba medicea 725, fol. 82v; F. Baldinucci n.d. [1678 ca.], BNCF, ms. II.II.110, fol. 351v; Inventario di Palazzo Pitti, 1688, ASF, Guardaroba medicea 932, fol. 129r; Inventario di Palazzo Pitti, 1716–1723, Biblioteca degli Uffizi, ms. 79, fol. 105; Inventario di Palazzo Pitti, 1761, ASF, Guardaroba medicea appendice 94, fol. 537v

*Bibliography*
*Mostra del Ritratto* 1911, p. 212, no. 13; Bautier 1912b, pp. 39, 128, pl. XIII; Simar 1913, p. 136; Bautier 1926–1929, p. 318; Gamba 1927, p. 95, pl. XIII; Göz 1928, pp. 30–31, 34; Singer 1937–1938, I, 1937, p. 43, no. 1127; Langedijk 1981–1987, I, 1981, pp. 181, 248, no. 3/6; K. Langedijk, in *Sustermans* 1983, p. 29, no. 9; S. Meloni Trkulja and G. Butazzi, in *I principi bambini*, 1985, p. 54 , no. 20; M. Mosco, in *Natura viva* 1985, p. 90, sub no. 25, fig.; L. Goldenberg Stoppato, in *Il Seicento fiorentino* 1986, *Biografie*, p. 168; Danesi Squarzina 1990, pp. 89, 90 (fig. 75), 94, note 9; Danesi Squarzina 1995, p. 13, note 2; L. Goldenberg Stoppato, in Turner 1996, p. 40; *Crafting the Medici* 1999, pp. 40–41, no. 9; *I Volti del Potere* 2002, pp. 86–87, no. 24; L. Goldenberg Stoppato, in *I gioielli dei Medici* 2003, pp. 150–151, no. 80; L. Goldenberg Stoppato, in *Il viaggio a Compostela* 2004, pp. 75, 89–90 (notes 36–38), 101, no. 2

**5** *Ferdinand II von Habsburg (1578–1637), emperor of Austria*
1623–1624
Florence, Palazzo Pitti, Galleria Palatina, inv. 1912, no. 209
oil on canvas, cm 64 × 50

One of the paintings exhibited in the Suttermans room in Palazzo Pitti in 1688 was a portrait of Emperor Ferdinand II, the brother of the Grand Duchess of Tuscany Maria Maddalena. According to the inventory he was dressed in black and was wearing a ruff and a chain with the emblem of the order of the Golden Fleece:

> Un quadro in tela altro braccia 1 ⅛, largo ⅚, dipintovi il ritratto del-l'imperato[re] Ferdinando secondo con collare a lattughe, tosone al collo, vestito di nero ricamato d'oro, con adornamento intagliato e dorato n. 1

Like many of the works exhibited, the painting came from the collection of Cardinal Leopoldo de' Medici, the youngest of Maria Maddalena's sons. It is listed both in the inventory of Leopoldo's collection, which was compiled after his death in 1675, and in the Guardaroba journal where the possessions Cosimo III inherited from him were registered on 27 February 1676 [ab Incarnatione=1677 modern style]. According to another Guardaroba journal, the painting was officially consigned to the keeper of Palazzo Pitti on 30 August 1680.

This bust-length portrait of Emperor Ferdinand II and the similar portraits of his wife *Eleonora Gonzaga* and his brother *Karl von Habsburg* were probably painted by Suttermans during his visit to Vienna. This visit, which was mentioned by Filippo Baldinucci in his biography of the painter, began on 6 November 1623. Giusto's arrival in Vienna with his brother Jan was announced by Giovanni Altoviti, the Medici ambassador at the imperial court, to Curzio Picchena, Medici court secretary, by letter on the 11th of the same month: "Vennero li due fratelli pittori fin cinque giorni sono [. . .]"(ASF, Mediceo del Principato 4374a, fol. 214). Since Baldinucci claims that Giusto stayed in Vienna for a whole year, he may well have still been there on 1 October 1624 when Emperor Ferdinand II granted him and his brothers a patent of nobility (Vienna, Adelsarchiv, published by HAJDECKI 1905, pp. 6–7).

In another letter sent to secretary Picchena on 6 July 1624, Ambassador Altoviti mentions a set of paintings sent by Suttermans to the Medici court from Vienna. This set included portraits of Emperor Ferdinand II, his wife Eleonora Gonzaga, his brothers the Archdukes Karl and Leopold and his children Ferdinand, Leopold Wilhelm, Maria Anna and Cecilia Renata. Altoviti asks whether Maria Maddalena of Austria would be willing to have copies of the portraits sent to Florence made for Carlo Caraffa, nuncio to Vienna from 1621 to 1628 and bishop of Aversa (ASF, Mediceo del Principato 4375, unpaginated):

> Non so se la Serenissima Arciduchessa sia per contentarsi che si cavi copia dell'Imperatore et Imperatrice, degl'Arciduchi fratelli e figliuoli e delle Arciduchesse da gli originali ch'ha mandato costì il Suttermann pittore fiammingo. Io son pregato come Vostra Signoria Illustrissima vedrà dall'aggiunto viglietto da questo Monsignor Nunzio a farnela cavare da qualche buona mano [. . .]; signor Luigi mio fratello harà poi la cura di trovar, e sodisfar il pittore che gl'harà a fare [. . .]. Io havevo proposto al Nunzio di farseli far qua dal fratello [Jan Suttermans] che opera assai bene, e glieli harebbe fatti, ma egli ha opinione d'haver a essere servito meglo costì [. . .].

A written request from the bishop of Aversa was enclosed in the ambassador's letter. The bishop asks explicitly for full-length copies of the portraits, measuring eight palmi, of all the members of the emperor's family: "Prego Vostra Signoria Illustrissima a farmi favore di scrivere a Firenze per la copia del' infrascritti ritratti che siano tutti intieri del'altezza di otto palmi l'uno [. . .] l'Imperatore, Imperatrice, Arciducha Leopoldo, Arciducha Carlo, li dui archiduchi figli di Sua Maestà con le due Arciduchesse ancora figlie di Sua Maestà". The request was refused on 20 July 1624 by secretary Picchena, who claimed that the portraits had not yet arrived in Florence and that, in any case, Maria Maddalena Maddalena of Austria was not willing to have them copied: "[. . .] intorno a [. . .] i ritratti di cotesti principi, che ella dice essere stati mandati qua dal suo Pittore fiammingo, [. . .] l'Altezza Serenissima dice che [. . .] non sono mai comparsi [. . .]. Poi ha detto liberamente che non si contenta in modo alcuno, che da questi che verranno qua si cavino copie. [. . .]" (ASF, Mediceo del Principato 4486, unpaginated).

The three bust-length portraits of Habsburgs exhibited are not necessarily the portraits mentioned in these letters, which may well be the full-length portraits of the Emperor and the other members of his family that belong to the Gallerie fiorentine, all painted by Suttermans with the help of a workshop hand. These portraits, now in storage in a variety of museum deposits, were exhibited in the 17th century in the Villa del Poggio Imperiale, Maria Maddalena's suburban residence. They are listed without an attribution in the inventories of the villa compiled in 1624 (ASF, Guardaroba medicea 479, fols. 27s, 35s), between 1654 and 1655 (ASF, Guardaroba medicea 657, fol. 30) and in 1691 (ASF, Guardaroba medicea 991, fols. 77r, 87r-v). The set includes full-length portraits of *Emperor Ferdinand II von Habsburg* (inv. 1890, no. 4305, fig. 1), *Empress Eleonora Gonzaga* (inv. 1890, no. 4274, see cat. no. 6), *Archduke Karl von Habsburg* (inv. 1890, no. 2433, see cat. no. 7), *Archduke Leopold von Habsburg* (to be identified with one of two portraits that belong to the Florentine museums, inv. 1890, no. 2264, fig. 2, or inv. Poggio a Caiano, no. 145) and of the emperor's children, long believed to be members of the Medici family. The sitter in the portrait of the emperor's heir *Ferdinand III von Habsburg (1608–1657) as a young man* (inv. Poggio Imperiale "rosso", no. 971, fig. 3), believed to be don Lorenzo de' Medici, is clearly identified as an 'Emperor when he was young' by the 1691 inventory of the Villa del Poggio Imperiale (ASF, Guardaroba medicea 991, fol. 87r). Every detail of the portrait matches the painting listed

Fig. 1 - Giusto and Jan Suttermans, *Emperor Ferdinand II von Habsburg*, 1623–1624. Florence, Galleria degli Uffizi, inv. 1890, no. 4305
Fig. 2 - Giusto and Jan Suttermans, *Archduke Leopold von Habsburg*, 1623–1624. Florence, Galleria degli Uffizi, Inv. 1890, no. 2264
Fig. 3 - Giusto and Jan Suttermans, *Emperor Ferdinand III von Habsburg as a young man*, 1623–1624. Florence, Gallerie fiorentine, storage, inv. Poggio Imperiale "rosso", no. 971

by the inventory, which describes the sitter in armor and black hose, with his right hand on his hip and a helmet with red and white feathers on the table beside him: "Un Quadro simile alto braccia 3 ⅖, largo braccia 1 ⅔, dipintovi some sopra un Imperatore da giovane armato, calze nere, mano destra al fianco, e morione con penne incarnate e bianche sopra d'un tavolino [. . .]". The sitter in the portrait of the emperor's younger son *Leopold Wilhelm von Habsburg (1614–1662)* (inv. 1890, n. 4264, fig. 5) has been mistaken for Leopoldo de' Medici, but closely resembles Leopold Wilhelm as he was portrayed by Franz Luycz (see HEINZ–SCHÜTZ 1976, no. 115, fig. 175). The painting is described in great detail in the 1691 Poggio Imperiale inventory, as the portrait of a young prince wearing a long black gown with white cuffs and collar, holding his hat in his right hand on top of a table and a sprig of three yellow flowers in his left hand: "[. . .] un Principe da giovanetto in veste lunga nera che con la mano destra tiene il cappello posato su d'un tavolino, e con la sinistra una ciocca di tre fiorellini gialli, con collarino e manichi puri da prete [. . .]" (ASF, Guardaroba medicea 991, fol. 77r). He is clearly identified as Archduke Leopold, the brother of the ruling emperor, by the 1654–1655 inventory, which also mentions his clerical garb (ASF, Guardaroba medicea 657, fol. 30). The portraits of *Maria Anna (1610–1665)* and *Cecilia Renata (1611–1644) von Habsburg* (inv. 1890, nos. 4275, 2297, figs. 4, 6) have been considered portraits of Eleonora de' Medici, the daughter of Grand Duke Ferdinando I. They are instead clearly identified as Emperor Ferdinand II's daughters in the 1624 inventory of the Villa del Poggio Imperiale and as Emperor Ferdinand III's sisters in the 1654–1655 inventory. The portraits are described in great detail in the 1691 inventory of the same villa which identifies the princesses as the sisters "dell'Imperatore morto", of deceased Emperor Ferdinand III (ASF, Guardaroba medicea 991, fol. 87r). According to this inventory, one sister was holding a rose and a handkerchief, the other sister had her right hand on a table and her left hand touching the piece of jewelry on her chest, and both had a small dog at their feet, exactly like the young princesses in these portraits. The sitters do in fact resemble the two archduchesses as they appear in several portraits that belong to the Kunsthistorisches Museum in Vienna (see HEINZ–SCHÜTZ 1976, nos. 112, 113, 114, figs. 183, 169, 171).

A second full-length portrait of *Emperor Ferdinand II* belongs to Vienna's Kunsthistorisches Museum (inv. no. 6100, oil on canvas, cm 196 × 103). Since the quality of the brushwork is far lower, it probably was painted by Suttermans' brother Jan.

*Archival sources*

Inventario della Villa di Poggio Imperiale, 1624, ASF, Guardaroba medicea 479, fol. 58s; Inventario di Leopoldo de' Medici, 1675, ASF, Guardaroba medicea 826, fol. 76v, no. 361; Quaderno della Guardaroba generale 1674–1680, 27 February 1676 [ab Incarnatione=1677 modern style], ASF, Guardaroba medicea 799, fol. 191v, no. 361; Quaderno della Guardaroba generale 1679–1685, 30 August 1680, ASF, Guardaroba medicea 870, fol. 63r; Inventario di Palazzo Pitti, 1688, ASF, Guardaroba medicea 932, fol. 130v; Inventario di Palazzo Pitti, 1716–1723, Biblioteca degli Uffizi, ms. 79, fol. 81; (?)Inventario di Palazzo Pitti, 1761, ASF, Guardaroba medicea appendice 94, fol. 530v

*Bibliography*

G. Masselli, in BARDI 1837–1842, I, 1837, unpaginated; CHIAVACCI 1859, p. 100, no. 209; MICHIELS 1865–1878, IX, 1874, p. 28; LAFENESTRE–RICHTENBERGER, E., n.d. [1895?], p. 150, no. 209; WURZBACH 1906–1910, II, 1910, p. 676; BAUTIER 1912b, pp. 59–60; ZIMMERMANN 1912, p. 59; BAUTIER 1926–1929, p. 322; GÖZ 1928, p. 38; JAHN RUSCONI 1937, p. 287, no. 209; TARCHIANI 1939, p. 25; HEINZ 1963, pp. 148, 199 (sub no. 89), 202 (sub no. 112), 216 (sub no. 206); CIPRIANI 1966, p. 19, no. 209; HEINZ–SCHÜTZ 1976, pp. 125–126, sub no. 96; *La Galleria Palatina* 1982, p. 40; S. Meloni Trkulja, in *Sustermans* 1983, pp. 108, no. L; L. Goldenberg Stoppato, in *Il Seicento fiorentino* 1986, *Biografie*, p. 168; L. Goldenberg Stoppato, in TURNER 1996, p. 40; CHIARINI–PADOVANI 1999, p. 103, no. 37; S. Casciu, in CHIARINI–PADOVANI 2003, II, pp. 414–415, no. 682°; L. Goldenberg Stoppato, in *Il viaggio a Compostela* 2004, pp. 75, 104, no. 15

Fig. 4 - Giusto and Jan Suttermans, *Cecilia Renata von Habsburg (1611–1644)*, 1623–1624. Florence, Gallerie fiorentine, storage, inv. 1890, no. 2297
Fig. 5 - Giusto and Jan Suttermans, *Archduke Leopold Wilhelm von Habsburg*, 1623–1624. Florence, Gallerie fiorentine, storage, inv. 1890, no. 4264
Fig. 6 - Giusto and Jan Suttermans, *Maria Anna von Habsburg (1610–1665)*, 1623–1624. Florence, Gallerie fiorentine, storage, inv. 1890, no. 4275

**6** *Eleonora Gonzaga (1598–1655), empress of Austria*
1623–1624
Florence, Palazzo Pitti, Galleria Palatina, inv. 1912, no. 203
oil on canvas, cm 64.7 × 50.2

One of the paintings exhibited in the Suttermans room in Palazzo Pitti in 1688 was a bust-length portrait of Eleonora, the daughter of Vincenzo I Gonzaga and the second wife of Emperor Ferdinand II. According to the inventory Eleonora was wearing a black embroidered dress with jewelry and a ruff:

> Un simile alto braccia 1 ⅛, largo ⅗, dipintovi di mano del suddetto il ritratto dell'imperatrice Eleonora con collare a lattughe, veste nera ricamata tutta gioiellata, con adornamento simile al suddetto  n. 2

Like the portraits of Emperor Ferdinand II and of Archduke Karl von Habsburg, this portrait came from the collection of Cardinal Leopoldo de' Medici. It is described in great detail both in the inventory of his collection which was compiled after his death in 1675, and in a Guardaroba journal on 27 February 1676 [ab Incarnatione=1677 modern style] when the cardinal's possessions entered Cosimo III's collection. According to a second journal, the painting was officially entrusted to the keeper of Palazzo Pitti on 30 August 1680.

Like the other two Habsburg portraits exhibited, the one portraying Empress Eleonora was probably painted during Giusto Suttermans' stay in Vienna between 1623 and 1624 (see cat. no. 5 for further information about the visit). A second, full-length version belongs to the Gallerie fiorentine (in storage, inv. 1890, no. 4274, oil on canvas, cm 190 × 110, fig. 1). A third full-length replica in the Kunsthistorisches Museum in Vienna can be attributed to Giusto's brother Jan, who accompanied him to the imperial court (inv. no. 1734, oil on canvas, cm 207 × 108). A miniature portrait of Eleonora in the same collection can be considered an autograph work (inv. no. 5436, oil on panel, cm 5 × 4.8).

The presence of a portrait of Eleonora Gonzaga in a Medici collection is not at all surprising. Eleonora was a close relation: she was both the daughter of Eleonora de' Medici and the sister-in-law of Grand Duchess Maria Maddalena. The relationship went even deeper: Maria Maddalena had played matchmaker to the marriage between Eleonora of Mantua and Ferdinand II of Austria. In December 1617 she proposed the idea of the marriage to Duke Ferdinando Gonzaga, Eleonora's brother and in January 1618 sent the Florentine painter Tiberio Titi to Mantua expressly to portray the prospective bride. Archival sources mention both a small portrait of Eleonora and a large one by Titi sent to Vienna to present her to the emperor. Titi's larger painting may well be the portrait of *Eleonora Gonzaga* which is now exhibited at the Hofburg in Vienna (inv. no. 3477, oil on canvas, cm 129 × 101.5, fig. 2). When the marriage agreement was signed three years later, at the end of 1621, Suttermans himself was sent to Mantua by Maria Maddalena Maddalena of Austria to paint an up-to-date portrait of the bride. According to a letter sent by Maria Maddalena to Caterina de' Medici, the wife of Ferdinando Gonzaga, on 5 January 1621 [ab Incarnatione=1622 modern style], she intended to send this portrait to the emperor. However, since Eleonora had already sent him a portrait, Maria Maddalena decided to keep the one Suttermans painted (see ASF, Miscellanea medicea 18, insert 2, fol. 8; Mediceo del Principato 6108, fol. 53). Further correspondence makes it clear that Giusto brought back to Florence not only the portrait of Eleonora, but also two portraits of Duchess Caterina. The larger of the two portraits of Caterina (the smaller one was a gift for Dowager Grand Duchess Christine of Lorraine) and the one portraying Eleonora were registered in the Guardaroba inventory on 10 January 1621 [ab Incarnatione=1622 modern style] and sent to the keeper of Palazzo Pitti (Inventario della Guardaroba medicea, 1618–1624, ASF, Guardaroba medicea 373, fols. 297s-d). The inventory specifies that Eleonora and Caterina were portrayed "sino a ½ cintola", to mid-waist, and Maria Maddalena refers to them as half-length portraits. Thus the portrait of *Eleonora Gonzaga as a bride* by Suttermans might well be the half-length portrait which was sold by the antiques dealer Durand-Ruel in Paris by 1952 (oil on canvas, cm 72 × 58, see the photograph by T. Sardnal in the Frick Art Reference Library in New York, fig. 3).

*Archival sources*
Inventario di Leopoldo de' Medici, 1675, ASF, Guardaroba medicea 826, fol. 76v, no. 362; Quaderno della Guardaroba generale 1674–1680, 27 February 1676 [ab Incarnatione=1677 modern style], ASF, Guardaroba medicea 799, fol. 191v, no. 362; Quaderno della Guardaroba generale 1679–1685, 30 August 1680, ASF, Guardaroba medicea 870, fol. 63r; Inventario di Palazzo Pitti, 1688, ASF, Guardaroba medicea 932, fol. 131v; Inventario Palazzo Pitti, 1716–1723, Biblioteca degli Uffizi, ms. 79, fol. 81; (?)Inventario di Palazzo Pitti, 1761, ASF, Guardaroba medicea appendice 94, fol. 530v

*Bibliography*
G. Masselli, in BARDI 1837–1842, I, 1837, unpaginated; CHIAVACCI 1859, p. 100, no. 203; MICHIELS 1865–1878, IX, 1874, p. 28; LAFENESTRE–RICHTENBERGER n.d. [1895?], p. 149, no. 203; WURZBACH 1906–1910, II, 1910, p. 676; BAUTIER 1912b, pp. 59–60; ZIMMERMANN 1912, p. 59; BAUTIER 1926–1929, p. 322; GÖZ 1928, p. 38; JAHN RUSCONI 1937, p. 287, no. 203; *Mostra Iconografica Gonzaghesca* 1937, p. 47, no. 213; J. Lavalleye, in THIEME–BECKER 1907–1950, vol. XXXII, 1938, p. 324; TARCHIANI 1939, p. 25; HEINZ 1963, pp. 148, 202 (sub no. 112), 216 (sub no. 206); CIPRIANI 1966, p. 19, no. 203; HEINZ–SCHÜTZ 1976, p. 273, sub no. 242; *Rubens e la pittura fiamminga* 1977, p. 196, sub no. 79; MATTIOLI 1977, p. 81, sub nos. F 16, F 17; *La Galleria Palatina* 1982, p. 40; S. Meloni Trkulja, in *Sustermans* 1983, p. 114, no. LXX; L. Goldenberg Stoppato, in *Il Seicento fiorentino* 1986, *Biografie*, p. 168; L. Goldenberg Stoppato, in TURNER 1996, p. 40; CHIARINI–PADOVANI 1999, p. 104, no. 42; S. Casciu, in CHIARINI–PADOVANI 2003, II, pp. 414–415, no. 682; L. Goldenberg Stoppato, in *Il viaggio a Compostela* 2004, pp. 75, 105–106, no. 19

Fig. 1 - Giusto and Jan Suttermans, *Empress Eleonora Gonzaga*, 1623–1624. Florence, Gallerie fiorentine, storage, inv. 1890, no. 4274
Fig. 2 - Tiberio Titi, *Eleonora Gonzaga*, 1618. Vienna, Hofburg, inv. no. 3477
Fig. 3 - Giusto Suttermans, *Eleonora Gonzaga as a bride*, 1621. Formerly Paris, Galerie Durand-Ruel

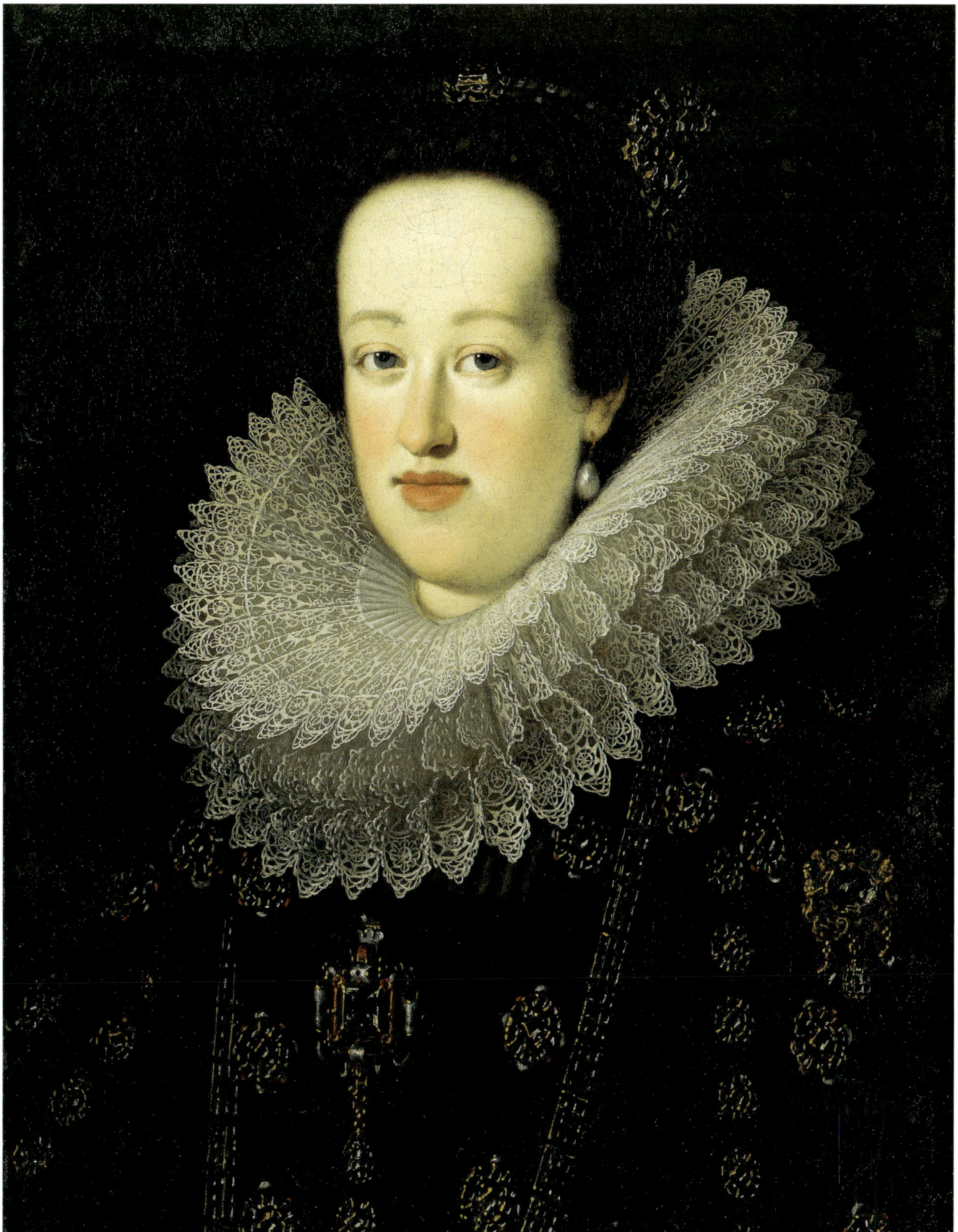

**7** *Karl von Habsburg (1590–1624), archduke of Austria*
1623–1624
Florence, Palazzo Pitti, Galleria Palatina, inv. 1912, no. 293
oil on canvas, cm 67 × 52.5

One of the portraits exhibited in the Suttermans room on the second floor of Palazzo Pitti in 1688 was the bust-length portrait of an unspecified archduke of Austria. According to the inventory the archduke was wearing a cape with a large cross on it and another cross was hanging from a chain around his neck:

> Un quadro in tela alto braccia 1 ⅛, largo ⅝, dipintovi il ritratto dell'Arciduca N: con croce grande al ferraiolo con collana al collo attaccatovi una croce, di mano di Giusto Suttermanni, con adornamento intagliato, e dorato n. 1

The description and the size of the painting (1 Florentine braccio=58,3 centimeters) make a perfect match with a portrait which is still in Palazzo Pitti today, exhibited in the Galleria Palatina. Like the bust-length portraits of *Emperor Ferdinand II von Habsburg* and *Empress Eleonora Gonzaga* in the same museum, this painting came from the collection of Cardinal Leopoldo de' Medici. It is described in great detail in the inventory of his possessions which was compiled after his death 1675:

> Un quadro simile in tela dipintovi il ritratto dell'Arciduca [spazio vuoto] con croce grande al ferraiolo, con collana al collo, attaccatovi una croce, e nella mano destra tiene una pezzuola turchesca di mano di Giusto senza adornamento n.° 1

The name of the archduke does not appear even in the two Guardaroba journals which register the entrance of Leopoldo's possessions in Cosimo III's collection on 27 February 1676 [ab Incarnatione=1677 modern style] and the official consignment to the keeper of Palazzo Pitti on 30 August 1680. Not even the 1716–1723 inventory of Palazzo Pitti supplies his name.

The identity of the sitter has thus been a subject of great debate for art historians. He was identified in the 1859 catalogue of the Galleria Palatina by Chiavacci as Odoardo I Farnese, duke of Parma, perhaps because a portrait of Odoardo's wife *Margherita de' Medici* by Suttermans belongs to the same gallery (see cat. no. 18). Hermann Voss (see GIGLIOLI 1909) correctly recognized the same sitter in a miniature portrait in the Kunsthistorisches Museum in Vienna (inv. no. 5473, oil on paper, cm 7 × 5; see KENNER 1893, pp. 168–169, fig. 207), who was believed to be Archduke Maximilian von Habsburg (1558–1618), grand master of the Teutonic Knights. The sitter is indeed wearing the cross of this military order, but certainly cannot be identified with Maximilian who died in 1618, five years before Suttermans reached Austria.

His identity can now be established without doubt thanks to an unpublished letter sent by Giovanni Altoviti, Medici ambassador to the imperial court, to Curzio Picchena, Medici court secretary, on 11 November 1623. Ambassador Altoviti, who was writing to secretary Picchena to inform him that the two Suttermans brothers had arrived in Vienna five days earlier, specifies that the older of the brothers, namely Giusto, had already started to paint a portrait of Archduke Karl von Habsburg (1590–1624), a brother of Emperor Ferdinand II and of the Grand Duchess of Tuscany Maria Maddalena (ASF, Mediceo del principato 4374a, fol. 214):

> Vennero li due fratelli pittori fin cinque giorni sono. Ha il maggiore già fatto il ritratto del viso del serenissimo arciduca Carlo ch'è stato il primo rispetto alla sua partenza, per far ora gl'altri sci vorrà del tempo, non havendo trovato né tele, né telari in ordine, e dubito che bisognerà che ci svernino ambedue [...]

Since Karl was named grand master of the Teutonic Knights after the death of Maximilian, he clearly must be the sitter in the Galleria Palatina portrait.

A second, full-length version of Archduke Karl's portrait belongs to the Gallerie fiorentine (in storage, inv. 1890, no. 2433, oil on canvas, cm 192 × 111). It comes from a set of full-length portraits of members of Emperor Ferdinand II's family sent to Florence by Suttermans in 1624 and mentioned in a letter sent by ambassador Altoviti to secretary Picchena on 6 July of the same year (see cat. no. 5 for a full transcription of the letter).

*Archival sources*
Inventario di Leopoldo de' Medici, 1675, ASF, Guardaroba medicea, 826, fol. 76v, no. 363; Quaderno della Guardaroba generale 1674–1680, 27 February 1676 [ab Incarnatione=1677 modern style], ASF, Guardaroba medicea 799, fol. 191v, no. 363; BALDINUCCI n.d. [1678 ca.], BNCF, ms. II, II, 110, fol. 350; Quaderno della Guardaroba generale 1679–1685, 30 August 1680, ASF, Guardaroba medicea 870, fol. 63r; Inventario di Palazzo Pitti, 1688, ASF, Guardaroba medicea 932, fol. 130r; Inventario di Palazzo Pitti, 1716–1723, Biblioteca degli Uffizi, ms. 79, fol. 82; (?)Inventario di Palazzo Pitti, 1761, ASF, Guardaroba medicea appendice 94, fol. 530v

*Bibliography*
P. Tanzini, BARDI 1837–1842, II, 1838, unpaginated; CHIAVACCI 1859, p.135, no. 293; GIGLIOLI 1909, p. 154, no. 293; BAUTIER 1912b, pp. 65, 127; ZIMMERMANN 1912, pp. 60, 61; BAUTIER 1926–1929, p. 322; GÖZ 1928, p. 48; JAHN RUSCONI 1937, pp. 288–289, no. 293; TARCHIANI 1939, p. 25; CIPRIANI 1966, p. 126, no. 293; S. Meloni Trkulja, in *Sustermans* 1983, p. 108, sub no. LI; L. Goldenberg Stoppato, in *Il Seicento fiorentino*, 1986, *Biografie*, p. 168; L. Goldenberg Stoppato, in TURNER 1996, p. 40; S. Casciu, in CHIARINI–PADOVANI 2003, II, pp. 416–417, no. 685; L. Goldenberg Stoppato, in *Il viaggio a Compostela* 2004, pp. 75–78, 90 (notes 39–43), 104, no. 12

Fig. 1 - Giusto and Jan Suttermans, *Archduke Karl von Habsburg*, 1623–1624. Florence, Gallerie fiorentine, storage, inv. 1890, no. 2433

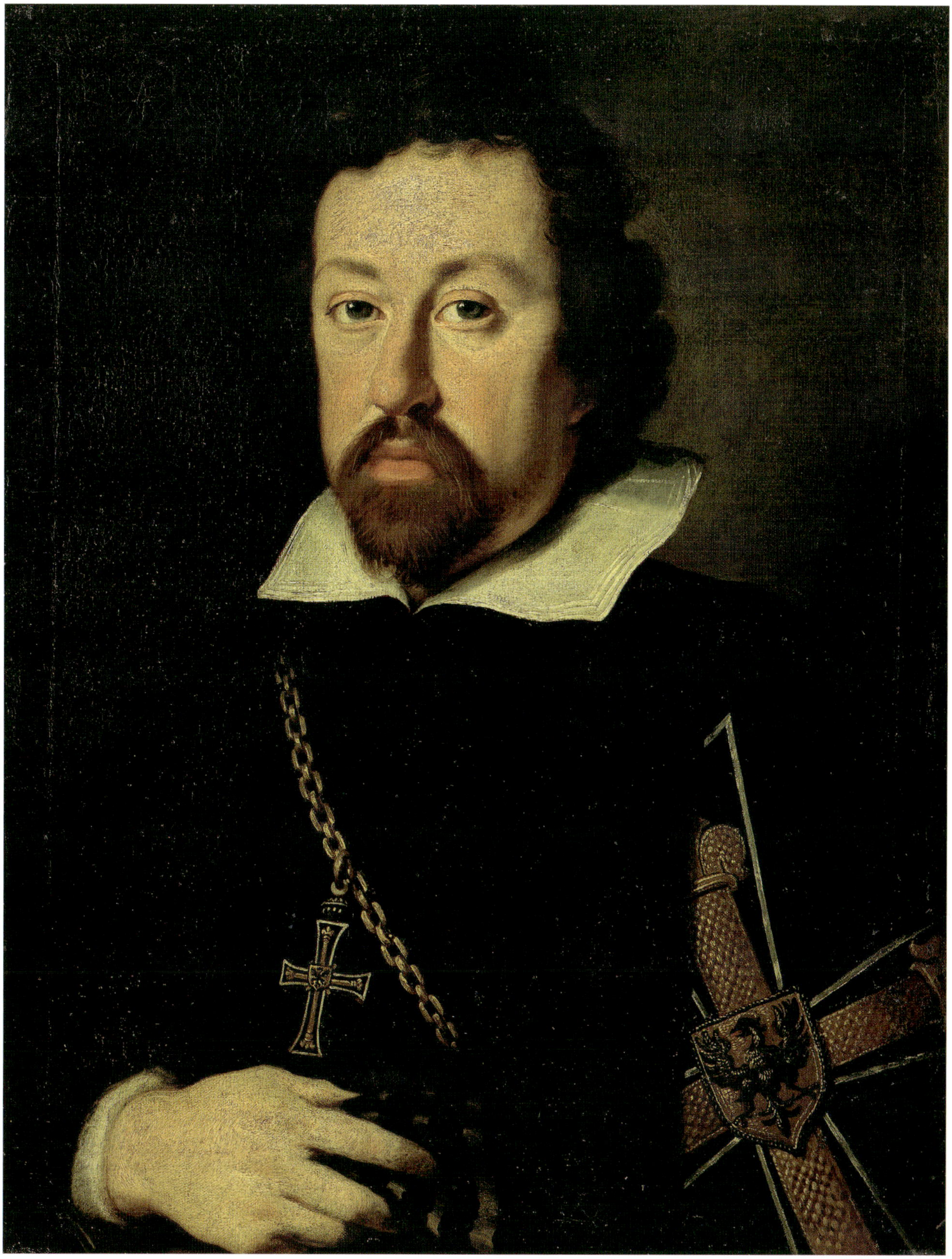

**8** *Leopoldo de' Medici (1617–1675) as a boy in canonicals*
1627
Florence, Galleria degli Uffizi, storage, inv. 1890, no. 3762
oil on canvas, cm 182 × 132.5 (cut down)

One of the paintings exhibited in the Suttermans room on the second floor of Palazzo Pitti was a portrait of Leopoldo de' Medici as a boy. According to the 1688 inventory of the palace, which mistook him for his brother Mattias (1613–1667), he was dressed in clerical garb and was reaching for a hat placed on a table:

> Due quadri in tela alti braccia 3 in circa larghi braccia 2 in circa dipintovi di mano di Giusto Suttermanni, in uno il ritratto del serenissimo principe Mattias figura intera vestito da prete, che con la mano destra posa sopra d'un tavolino coperto di panno rosso in atto di pigliare il cappello, che vi è sopra; e nell'altro il ritratto del serenissimo cardinale Francesco Maria da prete in età giovenile, che con la mano destra posa sopra la testa d'un cane, e con la destra tiene un foglio: con adornamenti intagliati, e dorati n. 2

The mistaken identity was repeated in the palace inventories compiled between 1716 and 1723 and in 1761 and has been taken at face value by modern art historians. The young sitter is in fact identified as Mattias de' Medici both by Silvia Meloni Trkulja in the 1979 catalogue of the Galleria Uffizi and by Karla Langedijk in 1983 in her census of Medici portraiture. Both quoted the 17th-century inventories as their sources of information. It has even been proposed (see the catalogue of the exhibition *I principi bambini* 1985) that this painting was the portrait of Mattias missing from the set of portraits of Medici children painted by Suttermans nel 1622 and exhibited in the Villa del Poggio Imperiale in the 17th century (see cat. nos. 3–4). The hypothesis is not tenable, since the details of this painting do not match the description of the 1622 portrait of Mattias, which appears in the 1691 inventory of this villa. According to this inventory, Mattias had a handkerchief in his left hand and his right hand on a breviary which was lying on the table beside him with a clock (see Inventario della Villa del Poggio Imperiale, 1691, ASF, Guardaroba medicea 991, fol. 88r).

The sitter cannot even be identified with Giovan Carlo de' Medici (1611–1663), whose name was proposed in the catalogue of the exhibition *Mostra del Ritratto* in 1911. Giovan Carlo was destined to a military career by his mother and at age eleven had already been named to the Military Order of Saint John of Jerusalem. According to the books of the Guardaroba, which provide detailed descriptions of the clothing of each member of the family, Giovan Carlo was never dressed in clerical robes during his childhood. He reoriented his career choices and was named cardinal in 1644, only after the failure of the negotiations aimed at marrying him to Anna Carafa, heiress both to the Principality of Stigliano and to the Duchy of Sabbioneta.

As Carlo Gamba recognized in 1927, the sitter is in truth Leopoldo de' Medici, the youngest son of Grand Duke Cosimo II and Archduchess Maria Maddalena. He is clearly identified in an inscription on the back of a small, oval version of the portrait which belongs to the Musée du Louvre in Paris (inv. M.I. 984, oil on canvas, cm 37 × 28, see LANGEDIJK 1981–1987, II, 1983, p. 1315, no. 92/21a): "Leopoldo de Medici, Figliuolo di Cosimo II. Gran Duca, Canonico di Colonia, Creato Cardinale da Clemente IX nel 1667". This small replica comes from a set which included two oval portraits of his mother *Maria Maddalena of Austria* and his brother *Francesco de' Medici (1614–1634)*. These paintings not only resemble the Louvre portrait in format and size, but also have similar inscriptions on the back (see L. Goldenberg Stoppato, in *Pitture fiorentine del Seicento* 1987, pp. 106–108, nos. 37–38).

The portrait of Leopoldo exhibited in the Suttermans room came from a set of full-length portraits of the five sons of Cosimo II de' Medici. This set is cited in 1627 by an inventory of the grand ducal Guardaroba which was called to public attention by Karla Langedijk (1981–1987, vol. II, 1983, p. 779, no. 38/31a). The inventory lists portraits of Ferdinando II in armor, Giovan Carlo and Francesco in embroidered hose and Mattias and Leopoldo in clerical gowns, all delivered to their mother the Archduchess Maria Maddalena of Austria on 8 April 1627:

> [fol. 170s] Cinque quadri in tela alti braccia 3 ½, larghi braccia 2, che vi sono dentro dipinti interi al naturale in uno il Serenissimo nostro Granduca Ferdinando secondo in calza intera e busto armato con elmo e pennachiera in sul tavolino e in dua che in uno il Serenissimo principe Giovan Carlo e Francesco in calze intere recamate e in dua altri, signori principi Mattias e Leopoldo in abito lungo neri da preti con panni pendenti [. . .], / [fol. 170d] [. . .] e tavolini imitati a velluto rosso, mandati con altri dipinti alla arciduchessa d'Austria addì 8 di aprile [1627] [. . .]

The details of the description help us recognize this portrait of Leopoldo and three other paintings from the same series, portraits of the young *Grand Duke Ferdinando II (1610–1670)*, *Mattias (1613–1667) in canonicals* and *Francesco de' Medici (1614–1634)* which are currently exhibited in Palazzo Pitti's Appartamenti reali (Florence, inv. Poggio a Caiano, nos. 138, 136, 140, oil on canvas, cm 201 × 117, 202 × 117, 205 × 119, figs. 1–3; see S. Casciu, in CHIARINI–PADOVANI 2003, II, pp. 430, 432–433, nos. 710, 712, 713). Leopoldo's portrait is listed with the rest of the set by the Palazzo Pitti inventories compiled in 1638 (in the hall of his own apartment) and between 1663 and

Fig. 1 - Giusto Suttermans, *Ferdinando II de' Medici (1610–1670)*, 1627. Florence, Palazzo Pitti, Appartamenti reali, inv. Poggio a Caiano, no. 138
Fig. 2 - Giusto Suttermans, *Mattias de' Medici (1613–1667)*, 1627. Florence, Palazzo Pitti, Appartamenti reali, inv. Poggio a Caiano, no. 136
Fig. 3 - Giusto Suttermans, *Francesco de' Medici (1614–1634)*, 1627. Florence, Palazzo Pitti, Appartamenti reali, inv. Poggio a Caiano, no. 140
Fig. 4 - Giusto Suttermans, *Giovan Carlo de' Medici (1611–1663)*, 1627. Tel Aviv, Museum of Art, formerly London, Speelman collection

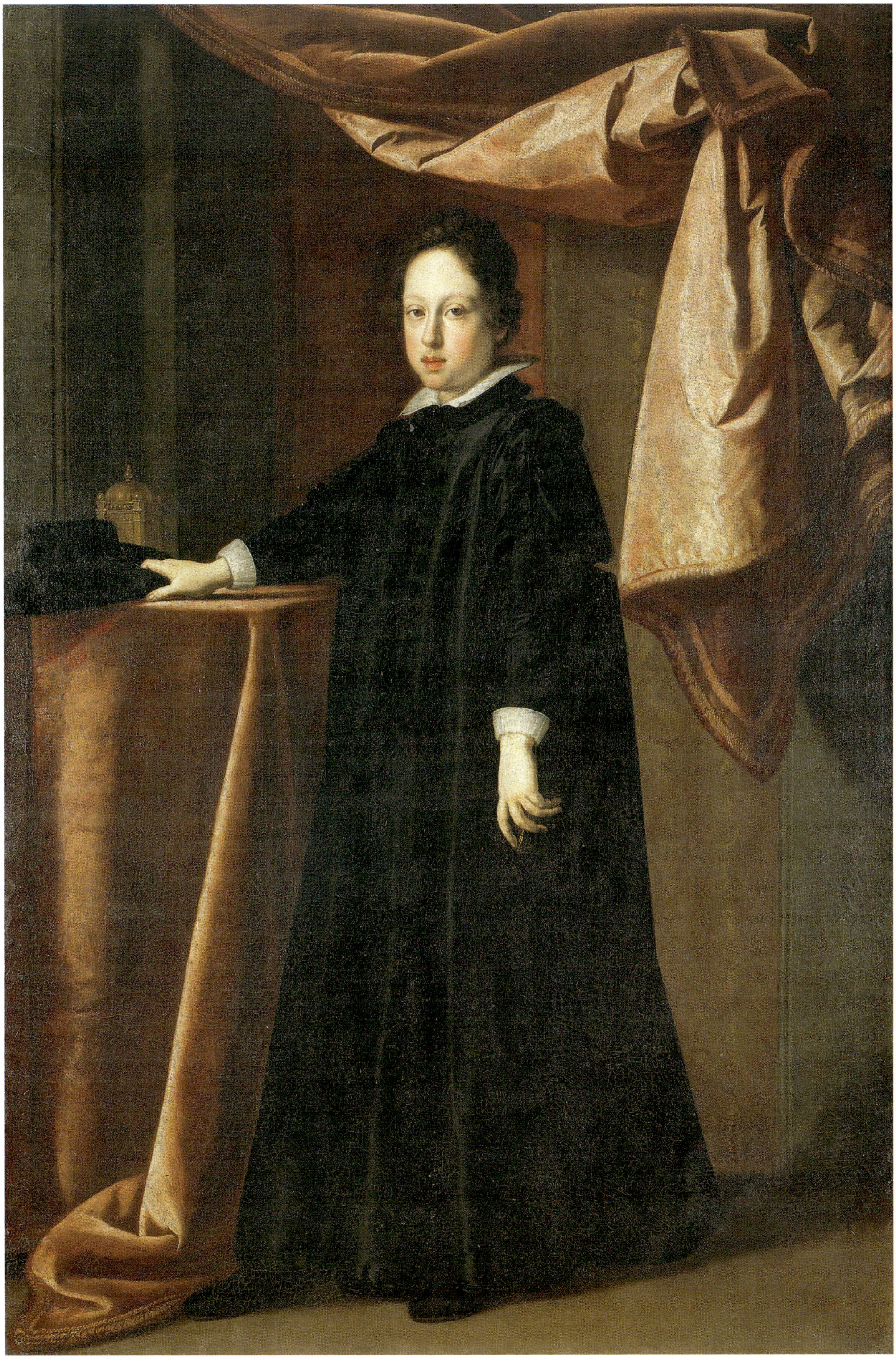

1664 (in Cardinal Carlo de' Medici's apartment, in a room on the left with two windows overlooking Piazza Pitti). It was separated from rest of the set in 1678 to be sent to the Suttermans room, where it was hanging in 1688 as a 'pendant' to the portrait of Leopoldo's nephew *Francesco Maria de' Medici as a boy with his dog* (see cat. no. 20). Three of the other portraits painted in 1627, the ones portraying *Ferdinando II, Mattias* and *Francesco de' Medici*, are described in the 1688 inventory of Palazzo Pitti on the first floor, in the first room on the left with windows overlooking Piazza Pitti, which was used as antechamber by Grand Prince Ferdinando (Inventario di Palazzo Pitti, 1688, ASF, Guardaroba medicea 932, fol. 50v), along with several other full-length Medici portraits. All these portraits were sent to the Medici Villa di Poggio a Caiano in 1866 and brought back to Florence for the portrait exhibition *Mostra del Ritratto* held in Palazzo Vecchio in 1911 (inv. Poggio a Caiano, nos. 146, 142, 145, 143 and 139). The fifth portrait in the 1627 set, which portrayed Giovan Carlo de' Medici (1611–1663), had already been separated from the other four portraits when the first 17th-century inventory of Palazzo Pitti's furnishings was compiled in 1638. It may well have been given in the meantime to Giovan Carlo. A full-length portrait of "Sua Altezza Reverendissima quando era giovane secolare", of 'His Most Reverend Highness' when he was a young layman, is mentioned by the 1663 inventory of Cardinal Giovan Carlo's possessions in the Villa di Castello (ASF, Miscellanea medicea 31, insert 10, fol. 121r). Since the cardinal's collection was sold off after his death, the missing canvas in the 1627 set might well be the portrait of *Giovan Carlo de' Medici (1611–1663) as a youth* given by Edward Speelman to the Tel Aviv Museum in 1953 (see fig. 4; LANGEDIJK 1981–1987, vol. II, 1983, pp. 790–791, no. 38/42; LURIE 1995, pp. 96–97, 208–209, no. 58). The young sitter in the Tel Aviv portrait has been mistaken in the past for Ferdinando II de' Medici, but is clearly identified by the white cross of the Order of Saint John of Jerusalem he is wearing. As mentioned above, Giovan Carlo was admitted to this military order when he was a child and was portrayed by Suttermans in 1622 with the cross of the order on his chest.

*Archival sources*
Inventario della Guardaroba generale 1624–1638, 8 April 1627, ASF, Guardaroba medicea 435, fols. 170s-d; Inventario di Palazzo Pitti, 1638, ASF, Guardaroba medicea 525, fol. 62v; Inventario della Guardaroba di Palazzo Pitti, 1638, ASF, Guardaroba medicea 535, fol. 90s; Entrata e Uscita di Palazzo Pitti, 1638–1648, ASF, Guardaroba medicea 530, fol. 166s; Inventario di Palazzo Pitti, 1663–1664, ASF, Guardaroba medicea 725, fol. 41r; Inventario di Palazzo Pitti, 1688, ASF, Guardaroba medicea 932, fol. 131r; Inventario di Palazzo Pitti, 1716–1723, Biblioteca degli Uffizi, ms. 79, fol. 104; Inventario di Palazzo Pitti, 1761, ASF, Guardaroba medicea appendice 94, fol. 537v

*Bibliography*
Mostra del Ritratto 1911, p. 212, no. 12; BAUTIER 1912b, pp. 31, 39; VENTURI 1913, p. 148 PIERACCINI 1924–1925, II, 1925, p. 555, note a; GAMBA 1927, p. 95, pl. XIII; GÖZ 1928, pp. 25–26, 34; SINGER 1937–1938, III, 1938, p. 239, no. 23987; J. Lavalleye, in THIEME–BECKER 1907–1950, vol. XXXII, 1938, p. 324; S. Meloni Trkulja, in *Gli Uffizi* 1979, ed. 1980, p. 757, no. Ic1028; LANGEDIJK 1981–1987, I, 1981, p. 248, sub no. 3/6, II, 1983, pp. 1314–1315, no. 92/21; S. Meloni Trkulja, in *Sustermans* 1983, pp. 99 (sub no. XXIV), 105, no. XLIII; S. Meloni Trkulja and G. Butazzi, in *I principi bambini* 1985, pp. 53 (sub no. 19), 54 (sub no. 20), 57 (sub no. 23, fig.); L. Goldenberg Stoppato, in *La pittura in Italia. Il Seicento* 1988 ed. 1989, II, p. 895; DANESI SQUARZINA 1990, p. 94 (note 9); L. Goldenberg Stoppato, in TURNER 1996, p. 40; L. Goldenberg Stoppato, in *Il viaggio a Compostela* 2004, pp. 78, 90–91 (notes 46–50), 105, no. 16

## 9 *Leonardo Gamucci (1573-post 1638)*
1626–1630 ca.
Florence, Palazzo Pitti, Galleria Palatina, inv. 1912, no. 419
oil on canvas, cm 99.5 × 78.5

One of the paintings exhibited in the Suttermans room on the second floor of Palazzo Pitti was a portrait of Leonido, a steward of the Dispensa, the grand ducal larder. The 1688 inventory of the palace specifies that he was holding his handkerchief in his hand:

> Un quadro in tela alto braccia 1 ½ buona misura largo braccia 1 ¼ dipintovi di mano di Giusto Suttermanni, il ritratto di messer Leonido di dispensa di Sua Altezza Serenissima con fazzoletto in mano; con adornamento intagliato, straforato, e dorato n. 1

As Silvia Meloni Trkulja noted in 1980, the painting can easily be identified with the Galleria Palatina's painting no. 419. The portrait of "messer Leonido" is also described by the 1716–1723 inventory of the palace, which specifies its provenance from the collection of Cardinal Leopoldo de' Medici. A "mezza figura di messere Leonido di dispensa", a half-length portrait of Leonido of the larder, is in fact mentioned by the inventory of Leopoldo's possessions compiled after his death in 1675. It is also cited by two Guardaroba journals: the first one documents the entrance of the cardinal's possessions in Cosimo III's collection on 27 February 1676 [ab Incarnatione=1677 modern style] and the second one registers the official consignment to the keeper of Palazzo Pitti on 30 August 1680. The portrait is also mentioned without the sitter's name in the 1761 inventory of the same palace. The inventory describes it as a three quarter-length portrait of an old man dressed in black with a white collar and a white beard, holding his handkerchief in his right hand:

> Un Quadro in tela alto braccia 1 ⅔, largo braccia 1 soldi 6, dipintovi, dicesi di mano di Monsieur Giusto, un ritratto d'uomo vecchio mezza figura fino al ginocchio con veste e manto nero, con collana bianca, barba bianca corta, tiene nella mano destra un fazzoletto, con adornamento intagliato, straforato, e tutto dorato segnato n.° 460

The last name of the steward appears in two handwritten lists of debtors and creditors for objects delivered to various members of the court staff by the Medici Guardaroba. "Lionardo Gammucci di Dispensa" is mentioned as a debtor for "un piatto di stagnio", a tin plate, delivered to him on 19 June 1636 (see Debitori e creditori della Guardaroba generale, 1618–1638, ASF, Guardaroba medicea 365, fol. 131s). The debt for the plate in the name of "Leonido Gamucci di Dispensa" was still standing on 28 April 1638 (see Debitori e creditori della Guardaroba generale, 1633–1638, ASF, Guardaroba medicea 476, fol. 210s). This Medici steward might be "Lionardo di Salvestro di Francesco Ganucci", who was born on 6 June 1573 in the Florentine parish of San Marco and baptized on the following day with Piero di Antonio Berti standing as godfather (see Registro dei Battezzati, Maschi, 1571–1577, Florence, Archivio dell'Opera di Santa Maria del Fiore, Registro 16, fol. 16).

The portrait probably was painted by Suttermans towards the end of the 1620's. Both the style of painting and the intense contrast between light and shadow recall the painter's manner in the portrait of *Leopoldo de' Medici as a boy in canonicals* he painted in 1627 (see cat. no. 8).

*Archival sources*
Inventario di Leopoldo de' Medici, 1675, ASF, Guardaroba medicea 826, fol. 85v, no. 496; Quaderno della Guardaroba generale 1674–1680, 27 February 1676 [ab Incarnatione=1677 modern style], ASF, Guardaroba medicea 799, fol. 203v, no. 496; Quaderno della Guardaroba generale 1679–1685, 30 August 1680, ASF, Guardaroba medicea 870, fols. 72v–73r; Inventario di Palazzo Pitti, 1688, ASF, Guardaroba medicea 932, fol. 129v; Inventario Palazzo Pitti, 1716–1723, Biblioteca degli Uffizi, ms. 79, fols. 91–92; Inventario di

Palazzo Pitti, 1761, ASF, Guardaroba medicea appendice 94, fol. 534v

*Bibliography*
INGHIRAMI 1834, p. 59, no. 419; P. Thouar, in BARDI 1837–1842, III, 1840, unpaginated; CHIAVACCI 1859, p. 182, no. 419; BAUTIER 1912b, pp. 86, 127; JAHN RUSCONI 1937, p. 291, no. 419; TARCHIANI 1939, p. 25; *Al servizio del granduca* 1980, p. 34, no. V, 16; S. Meloni Trkulja, in *Sustermans* 1983, p. 112, no. LXII; FRATELLINI 1993, p. 156; CHIARINI–PADOVANI 1999, p. 67, no. 26; S. Casciu, in CHIARINI–PADOVANI 2003, II, p. 420, no. 692; L. Goldenberg Stoppato, in *Il viaggio a Compostela* 2004, p. 102, no. 5

**10** *Domenico Cresti, known as Passignano (1559–1638)*
1630–1632 ca.
Florence, Palazzo Pitti, Galleria Palatina, inv. 1890, no. 565
oil on canvas, cm 62 × 46

This painting was long believed to be a self-portrait of the painter Domenico Cresti and was exhibited with the Uffizi's collection of self-portraits. It was Odoardo GIGLIOLI (1909) who first recognized it as the portrait of Passignano painted by Giusto Suttermans, quoting the 1675 inventory of Cardinal Leopoldo de' Medici's collection as his source of information. Every detail of the painting matches the description of the portrait in this inventory, which specifies that Passignano was portrayed by the Fleming in his old age with a bald head and a white beard and was dressed in black with a slender gold chain hanging around his neck:

> Un Quadro in tela alto braccia 1 ⅓, largo 1 ⅛, dipintovi di mano di Giusto il ritratto del Passignano da vecchio, con capo calvo e scoperto, barba bianca, vestito di nero, senza mani, e si vede l'orecchio destro, con catenuzza d'oro al collo, senz'adornamento

After the cardinal's death his possessions, including this painting, entered the collection of his nephew Grand Duke Cosimo III and were registered in a journal of the grand ducal Guardaroba on 27 February 1676 [ab Incarnatione=1677 modern style]. According to another Guardaroba journal, the painting was officially entrusted to the keeper of Palazzo Pitti on 30 August 1680. These 'transfers' were of a purely administrative nature. The portrait, like many of Leopoldo's other paintings, never left the cardinal's apartment on the second floor of Palazzo Pitti. It was only moved from the room Leopoldo used as Guardaroba to another room in the same apartment for the exhibition in Suttermans' honor. Filippo Baldinucci in fact mentioned it in the Suttermans room in his *Notizie del cav. Domenico Passignani*, the biography of the Tuscan painter he published in 1681:

> Venendo ora al fine di questa narrazione, dico che un ritratto del Passignano [...] veramente bellissimo ha il serenissimo granduca fatto al vivo per mano di Giusto Subtermans, che si conserva nel palazzo de' Pitti, nella stanza de' ritratti e pitture di mano dello stesso Giusto.

The 1688 inventory of Palazzo Pitti also listed this portrait among the thirty paintings by the Fleming exhibited together on the second floor of the palace:

> Un quadro in tela alto braccia 1 ⅓ largo, braccia 1 ⅛, dipintovi di mano di Giusto Suttermanni, il ritratto del Passignano da vecchio con capo calvo scoperto, barba bianca, vestito di nero, senza mani, e si vede l'orecchio destro con catenuzza d'oro al collo, con adornamento intagliato, e tutto dorato       n. 1

The sitter closely resembles Passignano as he appears in two other portraits that belong to the Galleria degli Uffizi, a copy bearing his name at the top of the canvas "DOMENICO PASSIGNIANI" (inv. 1890, no. 3102, oil on canvas, cm 62 × 46, see M. Mosco, in *Gli Uffizi* 1979, ed. 1980, p. 720, no. Ic766) and the *Self-portrait* he painted when he was younger (inv. 1890, no. 1695, oil on canvas, see S. Meloni Trkulja, in *Gli Uffizi* 1979, ed. 1980, p. 952, no. A674).

Nel 1909 Giglioli suggested that Suttermans may have been a student of Passignano. His hypothesis was based on the entry for the portrait of *Simone Paganucci* in an inventory of Palazzo Pitti compiled during the first decade of the 18th century (*Quadri del R. Palazzo Pitti*, n.d., ASF, Guardaroba medicea 1185, fol. 379s, no. 520). The portrait of Paganucci is listed in the inventory, which cites the works in alphabetical order by author, next to last in the list of paintings by "Monsù Giusto":

> 520 Un quadro del medesimo autore fatto nel tempo che uscì dalla scuola del Passignano, entrovi un Ritratto al naturale sino al ginocchio di Simone Paganucci vestito di nero [...] che tiene un fazzoletto in una mano e nell'altra una lettera con la sopra scritta seguente, All'Illustrissimo signore Simone Paganucci [...]

In short, the inventory states that the portrait of Paganucci, who had a handkerchief in one hand and a letter in the other one, was painted by the same artist at the time he had just left Passignano's school. On this basis, Claudio Pizzorusso (in *Sustermans* 1983) hypothesized that Suttermans studied with this painter shortly after he first arrived in Florence. Unfortunately the hypothesis is based on an error made by the scribe who compiled the 18th-century inventory. The portrait of *Simone Paganucci* can easily be identified with a canvas in the Galleria Palatina, since his name appears on the letter the sitter is holding (inv. 1912, no. 117, oil on canvas, cm 117 × 88; see GOLDENBERG STOPPATO 2004, pp. 168, 197–198, note 38, fig. 4). This canvas, once attributed to Suttermans, was actually painted by the Florentine portraitists Domenico and Valore Casini. It closely resembles the manner of painting in the portraits of *Lorenzo della Robbia* and his mother *Ginevra Popoleschi* in the Florentine church of Santa Maria in Campo, one of the few works by Valore Casini cited by Filippo BALDINUCCI (1681–1728, ed. 1845–1847, vol. III, 1846, pp. 450–451). Thanks to the brief biography published by Baldinucci, we know that the Casini brothers "uscirono", or came, from Passignano's school. Thus the scribe who penned the 18th-century inventory probably was referring to one of the Casini brothers when he mentioned the author of Paganucci's portrait, which somehow got added to the wrong list of paintings. Baldinucci's biography of Suttermans, which was based on information dictated to him by the painter, makes absolutely no reference to a period of study under Passignano. There is also no evidence of such a relationship in the Fleming's earliest Florentine works, which derive directly from the model set by Frans Pourbus the younger (see for example the portraits of *Margherita* and *Anna de' Medici* on exhibit, cat. nos. 3–4).

As Marco Chiarini suggested, the style of painting in the portrait of Passignano seems to date from 1630–1631, a date also appropriate for the sitter's apparent age.

*Archival sources*
Inventario di Leopoldo de' Medici, n.d. [1663–1671?], Firenze, Biblioteca Riccardiana, ms. Riccardi 2443, fol. 120; Inventario di Leopoldo de' Medici, 1675, ASF, Guardaroba medicea 826, fol. 90v, no. 601; Quaderno della Guardaroba generale 1674–1680, 27 febbraio 1676 [ab Incarnatione=1677 modern style], ASF, Guardaroba medicea 799, fol. 210v, no. 601; Quaderno della Guardaroba generale 1679–1685, 30 August 1680, ASF, Guardaroba medicea 870, fol. 77v; Inventario di Palazzo Pitti, 1688, ASF, Guardaroba medicea 932, fol. 129v; Inventario Palazzo Pitti, 1716–1723, Biblioteca degli Uffizi, ms. 79, fols. 251–252; (?)Inventario di Palazzo Pitti, 1761, ASF, Guardaroba medicea appendice 94, fol. 530v

*Bibliography*
BALDINUCCI 1681–1728, ed. 1845–1847, III, 1846, p. 451; GIGLIOLI 1909, pp. 332–333; BAUTIER 1926–1929, p. 319; JAHN RUSCONI 1937, p. 291, no. 565; TARCHIANI 1939, p. 25; FRANCINI CIARANFI 1964, p. 7; CIPRIANI 1966, p. 14, no. 565; PRINZ 1971, p. 236, under document 216; M. Chiarini, in *Gli Uffizi* 1979, ed. 1980, p. 1014, no. A919; C. Pizzorusso, in *Sustermans* 1983, p. 50, no. 27; L. Goldenberg Stoppato, in *Il Seicento fiorentino* 1986, *Pittura*, pp. 321–322, no. 1166, fig.; *Fifty Paintings* 1993, p. 76, sub no. 15; CHIARINI–PADOVANI 1999, p. 100, no. 26; S. Casciu, in CHIARINI–PADOVANI 2003, II, p. 422, no. 695; L. Goldenberg Stoppato, in *Il viaggio a Compostela* 2004, pp. 79, 101–102, no. 4

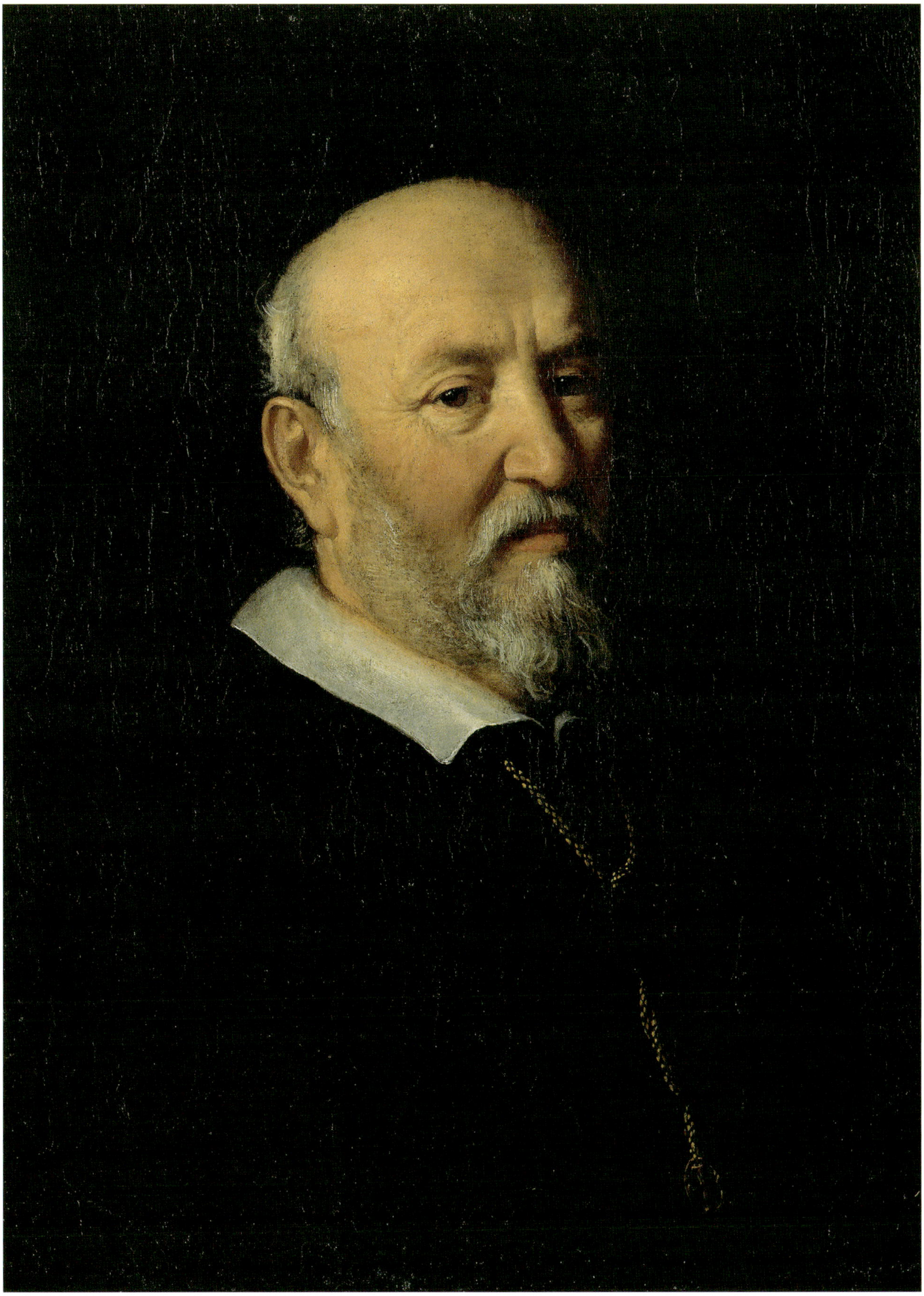

**11** *Charles of Lorraine (1571–1640), duke of Guise*
1632–1638
Florence, Palazzo Pitti, storage, inv. 1890, no. 2341
oil on canvas, cm 65 × 52

One of the paintings exhibited in the Suttermans room on the second floor of Palazzo Pitti in 1678 was a portrait of the duke of "Visa". According to the 1688 inventory of the palace the sitter was wearing armor, a white scarf and a lace-trimmed collar:

> Un quadro in tela alto braccia 1 soldi 2, largo ⅞ dipintovi, di mano del suddetto, si crede il ritratto del Duca di Visa in faccia, armato, con ciarpa bianca e collare di trina, con adornamento scorniciato liscio e tutto dorato          n. 1

The garbled title "Visa", which also appears in the 1716–1723 inventory of the palace, is written in a more comprehensible form in the inventories of the palace compiled in 1638 and between 1663 and 1664, which refer to the sitter as the "Duca di Ghisa" without specifying the name of the painter. Filippo Baldinucci also refers to him as the "Duca di Guisa" in the census of works by "Monsù Giusto" he compiled while he was planning the exhibition in 1678 and in the 1761 inventory of Palazzo Pitti. The sitter thus can be identified as Charles of Lorraine, duke of Guise, a distant relative of Dowager Grand Duchess Christine of Lorraine. The duke, who was forced out of France by Cardinal de Richelieu, found refuge in Tuscany in the early 1630's. He died in Cuna, in the province of Siena, on 30 September 1640 and was conceded the honor of burial in the Florentine church of San Lorenzo, where his corpse was interred on 3 October 1640 (see Morti della Grascia, 1626–1669, ASF, Ufficiali poi Magistrato della Grascia 195, fol. 98r).

The portrait was painted by 1638 when it was first described in an inventory of Palazzo Pitti. It may have been painted several years earlier since we know that Charles of Lorraine stood godfather for Suttermans' first-born son, Carlo, on 22 August 1632 (Atti Battesimali del Fonte di S. Giovanni di Firenze, Maschi, 1631–1634, Florence, Archivio dell'Opera di Santa Maria del Fiore, Registro 39, fol. 19v, cited by BATTISTINI 1930, p. 192). Suttermans owned a second version of this portrait, which was hanging in the living room of his villa in the parish of San Leonardo in Arcetri when he died in 1681 (see the inventory taken after his death, ASF, Pupilli del Principato 2722, fol. 304v, transcribed by M. C. Guidotti, in *Sustermans* 1983, p. 131, no. 654).

Two versions of the portrait still exist: the first one belongs to the Drury-Lowe collection at Locko Park in England, where the sitter has been mistaken for Ottavio Piccolomini (oil on canvas, cm 61 × 48.3, see *National Exhibition Leeds* 1868, p. 49, no. 703; GRAVES 1913–1915, III, 1914, p. 1278). Judging from the photograph in the Witt Library (Courtauld Institute, London, no. B73/1202), it seems to be of better quality than the painting we are exhibiting and may well be an autographic work. The second version, painted with the help of a workshop hand, belongs to the Kunsthaus in Zürich (inv. no. 1634, oil on canvas, cm 66 × 51, see J. Lavalleye, in THIEME–BECKER, 1907–1950, vol. XXXII, 1938, p. 324; *Kunsthaus Zürich* 1958, p. 64, no. 1634). The same assistant also painted the clothes in a portrait of the duke of Guise's son *François of Lorraine (1612–1639), prince of Joinville* in Florence (Gallerie fiorentine, inv. 1890, no. 2447, oil on canvas, cm 64 × 44, see S. Meloni Trkulja, in *Sustermans* 1983, p. 109).

*Archival sources*
Inventario di Palazzo Pitti, 1638, ASF, Guardaroba medicea 525, fol. 38r; Inventario della Guardaroba di Palazzo Pitti, 1638, ASF, Guardaroba medicea 535, fol. 51s; Entrata e Uscita di Palazzo Pitti, 1638–1648, ASF, Guardaroba medicea 530, fol. 135s; Inventario di Palazzo Pitti, 1663–1664, ASF, Guardaroba medicea 725, fol. 59r; F. BALDINUCCI n.d. [1678 ca.], BNCF, ms. II.II.110, fol. 350; Inventario di Palazzo Pitti, 1688, ASF, Guardaroba medicea 932, fol. 129r; Inventario di Palazzo Pitti, 1716–1723, Biblioteca degli Uffizi, ms. 79, fol. 101; Inventario di Palazzo Pitti, 1761, ASF, Guardaroba medicea appendice 94, fol. 534v

*Bibliography*
(?)NAGLER 1835–1852, XVIII, 1848, p. 6; RIDOLFI 1896, pp. 6–7; PIERACCINI 1910, p. 115, no. 1391; BAUTIER 1912a, p. 12; BAUTIER 1912b, pp. 340, 115, 126; BAUTIER 1926–1929, p. 319; GÖZ 1928, pp. 47; J. Lavalleye, in THIEME–BECKER 1907–1950, vol. XXXII, 1938, p. 324; S. Meloni Trkulja, in *Pittura Francese* 1977, p. 261, sub no. 207; M. Chiarini, in *Gli Uffizi* 1979, ed. 1980, pp. 530–531, nos. P1649, P1653; S. Meloni Trkulja, in *Sustermans* 1983, p. 109, no. LIV; K. Schütz, in *Die Pracht der Medici* 1998–1999, I, p. 158, no. 193; L. Goldenberg Stoppato, in *Il viaggio a Compostela* 2004, pp. 79, 80, 91 (notes 58–62), 101, no. 3

**12** *Elia da Zia, pilot master of the Capitana galley*
*(active 1606–1641)*
1634–1635 ca.
Florence, Palazzo Pitti, Galleria Palatina, inv. 1912, no. 119
oil on canvas, cm 69 × 56

One of the works exhibited in the Suttermans room on the second floor of Palazzo Pitti in 1678 was a portrait of Elia, the pilot master of one of the grand duke's galleys. According to the 1688 inventory, the sitter had a white beard, was wearing a red scarf and was holding a bamboo staff:

> Un simile alto braccia 1 soldi 4, largo soldi 18, dipintovi di mano del suddetto Elia comito reale delle galere di Sua Altezza Serenissima con barba a spazzola bianca, ciarpa rossa e canna d'India nelle mani, con adornamento simile al suddetto    n. 1

Thanks to this description, the portrait can easily be identified with this painting still on exhibit in Palazzo Pitti. Its presence in the palace is documented from 1638 on, when it was described both in two inventories and in a journal of outgoing and incoming objects started the same year. The painting is listed without an attribution both in these books and in the 1663–1664 inventory of the grand ducal residence. It is also mentioned in the 1716–1723 inventory of the palace in the room known as the "camera della Scarabattola d'Oro" in the apartment of Grand Prince Ferdinando, along with twelve other paintings attributed to "Giusto Sutterman". It can thus be recognized as one of the thirteen "Ritratti di Principi, Principesse, et altri suggetti", portraits of Princes, Princesses and other sitters, listed in the ninth room of the same apartment in the 1761 inventory of Palazzo Pitti. The portrait of Elia is also mentioned in an appendix to the 1768 inventory of the Villa del Poggio Imperiale. This appendix lists it with a group of paintings sent to the villa on 31 March 1780:

> Un Quadro in tela alto braccia 1 ⅕, largo soldi 19, dipintovi da Monsieur Giusto, ritratto fino a mezzo busto d'uomo vecchio, con capelli corti e barba canuta, collare bianco e veste nera con tracolla rossa, tiene nella destra bastone con palla d'argento, corniola e anello in dito, con adornamento intagliato e dorato, N: 876

The portrait was returned to Palazzo Pitti by 1837, when it was reproduced in Luigi Bardi's catalogue of the palace's gallery.
Gino Guarnieri mentioned the sitter "Elia da Zia piloto delle galere di Sua Altezza Serenissima in Livorno", the pilot of 'His Most Serene Highness' galleys in Livorno, in his study on the Knights of Saint Stephen, the military order founded by Cosimo I de' Medici. According to Guarnieri, Elia was the author of several reports concerning ports and landing places in the Mediterranean Sea. Two of these reports were presented to the Knights of Saint Stephen in March 1606 and in April 1611. The pilot master also translated several other reports presented in 1614, 1615 and 1617 from Greek to Italian. These translations refer to him as the pilot of the grand ducal galley known as "la Capitana" (see GUARNIERI 1965, pp. 116–120, 131–132). Pilot Elia was born on the Cycladic isle known as Zéa or Kéa and was still alive in 1641, when he was listed among the members of the Greek confraternity dedicated to the Santissima Annunziata in Livorno (see PANESSA 2001, p. 53; S. Casciu, in CHIARINI–PADOVANI 2003, II, p. 412).

The painting probably dates from the mid–1630's, since it is quite close in style to the portrait of *Madonna Domenica dalle Cascine, Cecca di Pratolino and Pietro Moro*, which is cited in a document from 1634 (see cat. no. 13).

*Archival sources*
Inventario di Palazzo Pitti, 1638, ASF, Guardaroba medicea 525, fol. 38v; Inventario della Guardaroba di Palazzo Pitti, 1638, ASF, Guardaroba medicea 535, fol. 51s; Entrata e Uscita di Palazzo Pitti, 1638–1648, ASF, Guardaroba medicea 530, fol. 136s; Inventario di Palazzo Pitti, 1663–1664, ASF, Guardaroba medicea 725, fol. 54v; F. Baldinucci n.d. [1678 ca.], BNCF, ms. II.II.110, fol. 350; Inventario di Palazzo Pitti, 1688, ASF, Guardaroba medicea 932, fol. 131v; Inventario di Palazzo Pitti, 1716–1723, Biblioteca degli Uffizi, ms. 79, fol. 88; (?)Inventario di Palazzo Pitti, 1761, ASF, Guardaroba medicea appendice 94, fol. 530v; Inventario della Villa del Poggio Imperiale, 1768, ASF, Imperiale e Reale Corte 4855, I Appendix, fol. 57r

*Bibliography*
G. Masselli, in BARDI 1837–1842, I, 1837, unpaginated; FÉTIS 1857, I, p. 451; CHIAVACCI 1859, p. 60, no. 119; MICHIELS 1865–1878, IX, 1874, p. 28; BAUTIER 1912b, pp. 81, 127, pl. XXIV; SIMAR 1913, p. 136; BAUTIER 1926–1929, p. 320; JAHN RUSCONI 1937, pp. 284–285, no. 119; J. Lavalleye, in THIEME–BECKER 1907–1950, vol. XXXII, 1938, p. 324; TARCHIANI 1939, pp. 25, 65, fig.; CIPRIANI 1966, p. 54, no. 119; *Al servizio del granduca* 1980, p. 31, no. V, 7; CHIARINI 1983, p. 270, fig. 9; M. Chiarini, in *Sustermans* 1983, pp. 12, 60; C. Pizzorusso, in *Sustermans* 1983, p. 56, no. 31; MEIJER 1983, p. 783, fig. 41; CHIARINI–PADOVANI 1999, p. 67, no. 29; M. Chiarini, in CHIARINI–PADOVANI 2003, I, p. 19; S. Casciu, in CHIARINI–PADOVANI 2003, II, p. 412, no. 678; L. Goldenberg Stoppato, in *Il viaggio a Compostela* 2004, p. 106, no. 21

**13** *Madonna Domenica dalle Cascine, Cecca di Pratolino and Piero Moro*

1634

Florence, Galleria degli Uffizi, inv. Poggio Imperiale "rosso", no. 1356

oil on canvas, cm 100 × 94

Filippo Baldinucci lists a portrait of "Menica" in the census of works by Monsù Giusto he compiled while planning the 1678 exhibition in the painter's honor. The portrait is also mentioned in the Suttermans room by the 1688 inventory of Palazzo Pitti, which specifies that there were three sitters, supplies their names and describes the simple, gilded frame:

> Un quadro in tela alto braccia 1 ⅚, largo braccia 1 soldi 8 dipintovi di mano di Giusto Suttermanni, madonna Domenica dalle Cascine, la Maria di Pratolino, e Piero moro con adornamento scorniciato liscio, e tutto dorato ___n. 1

The painting was already in the palace in 1638 when it was cited, without an attribution, by three inventories. It was hanging at that time in the fifth room of the new apartment facing Piazza Pitti:

> 76 Un quadro in tela entrovi dipinto Madonna Domenica dalle Cascine, la Maria di Pratolino e Pietro Moro con cornice tutte indorate alto braccia 2, largo braccia 1 ¾

It appears, duly attributed to Suttermans, in the inventories of Palazzo Pitti compiled between 1663 and 1664 and between 1716 and 1723. It is also described in the 1761 inventory of the palace, which was called to my attention by Paola Squellati. Though neither the painter's name, nor the identity of the sitters are indicated in this inventory, the painting can easily be recognized thanks to the detailed description, which mentions a black man with pearl earrings standing next to two elderly countrywomen, one holding a basket of grapes and the other one in a straw hat, holding a duck:

> Uno detto simile alto braccia 1 soldi 8, largo braccia 1 ½ dipintovi mezze figure due vecchie montanare, che una con cappello in capo di paglia con un'anatra in braccio, e l'altra con un panierino con uva dentro et un moro in disparte, con pendenti a pera di perle, con adornamento scorniciato e tutto dorato segnato di numero 1081

This painting has in the past been confused with a painting in the Galleria degli Uffizi that comes from the collection of Cardinal Carlo de' Medici, but after careful examination of the 17th-century documentation, it is now clear that there were two distinct versions of the same painting. The first one, which had a gold frame, was exhibited in Palazzo Pitti from 1638 to 1761 and was subsequently lost or sold off either by Grand Duke Leopold of Lorraine or by Napoleon's commissaries. The second version, which had a dark frame with gold edging, was listed in the 1667 inventory of the cardinal's collection, which supplies a different name for the second woman in the painting. While the inventories of Palazzo Pitti identify the second peasant woman as Maria from Pratolino, the inventory of the cardinal's collection calls her Cecca (an abbreviation for Francesca) from Pratolino.

Marco Chiarini attributed the Galleria degli Uffizi's painting to Suttermans in 1977 (it had been published with an attribution to Pietro Bellotti, see Cappi Bentivegna 1962-1964). As Chiarini noted, the painting in the Uffizi comes from the Villa del Poggio Imperiale and still has on the back of the canvas the number assigned to the painting by a 19th-century inventory of this villa outside Porta Romana, one of the gates to the city of Florence. It came to Poggio Imperiale in 1780 from another grand ducal villa. It is in fact listed with other paintings "provenienti dalla consegna del Guardaroba dell'Ambrogiana", from the consignment made by the keeper of the Ambrogiana, which were registered on 30 September 1780 in the appendix to the 1768 inventory of the Villa del Poggio Imperiale. The inventory describes both the walnut stained frame with gold edging and specifies that it depicted a black man and two old ladies, one carrying a basket of eggs and the other holding a duck:

> Uno detto in tela alto braccia 1 ⅔, largo braccia 1 ½, dipintovi da Monsieur Giusto Sutterman due vecchie che una con paniera di u[o]ve in mano ^e l'altra con anatra in mano e moro dietro^, ornamento tinto color di noce filettato d'oro - numero 14

The same painting is listed in the inventories of the Villa Ambrogiana compiled in 1732 and 1758, but not in the previous one that was compiled in 1683 (ASF, Guardaroba medicea 883bis). The canvas and the frame described in the 1732 inventory of the Ambrogiana were quite similar:

> Un simile [quadro in tela] alto braccia 1 ⅔, largo braccia 1 ½, dipintovi da Giusto Suttermanni due vec[c]hie, che una con paniere d'ova in mano e l'altra un'anitra e dietro si vede un moro, con adornamento tinto di color di noce e filettato d'oro

This painting probably came from the collection of Cardinal Carlo de' Medici. The 1667 inventory of his possessions in the Casino di San Marco describes just such a painting with a similar dark frame, edged with gold:

> Uno quadro in tela alto braccia 2 ½ - largo braccia 1 ⅝ entrovi Mona Domenica delle Cascine, la Ceccha di Pratolino e il Moro, dicesi mano di Mon[s]ù Giusto con adornamento nero filettato d'oro __ numero 1.

After the cardinal's death his possessions entered the grand duke's collection and were registered in the books of the Guardaroba generale on 30 June 1667.

Both paintings are mentioned in a letter sent by Giovan Carlo de' Medici (1611–1663) to his brother Mattias (1613–1667) from the Medici Villa di Pratolino on 30 September 1634 (called to my attention by Silvia Mascalchi). In this letter Giovan Carlo mentions portraits of local peasants painted by Suttermans and of a court dwarf painted by Giovanni da San Giovanni (1592–1636) to entertain the Medici court at rest in Pratolino:

> [. . .] Siamo stati fin'hora a Pratolino, facendo quelle cacce, che sono state copiose più di starne, che di lepri, e si poteva pigliarne senza numero, se havessimo voluto. Nell'hore della quiete havevamo la ricreazione delle pitture, Giusto faceva ritratti di quelle contadine, che si è portato esquisitamente. Giovanni da San Giovanni dipigneva a fresco, et è riuscito bravamente; in particolare in un tondo portatile ha dipinto Janni in forma di satiro che sia castrato da certe ninfe, e lo somiglia per eccellenza. [. . .]

Thanks to this letter we know that these rustic portraits were painted for recreational rather than purely artistic reasons. This purpose and the simultaneous presence at Pratolino of Giovanni da San Giovanni, who had a predilection for satirical painting, explain the unusual subject of these paintings. Above and beyond this source of inspiration, which was noted by Marco Chiarini, Suttermans draws from the cultural tradition of his native land. The works of Pieter Aertsen (1507/8–1575) and Joachim Bueckelaer (1533 ca.–1574) were aptly cited as iconographical models for this painting by Bert Meijer in 1983. The paintings by Jacob Jordaens (1593–1678) depicting *A Satyr with a Peasant* spring from the same cultural roots (see for example the painting in Brussels, Musées Royaux des Beaux Arts, inv. no. 6179).

The name of Monna Domenica or Menica dalle Cascine, also indicated as the Medici factoress at the Cascine, appears frequently in the lists of daily expenditures of Grand Duke Ferdinando II's Camera. These lists cite a great number of tips given to her for the geese, chicken and piglets she delivered. For example, in April 1622 a scudo was given to "mona Menica delle Cascine" (see *Ordini per il Serenissimo Gran Duca, l'Anno 1622*, Camera del Granduca 3b, fol. 10) and another scudo was given in October 1626 "A M.a Domenica delle Cascine che portò l'ocche", to monna Domenica from the Cascine who brought geese (see *Spese estraordinarie del Serenissimo Gran Duca dal primo di settembre 1626 a tutto agosto 1627*, Camera del Granduca 7b, fol. 6). Judging from some of the tips she received, it seems that Domenica also played a second role at court. In December 1635 she received a tip of three scudi for coming to the Villa di Poggio, "A monna Domenica delle Cascine che venne al Poggio tre scudi", and another scudo was given to her later the same month as a reward for coming back to play jester once again, "A monna Domenica che tornò di nuovo a fare il buffone" (see *Spese estraordinarie del Serenissimo Gran Duca cominciate il primo settembre 1635 a tutto agosto 1636*, Camera del Granduca 17b, fols. 17r, 18v). The name of Cecca di Pratolino also appears in the lists of the grand duke's expenses. For example, she is mentioned in the list of expenditures for the month of October 1632, when she received a tip for the "mele cotognie", or quince she brought (see *Spese estraordinarie del Serenissimo Gran Duca cominciate il primo di settembre 1632 a tutto agosto 1633*, ASF, Camera del Granduca 14b, fol. 13v), and in July 1634 she was given a tip for "una zana di cedratino", a basket of citrons (see *Spese estraordinarie del Serenissimo Gran Duca dal primo settembre 1633 a tutto agosto 1634*, Camera del Granduca 15b, fol. 48v).

*Archival sources for the lost painting*
Letter from Giovan Carlo de' Medici, to Mattias de' Medici, Florence, 30 September 1634, ASF, Mediceo del Principato 5392, fol. 252; Inventario di Palazzo Pitti, 1638, ASF, Guardaroba medicea 525, fol. 38v; Inventario della Guardaroba di Palazzo Pitti, 1638, ASF, Guardaroba medicea 535, fol. 51s; Entrata e Uscita di Palazzo Pitti, 1638–1648, ASF, Guardaroba medicea 530, fol. 136s; Inventario di Palazzo Pitti, 1663–1664, ASF, Guardaroba medicea 725, fol. 55r; BALDINUCCI n.d. [1678 ca.], BNCF, ms. II,II, 110, fol. 350; Inventario di Palazzo Pitti, 1688, ASF, Guardaroba medicea 932, fol. 132r; Inventario di Palazzo Pitti, 1716–1723, Biblioteca degli Uffizi, ms. 79, fol. 87; Inventario di Palazzo Pitti, 1761, ASF, Guardaroba appendice 94, fol. 648v

*Archival sources for the painting exhibited*
Letter from Giovan Carlo de' Medici, to Mattias de' Medici, Florence, 30 September 1634, ASF, Mediceo del Principato 5392, fol. 252; Inventario di Carlo de' Medici, 1667, ASF, Guardaroba medicea 758, fol. 26r; Quaderno della Guardaroba generale 1666–1674, I, 30 June 1667, ASF, Guardaroba medicea 750, fol. 73v; Inventario della Guardaroba generale 1666–1680, 30 June 1667, ASF, Guardaroba medicea 741, fol. 384s; Inventario della Villa Ambrogiana, 1732, ASF, Guardaroba medicea 1392, fol. 52r; Inventario della Villa Ambrogiana, 1758, ASF, Guardaroba medicea appendice 92, fol. 90r; Inventario della Villa del Poggio Imperiale, 1768, ASF, Imperiale e Reale Corte 4855, appendix VI, 30 September 1780, fol. 3v

*Bibliography*
CAPPI BENTIVEGNA 1962-1964, II, 1964, fig. 19; CHIARINI 1977a, pp. 38 (fig. 39), 40–41; M. Chiarini, in *Gli Uffizi* 1979, ed. 1980, p. 534, no. P1668; *Al servizio del granduca* 1980, p. 33, no. V, 14; M. Chiarini, in *Sustermans* 1983, pp. 54–55, no. 30; L. Goldenberg Stoppato, in *Sustermans* 1983, pp. 68, 81, sub no. 51; MEIJER 1983, p. 785; MOSCO 1983, p. 370; FRATELLINI 1993, p. 156, fig. 36; L. Goldenberg Stoppato, in *Il Viaggio a Compostela* 2004, pp. 79–80, 91–92 (notes 63–67), 107, no. 23; L. Goldenberg Stoppato, in *Luce e Ombra* 2005, pp. 86–89, no. 30

**14** Florentine painter of the 17th century
*Galileo Galilei (1564–1642)*
1635–1645 ca.
Florence, Gallerie fiorentine, inv. 1890, no. 5432, on loan to the
Domus galilaeana in Pisa since 1942
oil on canvas, cm 78 × 64

One of the paintings exhibited in 1678 in the Suttermans room on the second floor of Palazzo Pitti was a portrait of the famous scientist Galileo Galilei. The 1688 inventory of the palace describes the sitter dressed in black with an old fashioned collar, a telescope in his right hand and a ring on his left hand. It is interesting to note that, unlike the other paintings we are exhibiting, the inventory does not attribute the portrait to Suttermans:

> Un quadro in tela alto braccia 1 soldi 7, largo soldi 19, dipintovi il ritratto di Galileo Galilei vestito di nero con collare all'antica, e nella mano destra tiene un canocchiale e in un dito della mano sinistra vi ha un anello, con adornamento scorniciato liscio, e tutto dorato     n. 1

This portrait is also listed in the inventories of Palazzo Pitti compiled between 1663 and 1664, between 1716 and 1723 and in 1761. It also appears in an inventory of Grand Prince Ferdinando's paintings which dates from the first decade of the 18th-century and in the inventory compiled after his death in 1713. All these inventories specify that Galileo was portrayed with his telescope in his right hand and a ring on his left ring finger.

The painting exhibited thus cannot be the famous bust-length portrait in the Uffizi (inv. 1890, no. 745, oil on canvas, cm 66 × 56, see essay fig. 3), where he is portrayed without his hands. The portrait in the Uffizi is a documented work, painted by Suttermans between June and August 1635 and sent to France in October of the same year to Elia Diodati, a lawyer of Lucchese origins who corresponded regularly with Galileo. Diodati sent this portrait back to Florence in 1656 as a gift to Grand Duke Ferdinando II de' Medici. A letter sent to Diodati by Galileo's pupil Vincenzo Viviani on 4 December 1656 describes the presentation of the gift. According to Viviani, the grand duke judged Diodati's portrait a good likeness and immediately recognized it as a work of Monsù Giusto. He compared it to a portrait of Galileo already hanging in Palazzo Pitti:

> [. . .] Il concetto che ell'ebbe di far regalo a questo Serenissimo Granduca del ritratto del Signor Galileo, già da esso mandatole, fu degno veramente della sua generosità. [. . .] Il giorno di S. Andrea ne feci la presentazione a Sua Altezza Serenissima a nome di Vostra Signoria Eccellentissima [. . .]. Lo riconobbe subito per somigliantissimo e fatto da monsù Giusto pittore di gra' fama che vive ancora trattenuto qui di continuo da questa Serenissima Altezza, sebbene oggi si trovi appresso il Serenissimo Arciduca ~~Leopoldo~~ d'Inspruch domandato al Granduca per qualche mese. Mi ricercò di che età poteva esser fatto, risposi che era di cinque anni e mezzo in circa avanti la sua morte, così ritraendolo dalle lettere di Vostra Signoria Eccellentissima. Ne volle far paragone con altro fatto pure dal medesimo pittore nel tempo che io mi ritrovavo appresso il Signor Galileo, cioè quattro anni doppo quel di Vostra Signoria dell'età di sopra 76 anni, quale Sua Altezza ha tenuto continuamente con singolarità tra molte pitture di gran fama in un salone del suo apartamento per dimostrazione della stima che ha sempre fatto di questo eroe, oltre all'averne fatto collocare una copia nel luogo più cospicuo della sua galleria tra l'effigie delli huomini illustri o di grande memoria. Hebbe diletto di far la conferenza dell'uno e dell'altro ritratto sì per la diversa eletione del pittore sì per la variazione dell'effigie che vi scorge essere servita dentro a quattro anni, perché quel di Vostra Signoria lo dimostra assai vivace, pieno di carne, illuminato, in atto di contemplare, e l'altro di Sua Altezza lo fa piuttosto estenuato, già cieco et in posto di speculare, ma con ciglio più severo. La maniera poi della pittura è diversissima, perché il primo è finito con morbidezza e ritoccato con diligenza in modo che in ogni detalio dimostra l'esquisitezza dell'arte; il secondo è fatto di maniera più risoluta, tutto di colpi, con tinte che non si possono imitare et in modo che da vicino par strapazzato, ma veduto in distanza debita si rende amirabile. [. . .]

The portrait given to Ferdinando II by Diodati was still in Palazzo Pitti several years later, when the 1663–1664 inventory was compiled. This inventory in fact describes two portraits of Galileo. While the first one, which measured braccia 1 ¾ × 1, had no frame, the second portrait, which measured roughly 101.8 × 87,3 centimeters, had a gilded frame: "Un quadro in tela che entrovi dipinto il Galileo con adornamento tutto dorato, alto braccia 1 ¾ e largo braccia 1 ½ in circa" (see Inventario di Palazzo Pitti 1662–1663, ASF, Guardaroba medicea 725, fol. 54r). An unpublished entry in a Guardaroba journal mentions that this portrait, "dipintovi il Gallileo mano di Giusto Sutterman con adornamento dorato alto braccia 1 ¾, largo 1 ½" was sent by the keeper of Palazzo Pitti to the Guardaroba generale on 15 November 1677 and was forwarded from there to Giovanni Bianchi, the keeper of the Galleria degli Uffizi for the gallery's Tribuna (see Quaderno della Guardaroba generale 1674–1679, ASF, Guardaroba medicea 801, fol. 90v). Filippo Baldinucci mentions the portrait painted for Diodati precisely in the Tribuna (see BALDINUCCI 1681–1728, ed. 1845–1845, vol. IV, 1846, p. 508; for a list of the documents and the bibliography see L. Goldenberg Stoppato, in *I Della Rovere* 2004, pp. 496–498, no. XVI.7).

A third portrait is mentioned by Viviani in his 1656 letter. It is the copy that belongs to the Uffizi set of portraits of illustrious men, known as the Gioviana series. The copy bears at the top an inscription with the sitter's name "GALILE.ˢ GALILEI", (inv. 1890, no. 246, oil on canvas, cm 61 × 49, see *Gli Uffizi* 1979, ed. 1980, p. 630, no. Ic212). The presence of this painting in the gallery is documented starting from 1651, when it was mentioned in the gallery's journal. According to this manuscript, on 15 June 1651 the painting was sent to the workshop of the Florentine painter Benedetto Bossi to be copied, "[. . .] si portò a Benedetto Bossi ill ritratto del Galileo Galilei, portato in bottega per copiare", and was returned shortly afterwards. The same portrait was given to Niccolò Bernardi, one of the Medici keepers, on 10 July 1674 and was returned by him to the gallery on 27 October 1676 (see the Giornale della Galleria degli Uffizi, Florence, Biblioteca degli Uffizi, ms. 62, fols. 26, 110, 111).

The other portrait, which belongs to the Galleria Palatina, is also a bust-length portrait without hands (inv. 1912, no. 106, oil on canvas, cm 56 × 48) and thus cannot possibly be the painting that was exhibited in the Suttermans room. It has been identified with the portrait of Galileo, which Viviani saw in Palazzo Pitti in 1656 (see FAVARO 1913, pp. 1017–1018; C. Pizzorusso, in *Sustermans* 1983, pp. 58–59, no. 34; S. Casciu, in CHIARINI–PADOVANI 2003, vol. II, p. 436, no. 718), but actually came to Palazzo Pitti only in the mid-1700s. It is cited in an inventory of the palace for the first time in 1761. This inventory describes it in great detail, immediately after the portrait of Galileo with his telescope (see ASF, Guardaroba medicea appendix 94, fol. 593v). Maria Letizia Strocchi suggested that this portrait came from Grand Prince Ferdinando's collection of small paintings in the Villa di Poggio a Caiano (see STROCCHI 1976, p. 97, no. 74), but the date of the transfer of this collection to the "Galleria" in 1773 (Strocchi cites a document in the Archivio Storico della Soprintendenza, shelf no. VI, inserts 61, 96) is not compatible with the mention of the painting in the 1761 inventory of Palazzo Pitti.

The only portrait still in Tuscany which matches the description supplied in the 1688 inventory of Palazzo Pitti, was loaned by the Gallerie fiorentine to Pisa's Domus galilaeana in 1942. This painting cannot in any case be attributed to Suttermans. It is a 17th-century copy painted by an unknown and rather modest Florentine painter. The prototype probably was the excellent quality portrait of *Galileo Galilei* from the Lansdowne collection, which was auctioned off by Christie's in 1995 (oil on canvas, cm 80.5 × 59.4, see Christie's sale, London, 7 April 1995, pp. 78–79, no. 51, fig. 51). The Lansdowne *Galileo* is clearly an original work and may well be the prototype for most of the copies known today, including this replica in the Domus galilaeana and the copies that belong to the Galleria Palatina and the Gioviana series in the Uffizi. It was sold in 1995 with an attribution to Suttermans but, in spite of its quality, does not seem to have been painted by him. The same portrait was in fact engraved as a work of Domenico Cresti known as Passignano by Pietro Bettellini (1763–1829). The Lansdowne *Galileo* has a Florentine provenance. Henry, 3rd Marquis of Lansdowne, purchased it from W. Blundell Spence, an English antiques dealer active in Florence, by 1854 when the marquis loaned it to the British Institution for an exhibition (see GRAVES 1913–1915, vol. III, 1914, p. 1277). It came from the collection of Prince Stanislaus Poniatowski, who died in Florence in 1833 and was indicated as the owner on Bettellini's engraving. The portrait of *Galileo* attributed to Passignano was mentioned in 1849 by the inventory of the possessions of the prince's sons Carlo and Giuseppe Poniatowski in the Villa di Rovezzano, just outside Florence (see BUSIRI VICI 1971, p. 337). It probably was sold a few years later, like the rest of their collection.

Before concluding, we must reflect on the quality of the portrait of *Galileo* on exhibit. The mediocre quality of the painting could give rise to comprehensible doubts that it actually is the portrait that Ferdinando II de' Medici kept in the famous collection of paintings in his own apartment. It is however the only version that belongs to the Gallerie fiorentine and matches in every detail the portrait described by the 17th-century inventories of Palazzo Pitti. Thus, though it may offend our sense of esthetics, it represents the only plausible identification until evidence is found that links a better quality portrait, like the Poniatowski-Lansdowne *Galileo*, to the Medici-Lorraine collections.

*Archival sources*
Lettera di Vincenzo Viviani a Elia Diodati, Firenze, 4 December 1656, BNCF, Galileiano 97, fols. 7–9, published by FAVARO 1913, pp. 1014–1015; Inventario di Palazzo Pitti, 1663–1664, ASF, Guardaroba medicea 725, fol. 54v; F. BALDINUCCI n.d. [1678 ca.], BNCF, ms. II.II.110, fol. 350; Inventario di Palazzo Pitti, 1688, ASF, Guardaroba medicea 932, fol. 132v; Inventario dei quadri di Palazzo Pitti, n.d. [1702?], ASF, Guardaroba medicea 1185, fols. 376–377s, no. 317; Inventario di Ferdinando di Cosimo III de' Medici, 1713, ASF, Guardaroba medicea 1222, fol. 52v; Inventario di Palazzo Pitti, 1716–1723, Firenze, Biblioteca degli Uffizi, ms. 79, fol. 270; Inventario di Palazzo Pitti, 1761, ASF, Guardaroba medicea appendice 94, fols. 593r-v; Inventario di Palazzo Pitti, 1761, ASF, Guardaroba medicea appendice 94, fols. 593r-v

*Bibliography*
S. Meloni Trkulja, in *Sustermans* 1983, p. 111, no. LXI; L. Goldenberg Stoppato, in *Il Seicento fiorentino* 1986, I, p. 324, sub no. 1.167; *Scienziati a Corte* 2001, p. 68; L. Goldenberg Stoppato, in *Il viaggio a Compostela* 2004, pp. 86, 96 (notes 119–122), 109, no. 31; F. Tognoni, in *Galileo e Pisa* 2004, pp. 88, 92

Fig. 1 - 17th-century painter, *Galileo Galilei (1564–1642)*. Formerly England, Meikleour House, Lansdowne collection

**15** *Valdemar Kristian (1622–1656), prince of Denmark*
[currently on loan to exhibition *Specchio del Tempo*]
1638
Florence, Palazzo Pitti, Galleria Palatina, inv. 1912, no 190
oil on canvas, cm 71 × 53

One of the paintings that were sent to the keeper of Palazzo Pitti on 28 February 1678 [modern style] expressly for the Suttermans room was a portrait of a prince of Denmark. According to the 1688 inventory of the palace, he was wearing a breastplate with a white and turquoise sash across it:

> Un quadro simile senza ornamento alto braccia 1 ¼, largo braccia 1, dipintovi il ritratto del figlio del Re Danimarcha armato con ciarpa turchina e biancha di mano del suddetto 144

The portrait, cited simply as "1 Danimarca", also appears in the census of Suttermans' works compiled by Filippo Baldinucci while he was planning the exhibition in 1678, among the "Ritratti in mano al Bernardi", portraits held by keeper Bernardi. When the next inventory of Palazzo Pitti was compiled in 1688, the portrait had already been moved to another room on the same floor, the ninth and last chamber of the same apartment, which had a window overlooking the small courtyard and a door leading to the library. The portrait of the prince of Denmark is also mentioned by the 1716–1723 inventory of the palace. It was hanging in a room known as the "camera della Scarabattola d'oro" in the apartment of Grand Prince Ferdinando, along with twelve other portraits by the same painter. It thus is probably one of the thirteen "[. . .] Ritratti di Principi, Principesse, et altri suggetti", Portraits of Princes, Princesses and other sitters, painted by Giusto Suttermans, which are listed together in the ninth room of the same apartment in the 1761 inventory of Palazzo Pitti.

Francis Beckett identified the prince in 1895 as Valdemar Kristian, a son of King Kristian IV of Denmark (1622–1656). Danish chronicles of the period indicate that young Prince Valdemar Kristian left Denmark in 1637 for a long trip across Europe and stayed in Paris for eight months before he traveled to Italy and visited Florence. His arrival in the Tuscan capital is mentioned in Cesare Tinghi's third diary of the Medici court. According to Tinghi, the third son of the King of Denmark arrived in Florence in June 1638, accompanied by a brother-in-law, and stayed for the entire summer. Tinghi specifies that he was hosted by the court in the home of Giovan Carlo de' Medici in Via della Scala (see TINGHI 1623–1644, ASF, Miscellanea medicea 11, fol. 361v):

> Del mese di giugno 1638 arrivò in Firenze il figliuolo terzogenito del Re di Danimarca in compagnia d'un suo cognato e doppo essere stato alcuni pochi giorni incognito alla camera locanda, [. . .] si concertò con il messo di detto Albmair, che [. . .] fussi alloggiato e spesato incognitamente nella casa della via della Scala [. . .] e continuò di stare a Firenze tutta questa state [. . .].

Suttermans probably painted the portrait during Valdemar Kristian's visit to Florence. It is in fact a splendid example of the painter's style towards the end of the 1630's. Suttermans' brushwork and palette of this period seem to have been influenced by the arrival in 1638 of Pieter Paul Rubens' large painting depicting *The Consequences of War* and by the simultaneous presence in the city of Pietro da Cortona, who was painting frescoes on the first floor of Palazzo Pitti for Ferdinando II de' Medici.

The portrait of Valdemar Kristian is mentioned on 17 September 1640 by an inventory of the grand duke's Guardaroba:

> Un quadro in tela entrovi dipinto il figliuolo del Re d'Animarca con banda bianca e turchina, alto braccia 1, largo braccia ¾ incirca, senza ornamento

According to a list of consignments made by the Guardaroba, this portrait was loaned to Suttermans to be copied only a few days later, on 25 September 1640, "a Giusto pittore, datoli per copiare", and was returned on 25 January 1641 [ab Incarnatione=1642 modern style].

Copies of Valdemar Kristian's portrait can be found in the army headquarters at Santa Maria a Candeli outside Florence (on loan from the Gallerie fiorentine), in Frederiksborg near Hilleröd and in Schloss Hinterglauchau in Glauchau. Another copy belonged to a private collection in Alexandria in Egypt in 1993.

*Archival sources*
Inventario della Guardaroba generale, 1640, ASF, Guardaroba medicea 572, fol. 6v; Consegne della Guardaroba generale 1640–1642, 25 September 1640 and 25 January 1641 [ab Incarnatione=1642 modern style], ASF, Guardaroba medicea 711, insert 2, fol. 162; Inventario della Guardaroba generale 1640–1666, ASF, Guardaroba medicea 585, fols. 36s-d; BALDINUCCI n.d. [1678 ca.], BNCF, ms. II.II.110, fol. 350; Inventario della Guardaroba generale 1666–1680, 28 February 1678 modern style, ASF, Guardaroba medicea 741, fols. 144s-d, no. 65; Quaderno della Guardaroba generale 1674–1680, 28 February 1678 modern style, ASF, Guardaroba medicea 799, fol. 276v; Inventario di Palazzo Pitti 1688, ASF, Guardaroba medicea 932, fols. 149v–150r; Inventario di Palazzo Pitti 1716–1723, Biblioteca degli Uffizi, ms. 79, fols. 90–91; (?)Inventario di Palazzo Pitti, 1761, ASF, Guardaroba medicea appendice 94, fol. 530v

*Bibliography*
INGHIRAMI 1828, p. 43; INGHIRAMI 1834, p. 38; D. Gazzadi, in BARDI 1837–1842, I, 1837, unpaginated; NAGLER 1835–1852, XVIII, 1848, p. 6, BURCKHARDT 1855, ed. 1952, p. 1114; FÉTIS 1857, I, p. 451; CHIAVACCI 1859, p. 95; WAAGEN 1863–1864, II, 1863, p. 226; SIRET 1866, p. 898; MICHIELS 1865–1878, IX, 1874, p. 28; SEUBERT 1878–1879, III, 1879, p. 389; MICHIELS 1881, pp. 118–120; MICHIELS 1882, pp. 122, 189–190; WAUTERS n.d. [1883?], p. 356; VENTURI 1891, IV, p. 110, no. 190; BECKETT 1895, pp. 737–738; LAFENESTRE–RICHTENBERGER n.d. [1895?], p. 147–190; CROWE 1904, p. 301; *Bryan's Dictionary* 1904–1905, V, 1905, p. 145; JOURDAIN 1905, p. 245; SCHMERBER 1906, p. 105; WAUTERS 1910, p. 314; WURZBACH 1906–1910, II, 1910, p. 676; BAUTIER 1911b, p. 239; BAUTIER 1912a, pp. 6, 11–12; BAUTIER 1912b, pp. 41–42, 115, 127, pl. XV; BAUTIER 1912c, p. 378; TARCHIANI 1912, p. 2; FIERENS GEVAERT 1913, p. 60; BAUTIER 1914, p. 616; HOOGEWERFF 1915, pp. 3–5,7,10, 12, pl. 3; FRIZZONI 1919, pp. 2, 3 (fig.); Christie's Sale 22 February 1924, p. 75, sub no. 79; BAUTIER 1926–1929, p. 315; GAMBA 1927, p. 89; GÖZ 1928, pp. 47–48; *Exposition Internationale* 1930, p. 108, no. 282; CORNETTE 1930, p. 20; *Rubens et son temps* 1936, p. 167, no. 99; JAHN RUSCONI 1937, pp. 286–287, no. 190; J. Lavalleye, in THIEME–BECKER 1907–1950, vol. XXXII, 1938, p. 323; TARCHIANI 1939, p. 5, 25, 65 (fig.); MARANGONI 1951, pl. 43; FRANCINI CIARANFI 1955, p. 148; HEINZ 1963, p. 156; CIPRIANI 1966, p. 24, no. 190, pl. on pp. 16–17; *Mostra di Opere restaurate* 1972, p. 86, no. 4; S. Meloni Trkulja, in *Sustermans* 1983, p. 109, no. LIII; *Christian IV and Europe* 1988, p. 47, no. 117; L. Goldenberg Stoppato, in TURNER 1996, p. 41; S. Casciu, in CHIARINI–PADOVANI 2003, I, p. 272, pl. 212, II, p.414, no. 681; L. Goldenberg Stoppato, in *Il viaggio a Compostela* 2004, pp. 74, 75, 80, 81 (fig.), 92 (notes 73–76), 109, no. 32

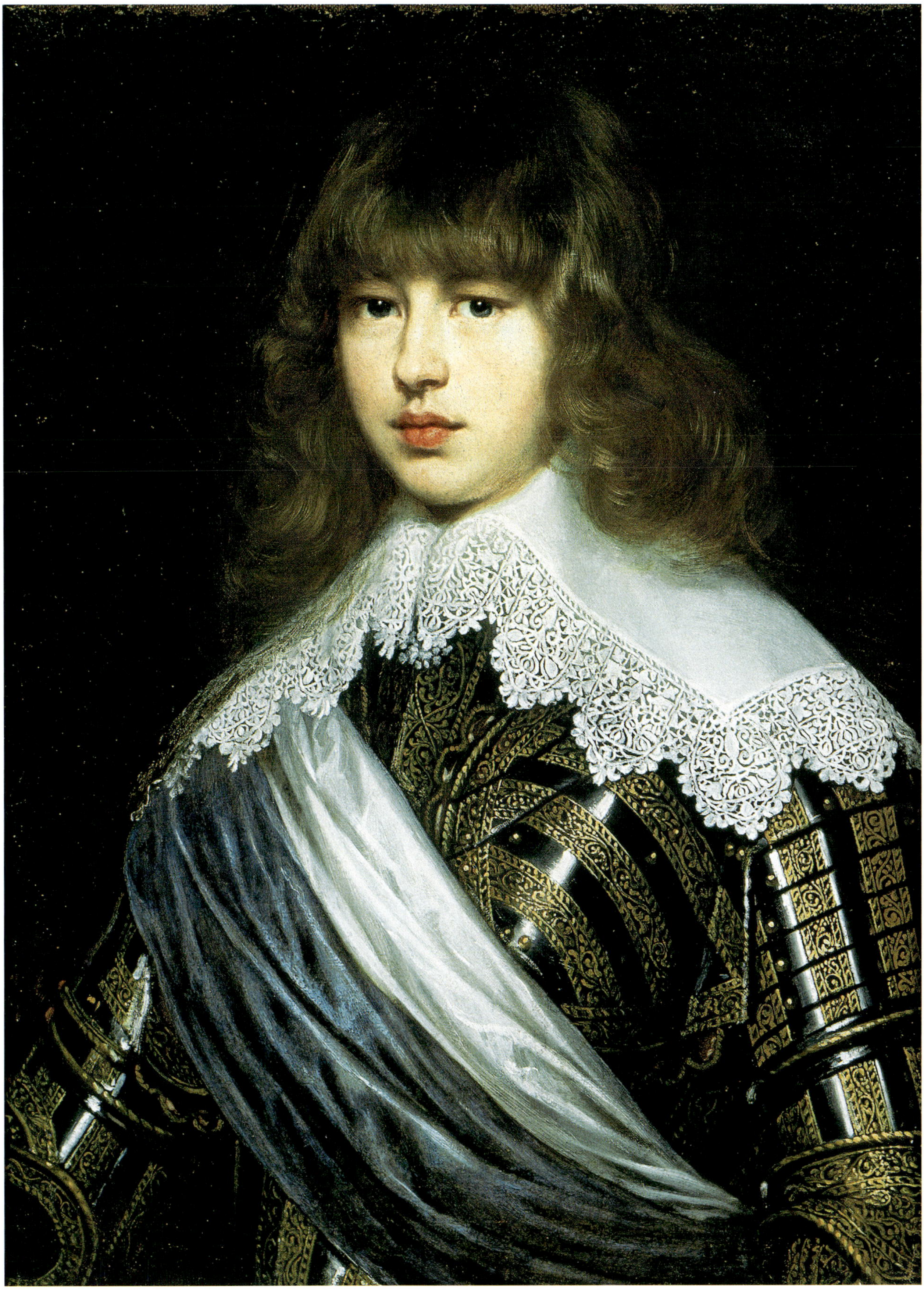

**16** *Meo Matto*
by 1640
Florence, Palazzo Pitti, storage, inv. 1890, no. 2187
oil on canvas, cm 62.5 × 51

Filippo Baldinucci cites a portrait of "Meo Matto" in the list of paintings by Giusto Suttermans he compiled while planning the 1678 exhibition in the painter's honor, specifically among the paintings entrusted to keepers Marmi and Bernardi in Palazzo Pitti. The portrait is also described in great detail by the 1688 inventory of the palace, which lists it among the paintings exhibited in the Suttermans room on the second floor of the palace. According to the inventory, Meo Matto, presumably a Medici court jester, was wearing a yellow and turquoise striped doublet and had his hair tied back:

> Un simile alto braccia 1 soldi 2, largo ⅞, dipintovi di mano del suddetto il ritratto di Meo Matto, vestito giallo e turchino a listre con capelli legati, et adornamento simile al suddetto ———— n. 1

The painting also appears in the 1716–1723 inventory of the palace, hanging with twelve other paintings by the Fleming in a room known as the "camera della Scarabattola d'Oro", in the apartment of Grand Prince Ferdinando de' Medici. It thus may well be one of the thirteen portraits listed together by the 1761 inventory of Palazzo Pitti in the ninth room of the same apartment:

> Tredici Quadri in tela alti braccia 1 soldi 2, larghi braccia 1 ⅚ in circa per ciascheduno, dipintovi dicesi di mano di Monsieur Giusto Suttermans, diversi Ritratti di Principi, Principesse et altri suggetti, che otto di uomini fino a mezzo busto e cinque di donne simili con adornamenti scorniciati tutti intagliati e dorati, segnati n.° 438

The portrait of *Meo Matto* came from the Guardaroba generale: both the journal and the inventory of the Guardaroba mention the transfer of the portrait on 30 April 1676 to the chamber of Grand Duke Cosimo III in Palazzo Pitti. Its presence in the Guardaroba is documented from 17 September 1640 on. On this date the painting appeared in three distinct Guardaroba inventories, listed without an attribution, immediately after the portrait of *Prince Valdemar Kristian of Denmark*. This date is a useful 'terminus ante quem' for the execution of the painting. It was Pierre BAUTIER (1912b) who first attributed the portrait of *Meo Matto* to Giusto Suttermans, citing the 1716–1723 inventory of Palazzo Pitti as the source of his attribution. Marco Chiarini (in *Gli Uffizi* 1979) came to the same conclusion, quoting the 1688 inventory of the palace. As Chiarini pointed out, the clothing and hairdo of the sitter in this painting match Meo Matto's in the portrait described by the inventory.

*Archival sources*
Copia dell'inventario della Guardaroba generale, 1640, ASF, Guardaroba medicea 571, fol. 5v; Inventario della Guardaroba generale, 1640, ASF, Guardaroba medicea 572, fol. 6v; Inventario della Guardaroba generale 1640–1666, ASF, Guardaroba medicea 585, fols. 36s-d, no. 69; Inventario della Guardaroba generale 1666–1680, 1666–30 April 1676, ASF., Guardaroba medicea 741, fols. 156s-d, no. 122; Quaderno della Guardaroba generale 1674–1680, 30 April 1676, ASF, Guardaroba medicea 799, fol. 43v; BALDINUCCI n.d. [1678 ca.], BNCF, ms. II.II.110, fol. 350; Inventario di Palazzo Pitti, 1688, ASF, Guardaroba medicea 932, fol. 130r; Inventario di Palazzo Pitti, 1716–1723, Biblioteca degli Uffizi, ms. 79, fol. 86; (?)Inventario di Palazzo Pitti, 1761, ASF, Guardaroba medicea appendice 94, fol. 530v

*Bibliography*
PIERACCINI 1910, p. 115, no. 3455; BAUTIER 1912b, pp. 40, 126; J. Lavalleye, in THIEME–BECKER 1907–1950, vol. XXXII, 1938, p. 324; M. Chiarini, in *Gli Uffizi* 1979, ed. 1980, p. 533, no. P1662; *Al servizio del granduca* 1980, p. 35, no. V, 17; M. Chiarini, in *Sustermans* 1983, p. 64, no. 39; MOSCO 1983, p. 370; FRATELLINI 1993, pp. 155–156, fig. 35; L. Goldenberg Stoppato, in *Il viaggio a Compostela* 2004, p. 103, no. 9

**17** *Alessandro Nomi (died 1644)?*
by 1644
Florence, Palazzo Pitti, storage, inv. 1890, no. 2335
oil on canvas, cm 63.5 × 46

One of the paintings exhibited in the Suttermans room on the second floor of Palazzo Pitti in 1688 was a small portrait of *Alessandro Nomi*, one of the grand duke's secretaries. According to the inventory compiled that year, Nomi was dressed in black with a simple white collar and had gray hair, beard and sideburns:

> Un quadro in tela alto braccia 1 ⅛, largo ⅝, dipintovi di mano del suddetto il ritratto d'Alessandro Nomi stato segretario di Sua Altezza Serenissima con barba, basette e capelli grigi, vestito di nero con collare puro, con adornamento intagliato e dorato _____ n. 1

Filippo Baldinucci mentions the portrait of "segretar Nomi" in the census of works by Monsù Giusto he compiled while he was planning the exhibition in 1678. The painting came from the collection of Cardinal Leopoldo de' Medici: it is described in the inventory of Leopoldo's possessions compiled after his death in 1675 and is listed with the rest of his collection when it entered the grand duke's Guardaroba on 27 February 1676 [ab Incarnatione=1677 modern style]. According to a second journal of the Guardaroba, the painting was officially entrusted to the keeper of Palazzo Pitti on 30 August 1680. The portrait is also mentioned by the inventory of the palace compiled between 1716 and 1723. At that time it was hanging with twelve other paintings by Suttermans in a room known as the "camera della Scarabattola d'Oro" in Grand Prince Ferdinando de' Medici's apartment. Thus the portrait of Nomi is probably one of the thirteen paintings by the same painter that were exhibited together in a room of the same apartment in 1761:

> Tredici Quadri in tela alti braccia 1 soldi 2, larghi braccia 1 ⅚ in circa per ciascheduno dipintovi dicesi di mano di Monsieur Giusto Suttermans diversi ritratti di principi, principesse, et altri suggetti, che otto di uomini fino a mezzo busto e cinque di donne simili con adornamenti scorniciati tutti intagliati e dorati, segnati n.° 438

The sitter, Alessandro Nomi, is mentioned as a secretary in the lists of Medici staff that date from the period between 1621 and 1644 (see *Cariche della Corte*, 18th century, ASF, Manoscritti 321, fols. 489, 574, 595). Further information appears in the notes of Carlo Sebregondi. According to Sebregondi, Alessandro di Niccolò di Giovanni Nomi was born in Borgo San Sepolcro. He was granted Florentine citizenship on 8 June 1628 and was given several short-term civic appointments during the period between 1629 and 1641 (see ASF, Raccolta Sebregondi 3853). Thanks to a legal document drawn up by the notary public Gherardo Gherardi on 28 October 1644, when Nomi delivered his last will and testament, we know that he lived in the parish of San Frediano (ASF, Notarile moderno 9361, fols. 66r–68r). According to an 18th-century transcription of this will "Alessandro Nomi, segretario di guerra di Sua Altezza Reale" named as heir his nephew Benedetto, the son of Francesco Giovagnoli from Borgo San Sepolcro, specifying that Benedetto had assisted him in his profession for many years. Starting in 1645, Benedetto is in fact listed in the books of the Decime Granducali, the grand duke's property tax office, as the owner of the property that had previously belonged to "messere Alessandro di Niccolò Nomi" in the Carro gonfalon of the Florentine quarter of Santa Croce (see ASF, Deputazione sopra la Nobiltà e Cittadinanza 48, insert 11, fols. 102, 106). Alessandro Nomi died in Florence on 11 November 1644 and was buried in the church of Santa Maria del Carmine (see Morti della Grascia, 1626–1669, ASF, Ufficiali poi Magistrato della Grascia 195, fol. 28v). His death date sets a 'terminus ante quem' for the portrait.

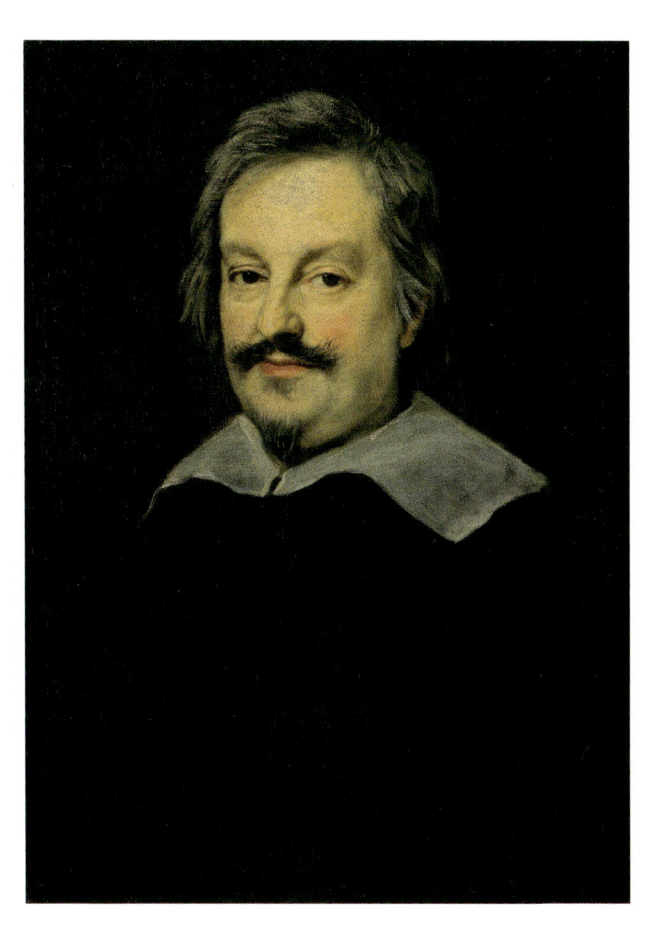

This 'terminus ante quem' helps us identify the portrait of *Alessandro Nomi*. It may well be the painting by Suttermans now in storage in Palazzo Pitti, which was exhibited in the Galleria degli Uffizi from 1896 to 1928 before being sent to the Galleria Palatina (see JAHN RUSCONI 1937). The attribution of this painting to Suttermans appeared in Pieraccini's catalogue of the Uffizi (see the 1910 ed.) and has been accepted in all the following studies. The elderly sitter in the painting is dressed in black clothing with a white collar, which matches the description of Nomi's clothing in the 1688 inventory. The size of the canvas is also similar to the size indicated by the inventory. Both the cut of the collar and the style of painting suggest a date in the late 1630's or in the early 1640's, which is perfectly appropriate for the portrait of Nomi.

*Archival sources*
Inventario della Guardaroba generale 1674–1680, 27 February 1676 [ab Incarnatione=1677 modern style], ASF, Guardaroba medicea 799, fol. 191v, no. 366; BALDINUCCI n.d. [1678 ca.], BNCF, ms. II.II.110, fol. 350; Quaderno della Guardaroba generale 1679–1685, 30 August 1680, ASF, Guardaroba medicea 870, fol. 63r; Inventario di Palazzo Pitti, 1688, ASF, Guardaroba medicea 932, fol. 132v; Inventario di Palazzo Pitti, 1716–1723, Firenze, Biblioteca degli Uffizi, ms. 79, fols. 82–83; (?)Inventario di Palazzo Pitti, 1761, ASF, Guardaroba medicea appendice 94, fol. 611v

*Bibliography*
PIERACCINI 1910, p. 115, no. 1190; BAUTIER 1912b, p. 86; JAHN RUSCONI 1937, pp. 292, no. 2335; TARCHIANI 1939, p. 25; *Artisti alla Corte Granducale* 1969, pp. 43, 44, no. 60, fig. 48; M. Chiarini, in *Gli Uffizi* 1979, ed. 1980, p. 533, no. P1663; S. Meloni Trkulja, in *Sustermans* 1983, p. 114, no. LXVIII; GODI–MINGARDI 1994, p. 44, sub no. 33; L. Goldenberg Stoppato, in *Il viaggio a Compostela* 2004, pp. 80, 92 (notes 68–72), 108, no. 29

**18** *Margherita de' Medici (1612–1679) as a widow*
1655–1656?
Florence, Palazzo Pitti, Galleria Palatina, inv. 1912, no. 298
oil on canvas, cm 64.9 × 50.9

One of the paintings exhibited in the Suttermans room on the second floor of Palazzo Pitti in 1688 was a portrait of the Duchess of Parma Margherita de' Medici, who also appeared at the 17th-century exhibition as a child in a second portrait (see cat. no. 3). The inventory describes the duchess with a white veil on her head and black string around her neck:

> Un simile alto braccia 1 ⅛, largo ⅚, dipintovi il ritratto della duchessa Margherita di Parma con velo bianco in capo e al collo con filetto nero che serve per vezzo, di mano del suddetto, con adornamento intagliato e dorato _____ n. 1

The painting described matches in each detail this portrait that belongs to the Galleria Palatina.

Like many of the paintings exhibited in 1688, this portrait of *Margherita de' Medici* comes from the collection of Cardinal Leopoldo de' Medici. It is listed in the inventory of his possessions compiled after his death in 1675:

> 365 Un quadro in tela simile, dipintovi il ritratto della Duchessa Margherita di Parma, vestita di nero, con veli bianchi in capo e al collo, con filettino nero che serve per vezzo, di mano di Giusto, senz'ornamento n.° 1

It also appears in a Guardaroba journal on 27 February 1676 [ab Incarnatione=1677 modern style], when Leopoldo's possessions entered Cosimo III's collection. A second journal registers the official consignment of the painting to the keeper of Palazzo Pitti on 30 August 1680. The portrait of "Duchessa Margherita di Parma" is also cited by the palace inventory compiled between 1716 and 1723, which describes the portrait in the third room of Prince Mattias' apartment. It might also be one of the thirteen bust-length portraits by Suttermans portraying "Principi, Principesse et altri suggetti, che otto di uomini fino a mezo busto e cinque di donne simili", Princes, Princesses and other sitters, eight of men and five of women, mentioned by the 1761 inventory of the palace, in the ninth room of Grand Prince Ferdinando's apartment.

Duchess Margherita is wearing widow's weeds. Thus, we can date the portrait after 11 September 1646 when her husband Odoardo Farnese died. Suttermans would have had a chance to portray the duchess either in early 1650, when he went to Parma from Modena, in 1655 during Margherita's visit to Florence, or in 1656 when the painter worked at the Farnese court from May to September. On 16 September 1656 Margherita wrote to her brother Leopoldo from Parma mentioning portraits painted by 'Giusto' during his visit (Letter from Margherita de' Medici to Leopoldo de' Medici, 16 September 1656, ASF, Mediceo del Principato 5503, fol. 276, published by PIERACCINI 1924–1925, II, 1925, pp. 530, 542, notes 4, 26):

> [. . .] Finalmente Giusto ha finito i ritratti che sono stati molti, perché ci ha ritratto tutti più d'una volta, essendoci valsi del occasione perché qui non habbiamo pittore che vaglia in questo mestiere. [. . .] Egli ha fatto esquisitamente in tutti, fuori che in quelli delle mie figlie, delle quali sono riusciti meglio i piccoli che egli porta per la serenissima Gran Duchessa, dicendo di così tenere ordine [. . .]

A date in the mid–1650's would be appropriate both for Margherita's apparent age and for the cut of her clothes.

*Archival sources*
Inventario di Leopoldo de' Medici, 1675, ASF, Guardaroba medicea 826, fol. 77r, no. 365; Quaderno della Guardaroba generale 1674–1680, 27 febbraio 1676 [ab Incarnatione=1677 modern style], ASF, Guardaroba medicea 799, fol. 191v, no. 365; Quaderno della Guardaroba generale 1679–1685, 30 August 1680, ASF, Guardaroba medicea 870, fol. 63r; Inventario di Palazzo Pitti, 1688, ASF, Guardaroba medicea 932, fol. 132r; Inventario di Palazzo Pitti, 1716–1723, Biblioteca degli Uffizi, ms. 79, fol. 268; (?)Inventario di Palazzo Pitti, 1761, ASF, Guardaroba medicea appendice 94, fol. 530v

*Bibliography*
INGHIRAMI 1834, p. 49, no. 298; CHIAVACCI 1859, p. 137, no. 298; BAUTIER 1912b, pp. 65, 127; PIERACCINI 1924–1925, II, 1925, p. 530, pl. LXXXIII, fig. XC; GÖZ 1928, pp. 30, 40; JAHN RUSCONI 1937, p. 289, no. 298; TARCHIANI 1939, p. 25; CIPRIANI 1966, p. 17, no. 298; LANGEDIJK 1981–1987, I, 1981, p. 193, II, 1983, p. 1223, no. 83/6; S. Meloni Trkulja, in *Sustermans* 1983, p. 102, no. XXXIV; L. Goldenberg Stoppato, in *Il Seicento fiorentino* 1986, I, p. 321, sub no. 1.165; GIUSTO 1994, pp. 184, 193, note 31; M. Pietrogiovanna, in LIMENTANI VIRDIS, 1997, p. 297; S. Casciu, in CHIARINI–PADOVANI 2003, II, p. 417, no. 686 ; L. Goldenberg Stoppato, in *Il viaggio a Compostela* 2004, pp. 83, 94 (note 91–94), 107, no. 25

**19** *Mattias de' Medici (1613–1667) in armor*
1668
formerly Milan, Crespi collection
oil on canvas, cm 115 × 87

This portrait of *Mattias de' Medici*, Grand Duke Ferdinando II's brother, is one of the paintings that were sent by the Guardaroba generale to the keeper of Palazzo Pitti on 28 February 1678, expressly for the "stanza de' quadri di Giusto Sutterman", the chamber of paintings by Giusto Suttermans. According to the journal entry it was a half-length portrait of the prince in armor with a red sash, holding a commander's staff:

> Un quadro in tela alto braccia 2,largo braccia 1 ½, dipintovi il serenissimo principe Mattias armato mezza figura, con bastone in mano e ciarpa rossa, di mano di Giusto suddetto [. . .]

By 1688, when the next inventory of the palace was compiled, the portrait had been moved from the Suttermans room on the second floor to the apartment of Grand Prince Ferdinando on the first floor, where it was hanging in the seventh chamber with the Fleming's *Vestal Tuccia* (inv. Palatina 1912, no. 116, essay fig. 6).
As Karla Langedijk pointed out in 1983, the portrait of Mattias was still on the first floor when the 1716–1723 inventory of Palazzo Pitti was compiled. This inventory describes the portrait of Mattias in greater detail. The sitter was wearing armor with a red sash, held a staff in his right hand and posed his left hand on his helmet, which was placed with a gauntlet on a table beside him:

> Un quadro in tela alto braccia 2, largo braccia 1 ½ circa, dipintovi il ritratto più che mezza figura del serenissimo principe Mattias tutto armato con ciarpa rossa, nella mano destra tiene il bastone del comando e la sinistra posa sopra un morione che è sopra un tavolino coperto di rosso, dove si vede un guanto di ferro, mano di Giusto Sutterman, con adornamento intagliato, e tutto dorato n. 1

This description allows us to identify the painting with a portrait formerly in the Crespi collection in Milan, which was published by Adolfo Venturi in 1900 as the portrait of an unidentified *Medici prince*. The Crespi portrait matches detail for detail the portrait described by the Palazzo Pitti inventories. The sitter is a sturdy, middle aged man in armor holding a staff in his right hand. His helmet and a gauntlet are placed on the table beside him. If one converts the measurements in braccia that appear in the inventories into centimeters (1 Florentine braccio=58.3 centimeters), even the size of the Crespi portrait makes a perfect match with the Pitti portrait. The Crespi collection was auctioned off in Paris on 4 June 1914 by the Galerie George Petit. Unfortunately, neither the portrait of *Mattias de' Medici*, nor the *Portrait of a Woman as a saint* by Suttermans, also published by Venturi (1900, pp. 309, 311), appear in the sales catalogue. The sitter in this second painting may well be *Vittoria della Rovere*.
An unpublished bill from Giusto Suttermans mentions the portrait of *Mattias de' Medici*. On 18 December 1668 the painter asked the Guardaroba generale for 50 scudi for a portrait of deceased prince Mattias delivered to Ferdinando II's chamber. He specifies that it was an original work, painted from life and portrayed the prince in armor with a red sash and other unspecified objects:

> Un ritratto del serenissimo principe Mattias felice memoria, fatto dal vivo, ultimo vero originale, in un quadro alto braccia 2 ½ e largo a proporzione si rapresente armano con ciarpe rosso et altri, consegniato in camera di Sua Altezza Serenissima --------------------- scudi 50

The painting was registered in the Guardaroba inventory two years later, on 30 December 1670.
It is not easy to determine when the portrait of Mattias was removed from Palazzo Pitti. It was still in the palace, in the apartment of deceased Grand Prince Ferdinando, when the 1761 inventory was taken. It may well have been dislocated when Grand Duke Pietro Leopoldo of Lorraine came to Florence in 1765. According to Marilena Mosco, Pietro Leopoldo chose Ferdinando's apartment as his residence in Palazzo Pitti and had the collection of paintings transferred to the northern wing of the palace, the one frescoed by Pietro da Cortona, now known as the Galleria Palatina (see *La Galleria Palatina* 1982, p. 55).

*Archival sources*
Bill from Giusto Suttermans 1668–1669, 18 December 1668, ASF, Guardaroba medicea 768, no. 327, fol. 519; Quaderno della Guardaroba generale 1666–1674, I, 30 December 1670, ASF, Guardaroba medicea 750, fol. 198r; BALDINUCCI n.d. [1678 ca.], BNCF, ms. II.II.110, fol. 350; Inventario della Guardaroba Generale 1666–1680, 30 December 1670, 28 February 1678 modern style, ASF, Guardaroba medicea 741, fols. 472s-d; Quaderno della Guardaroba generale 1674–1680, 28 February 1678 modern style, ASF, Guardaroba medicea 799, fol. 276; Inventario di Palazzo Pitti, 1688, ASF, Guardaroba medicea 932, fol. 68; Inventario di Palazzo Pitti, 1716–1723, Biblioteca degli Uffizi, ms. 79, fol. 61; Inventario di Palazzo Pitti, 1761, ASF, Guardaroba medicea appendice 94, fol. 590r, no. 786

*Bibliography*
VENTURI 1900, pp. 309–310; GÖZ 1928, p. 28, J. Lavalleye, in THIEME–BECKER 1907–1950, vol. XXXII, 1938, p. 324; LANGEDIJK 1981–1987, II, 1983, p. 1310, no. 92/13; K. Langedijk, in *Sustermans* 1983, p. 34, sub no. 13d; L. Goldenberg Stoppato, in *Il viaggio a Compostela* 2004, pp. 74, 75, 85, 95 (notes 108–112), 110, no. 33

**20** *Francesco Maria de' Medici (1660–1710) as a boy with his dog*
after November 1669
Florence, Galleria degli Uffizi, storage, inv. 1890, no. 9796
oil on canvas, cm 162 × 108.5

One of the paintings sent to Palazzo Pitti from the Medici Guardaroba on 28 February 1678 [modern style] expressly for the Suttermans room was a portrait of Cosimo III's young brother Francesco Maria de' Medici wearing canonicals, with his left hand on the head of a dog: "Un quadro simile alto e largo simile dipintovi il serenissimo Francesco vestito da prete, con la sinistra posa[ta] sopra la testa d'un cane". This same portrait of "Principe Franceschio" appears in the census of the painter's works compiled by Filippo Baldinucci while he was planning the 1678 exhibition, among the portraits he had found in the "Guardarobba Generale". It is described in great detail by the 1688 inventory of Palazzo Pitti, hanging with twenty-nine other paintings by Suttermans in a room on the second floor of the palace. The inventory describes it as a 'pendant' for the portrait of another young Medici prince dressed in canonicals. It mentions Francesco Maria's clerical attire, the dog beside him and a piece of paper in his left hand:

> Due quadri in tela alti braccia 3 in circa, larghi braccia 2 in circa, dipintovi di mano di Giusto Suttermanni, in uno il ritratto del serenissimo principe Mattias figura intera vestito da prete che con la mano destra posa sopra d'un tavolino coperto di panno rosso in atto di pigliare il cappello che vi è sopra; e nell'altro il ritratto del serenissimo cardinale Francesco Maria da prete in età giovenile che con la mano destra posa sopra la testa d'un cane e con la destra tiene un foglio, con adornamenti intagliati e dorati       n. 2

The portrait of Francesco Maria as a boy also appears in the 1716–1723 inventory of the palace. It was hanging at that time in the "Camera del Trucco", or gaming room, on the first floor, along with four other full-length portraits of young Medici princes. It thus may well be one of the five portraits of young princes, which are listed together in the eleventh room of an apartment on the same floor by the 1761 inventory of Palazzo Pitti. According to this inventory one of the five young princes was portrayed "con un cane tigrato", with a dog with a mottled coat, like the one in this portrait.

Since Francesco Maria seems to be roughly ten years old, the portrait may well be the one mentioned in two unpublished letters written on 12 November 1669. In the first letter Giusto Suttermans mentions an excise tax exemption granted him by Grand Duke Ferdinando II in exchange for portraits of his grandson Ferdinando and his sons Francesco Maria and Cosimo, still grand prince at that time:

> Il Serenissimo Granduca mi fa grazzia d'essere esente di pagare una gabella d'un podere compr[at]o, e che per tal grazzia devo io fare tre ritratti per Sua Altezza Serenissima, uno del Serenissimo Gran prencipe di Toscana, uno del Serenissimo prencipe Franciesco e un del Serenissimo principe Ferdinando. E per tanto prego Vostra Signoria Illustrissima [. . .] che quanto primo esegisci il comandamento di Sua Altezza Serenissima [. . .]

In the second letter, Valentino Farinola reassures an unspecified keeper of the Guardaroba generale that he had already written to the tax assessor about Suttermans' debt and asks him to draw up a written contract for the three portraits promised by the painter:

> Giusto è stato già conpiaciuto, havendo io scritto al signore Provveditore della gabella de' contratti che non lo molesti per il debito [. . .], perciò rimetto a Vostra Signoria Illustrissima l'obligo o sia scritto della sua promessa di fare li tre ritratti de' Serenissimi Principi Cosimo, Francesco Maria, e Ferdinando [. . .].

Other portraits of the young Medici princes were requested on 15 November 1669 by Margherita de' Medici, duchess of Parma (see ASF, Mediceo del Principato 5503, fol. 166, quoted by PIERACCINI 1924–1925, II, 1925, pp. 652, 659, note 115 and LANGEDIJK 1981–1987, II, 1983, p. 830, sub no. 39/24).

*Archival sources*
Letter from Giusto Suttermans, Florence, 12 November 1669, ASF, Guardaroba medicea 669 bis, fol. 703; Letter from Valentino Farinola, Florence, 12 November 1669, ASF, Guardaroba medicea 669 bis, fol. 702; Quaderno della Guardaroba generale 1674–1680, 28 February 1678 modern style, ASF, Guardaroba medicea 799, fol. 276v; BALDINUCCI n.d. [1678 ca.], BNCF, ms. II.II.110, fol. 351v; Inventario della Guardaroba generale 1660–1680, 28 February 1677 [ab Incarnatione=1678 modern style], ASF, Guardaroba medicea 741, fol. 560d; Inventario di Palazzo Pitti 1688, ASF, Guardaroba medicea 932, fol. 131r; Inventario di Palazzo Pitti 1716–1723, Biblioteca degli Uffizi, ms. 79, fols. 104–105; Inventario di Palazzo Pitti, 1761, ASF, Guardaroba medicea appendice 94, fol. 537v

*Bibliography*
*Mostra del Ritratto* 1911, p. 192, no. 14; BAUTIER 1912b, pp. 94–95, 128, pl. XXXII; NUGENT 1912, p. 34; TARCHIANI 1912, p. 2; PIERACCINI 1924–1925, II, 1925, pp. 695, 713, note 60; BAUTIER 1926–1929, p. 319; GAMBA 1927, pp. 96–97, pl. XVIII; GÖZ 1928, pp. 32, 35; HENDY 1931, p. 349; J. Lavalleye, in THIEME–BECKER 1907–1950, vol. XXXII, 1938, p. 324; KULTZEN 1977, pp. 38 (fig. 41), 40; LANGEDIJK 1981–1987, I, 1981, pp. 203–204, II, 1983, pp. 931–932, no. 45/8; S. Meloni Trkulja, in *Sustermans* 1983, p. 99, no. XXIII; M. Mosco, in *Natura viva* 1985, p. 89 (fig.); L. Goldenberg Stoppato, in *Il Seicento fiorentino* 1986, p. 169; L. Goldenberg Stoppato, in *La pittura in Italia. Il Seicento* 1988 ed. 1989, II, p. 895; L. Goldenberg Stoppato, in TURNER 1996, p. 42; M. Pietrogiovanna, in LIMENTANI VIRDIS 1997, p. 297; L. Goldenberg Stoppato, in *Il viaggio a Compostela* 2004, pp. 74, 84–85, 95 (notes 102, 105–106), 105, no. 17

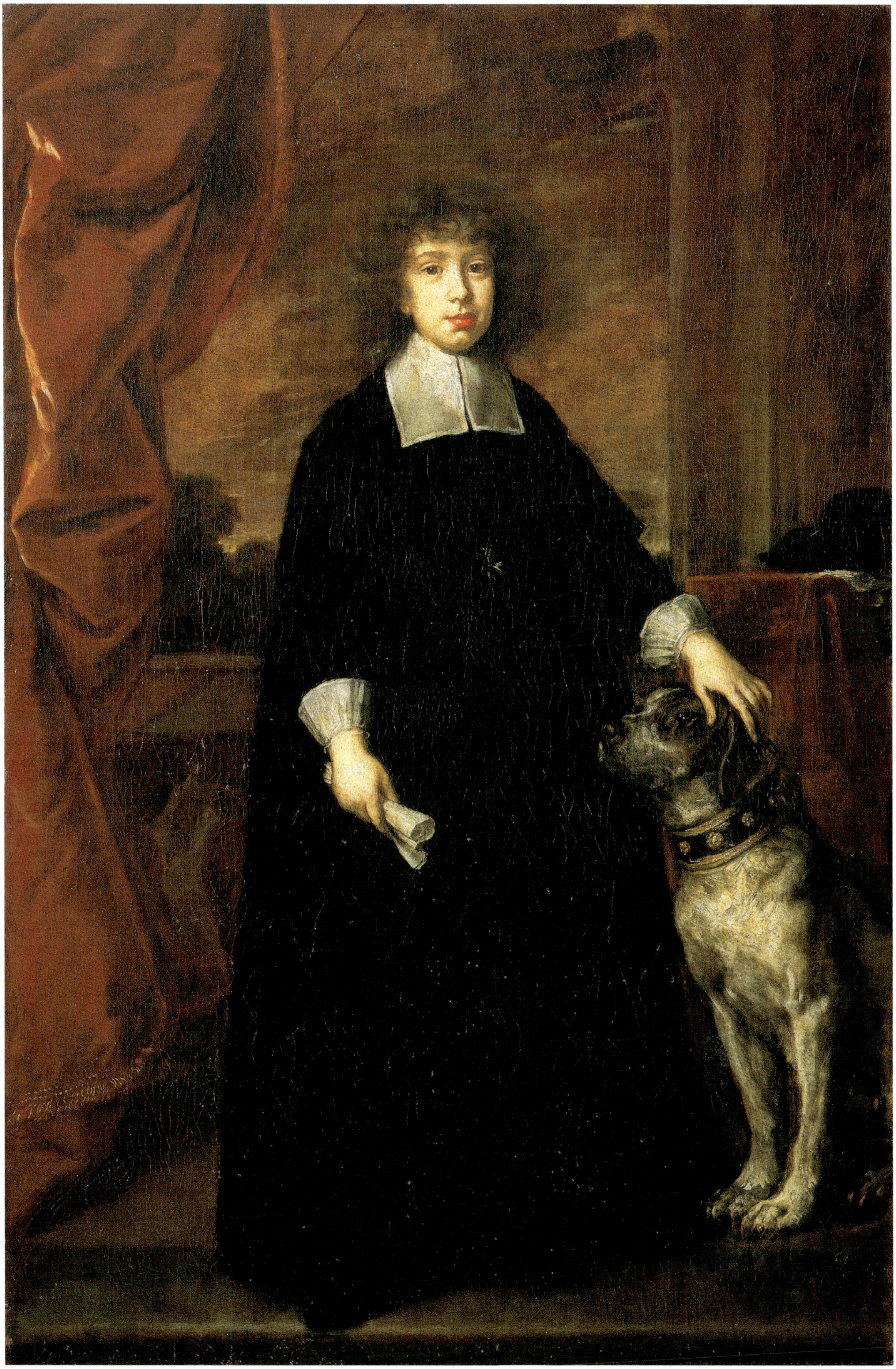

**21** *Grand Prince Ferdinando de' Medici (1663–1713) as a child*

by November 1670
Florence, Galleria degli Uffizi, storage, inv. 1890, no. 3761
oil on canvas, cm 187.5 × 125

One of the paintings sent to Palazzo Pitti by the Guardaroba on 28 February 1678 [modern style] expressly for the Suttermans room was a portrait of Grand Prince Ferdinando as a child dressed in red and white skirts and holding his hat: "Un quadro in tela senza adornamento altro braccia 2 ¾, largo braccia 1 ⅞, dipintovi il serenissimo principe Ferdinando da fanciullo, con gonnellino bianco e rosso, e berretta in mano". Filippo Baldinucci includes this portrait of "Principe Ferdinando", in the census of the painter's works he compiled while he was planning the exhibition, among the paintings in the "Guardarobba Generale". The portrait is also mentioned in the 1688 inventory of Palazzo Pitti hanging with twenty-nine other paintings by Monsù Giusto in a room on the second floor of the palace. The inventory describes it with the portrait of Ferdinando's sister *Anna Maria Luisa* (see cat. no. 22):

> Due quadri in tela alti braccia 2 soldi 16, larghi braccia 1 ⅝ dipintovi di mano di Giusto Suttermanni, in uno il ritratto del serenissimo principe Ferdinando da giovanetto con gonellino, con cappello sotto il braccio destro con penne rosse e bianche, e nell'altro la serenissima signora principessa Anna Maria Margherita Aluisa da bambina, vestita di rosso con una rosa nella mano destra, con adornamenti intagliati e tutti dorati

The portrait of Grand Prince Ferdinando is also described in the 1716–1723 inventory of Palazzo Pitti, which mentions it in the chamber of Grand Princess Violante of Bavaria, and in the inventory compiled in 1761.

Since Ferdinando is young enough to be dressed in skirts, the normal form of dress for little boys in the 17th century, the painting can be identified with one of the three portraits mentioned in an unpublished letter sent by "Giusto Suttermani" to an unspecified recipient on 12 November 1669. In the letter the painter mentions an excise tax exemption granted him by Grand Duke Ferdinando II in exchange for portraits of Cosimo III, who was still grand prince at that time, Francesco Maria and Ferdinando:

> Il Serenissimo Granduca mi fa grazzia d'essere esente di pagare una gabella d'un podere compr[at]o, e che per tal grazzia devo io fare tre ritratti per Sua Altezza Serenissima, uno del Serenissimo Gran prencipe di Toscana, uno del Serenissimo prencipe Franciesco e un del Serenissimo prencipe Ferdinando. E per tanto prego Vostra Signoria Illustrissima [. . .] che quanto primo esegisci il comandamento di Sua Altezza Serenissima [. . .]

The portraits are also mentioned in a letter sent on the same day by the grand duke's judge Valentino Farinola. Farinola informs an unspecified recipient, who probably was a keeper of the Medici Guardaroba, that he has already written to the tax officer about Suttermans' tax exemption and asks him to draw up a written contract for the three portraits:

> Giusto è stato già conpiaciuto, avendo io scritto al signore Proveditore della gabella de' contratti che non lo molesti per il debito [. . .], perciò rimetto a Vostra Signoria Illustrissima l'obligo o sia scritto della sua promessa di fare li tre ritratti de' Serenissimi Principi Cosimo, Francesco Maria, e Ferdinando [. . .].

Other portraits of the young Medici princes were requested by the Duchess of Parma Margherita de' Medici only a few days later, on 15 November 1669 (see ASF, Mediceo del Principato 5503, fol. 166, quoted by PIERACCINI 1924–1925, vol. II, 1925, pp. 652, 659, note 115; LANGEDIJK 1981–1987, II, 1983, p. 830, sub no. 39/24). As Karla Langedijk pointed out in 1983, the portrait of young prince Ferdinando was completed by 10 November 1670, when it was registered in an inventory of the Guardaroba generale, along with the portrait of his sister *Anna Maria Luisa*:

> Dua quadri in tela entrovi il ritratto fatti da Giusto Suttermano pittore, che in uno il ritratto del serenissimo principe Ferdinando vestito con mola di più colori e nell'altro il ritratto della serenissima principessa Anna Maria vestita d'incarnato, alti braccia 2 ¾ e larghi braccia 1 ⅞, dal signor Zanobi Betti ne' 10 novembre [1670]

*Archival sources*
Letter from Giusto Suttermans, Florence, 12 November 1669, ASF, Guardaroba medicea 669 bis, fol. 703; Letter from Valentino Farinola, Florence, 12 November 1669, ASF, Guardaroba medicea 669 bis, fol. 702; Quaderno della Guardaroba generale 1666–1674, 10 November 1670, ASF, Guardaroba medicea 751, fol. 205v; Inventario della Guardaroba generale 1666–1680, 10 November 1670, 28 February 1678, ASF, Guardaroba medicea 741, fols. 472s-d; BALDINUCCI n.d. [1678 ca.], BNCF, ms. II.II.110, fol. 351v; Quaderno della Guardaroba generale 1674–1680, 28 February 1678 modern style, ASF, Guardaroba medicea 799, fol. 276v; Inventario di Palazzo Pitti 1688, ASF, Guardaroba medicea 932, fol. 130r; Inventario di Palazzo Pitti 1716–1723, Biblioteca degli Uffizi, ms. 79, fol. 78; Inventario di Palazzo Pitti, 1761, ASF, Guardaroba medicea appendice 94, fol. 617r

*Bibliography*
*Mostra del Ritratto* 1911, p. 192, no. 13; BAUTIER 1912b, pp. 95, 128; NUGENT 1912, p. 34; BAUTIER 1926–1929, p. 319; GAMBA 1927, p. 97, pl. XVIII; GÖZ 1928, pp. 33, 35; SINGER 1937–1938, I, 1937, p. 44, no. 1134; M. Chiarini, in *Gli Ultimi Medici* 1974, p. 316, sub no. 187; LANGEDIJK 1981–1987, II, 1983, pp. 828–831, no. 39/24, fig. 39/24; S. Meloni Trkulja, in *Sustermans* 1983, p. 98, no. XXII; S. Meloni Trkulja and G. Butazzi, in *I principi bambini* 1985, p. 44, no. 10, fig.; L. Goldenberg Stoppato, in *Il Seicento fiorentino* 1986, p. 169; L. Goldenberg Stoppato, in *La pittura in Italia. Il Seicento* 1988 ed. 1989, II, p. 895; L. Goldenberg Stoppato, in TURNER 1996, p. 42; L. Goldenberg Stoppato, in *Il viaggio a Compostela* 2004, pp. 74, 84–85, 95 (notes 102, 104–107), 103, no. 10

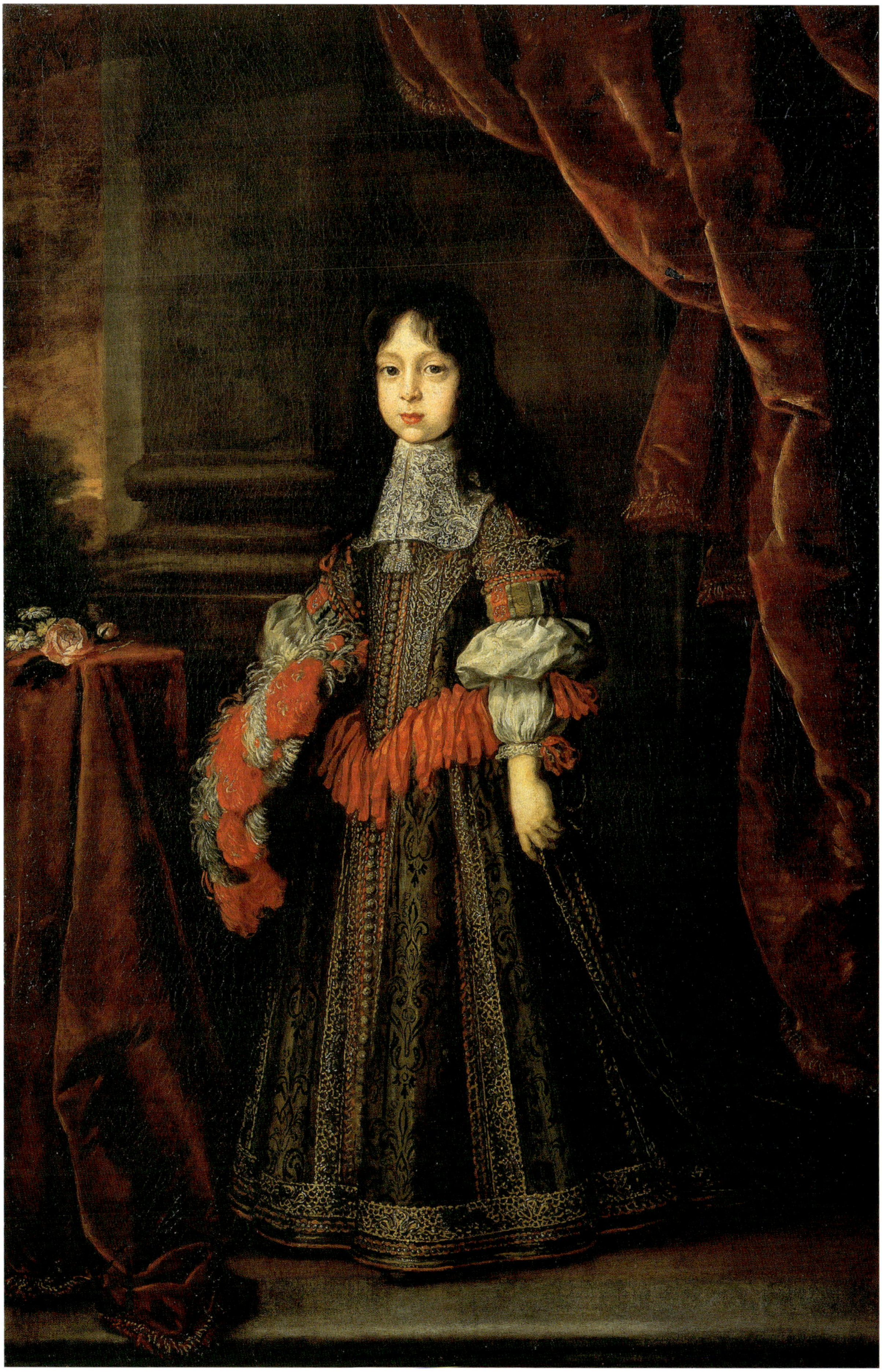

**22** *Anna Maria Luisa de' Medici (1667–1743) as a child*
by November 1670
Florence, Galleria degli Uffizi, storage, inv. 1890, no. 2504
oil on canvas, cm 139 × 106

One of the paintings exhibited in the Suttermans room was a portrait of *Anna Maria Luisa de' Medici*, Cosimo III's only daughter. The 1688 inventory of Palazzo Pitti describes it with its pendant, a portrait of her older brother *Grand Prince Ferdinando* (see cat. no. 21). According to the inventory, Anna Maria Luisa was dressed in red and was holding a rose in her right hand:

> Due quadri in tela alti braccia 2 soldi 16, larghi braccia 1 ⅝ dipintovi di mano di Giusto Suttermanni in uno il ritratto del serenissimo principe Ferdinando da giovanetto con gonellino con cappello sotto il braccio destro con penne rosse e bianche, e nell'altro la serenissima signora principessa Anna Maria Margherita Aliosa da bambina vestita di rosso con una rosa nella mano destra, con adornamenti intagliati, e tutti dorati

The portraits are also mentioned by the inventories of the palace compiled between 1716 and 1723 and in 1761.
Both paintings came from the grand duke's Guardaroba. The portrait of Ferdinando was one of the canvases sent to the keeper of Palazzo Pitti Diacinto Maria Marmi on 28 February 1678 [modern style] expressly for the Suttermans room (see Quaderno della Guardaroba generale 1674–1680, ASF, Guardaroba medicea 799, fol. 276v). According to a journal of the Guardaroba, the portrait of Anna Maria Luisa was sent to keeper Marmi on 20 May of the same year:

> a dì 20 Detto [May 1678] A Diacinto Maria Marmi
> Un Quadro in tela senza adornamento alto braccia 2 ¾, largo 1 ⅞, dipintovi la Serenissima Principessa Anna Maria di mano di Giusto come all'Inventario a 472 n.° 1

As Karla Langedijk pointed out in 1981, the portraits of both children were painted by 10 November 1670, when they were registered in the inventory of the Guardaroba generale:

> Dua quadri in tela entrovi il ritratto fatti da Giusto Suttermano pittore, che in uno il ritratto del serenissimo principe Ferdinando vestito con mola di più colori e nell'altro il ritratto della serenissima principessa Anna Maria vestita d'incarnato, alti braccia 2 ¾ e larghi braccia 1 ⅞ dal signor Zanobi Betti ne' 10 novembre [1670]

The date is entirely appropriate for Anna Maria Luisa's apparent age and for the style of painting. The brushwork is cursory and thin enough to let the dark under-painting show through, which is Suttermans' typical manner in the last phases of his career. The painting, though masterful, is pared down to bare essentials and thus betrays both the painter's flagging energy and his failing eyesight.
Anna Maria Luisa and Ferdinando were portrayed a second time by Suttermans in a painting that belongs to the Stibbert Museum in Florence. In this painting they appear together, wearing the same clothes and accompanied by their governess (see LANGEDIJK 1981–1987, I, 1981, p. 278, no. 6/57, II, 1983, p. 826, no. 39/21).

*Archival sources*
Quaderno della Guardaroba generale 1666–1674, 10 November 1670, ASF, Guardaroba medicea 751, fol. 205v; Inventario della Guardaroba generale 1666–1680, 10 November 1670, 20 May 1678, ASF, Guardaroba medicea 741, fols. 472s-d; Quaderno della Guardaroba generale 1674–1679, 20 May 1678, ASF, Guardaroba medicea 801, fol. 104r; Inventario di Palazzo Pitti 1688, ASF, Guardaroba medicea 932, fol. 130r; Inventario di Palazzo Pitti 1716–1723, Biblioteca degli Uffizi, ms. 79, fol. 104; Inventario di Palazzo Pitti, 1761, ASF, Guardaroba medicea appendice 94, fol. 537v

*Bibliography*
GÖZ 1928, p. 33; KÜHN STEINHAUSEN 1939, p. 141, no. 46, pl. 1, no. 2; KÜHN STEINHAUSEN 1967, pp. 20, 21; M. Chiarini, in *Gli Ultimi Medici* 1974, p. 316, sub no. 187; LANGEDIJK 1981–1987, I, 1981, p. 278, nos. 6/56 and 6/56a; S. Meloni Trkulja, in *Sustermans* 1983, p. 93, no. IV; S. Meloni Trkulja and G. Butazzi, in *I principi bambini* 1985, p. 44, sub no. 10, fig.; L. Goldenberg Stoppato, in *Il Seicento fiorentino* 1986, p. 169; L. Goldenberg Stoppato, in *La pittura in Italia. Il Seicento* 1988 ed. 1989, II, p. 895; DANESI SQUARZINA 1990, pp. 88, 93, fig. 79; L. Goldenberg Stoppato, in TURNER 1996, p. 42; L. Goldenberg Stoppato, in *Il viaggio a Compostela* 2004, pp. 84, 95 (notes 102–106), 103, no. 11

Fig. 1 - Giusto Suttermans, *Anna Maria Luisa and Ferdinando de' Medici with their governess*, 1670 ca. Florence, Stibbert Museum, inv. no. 4101

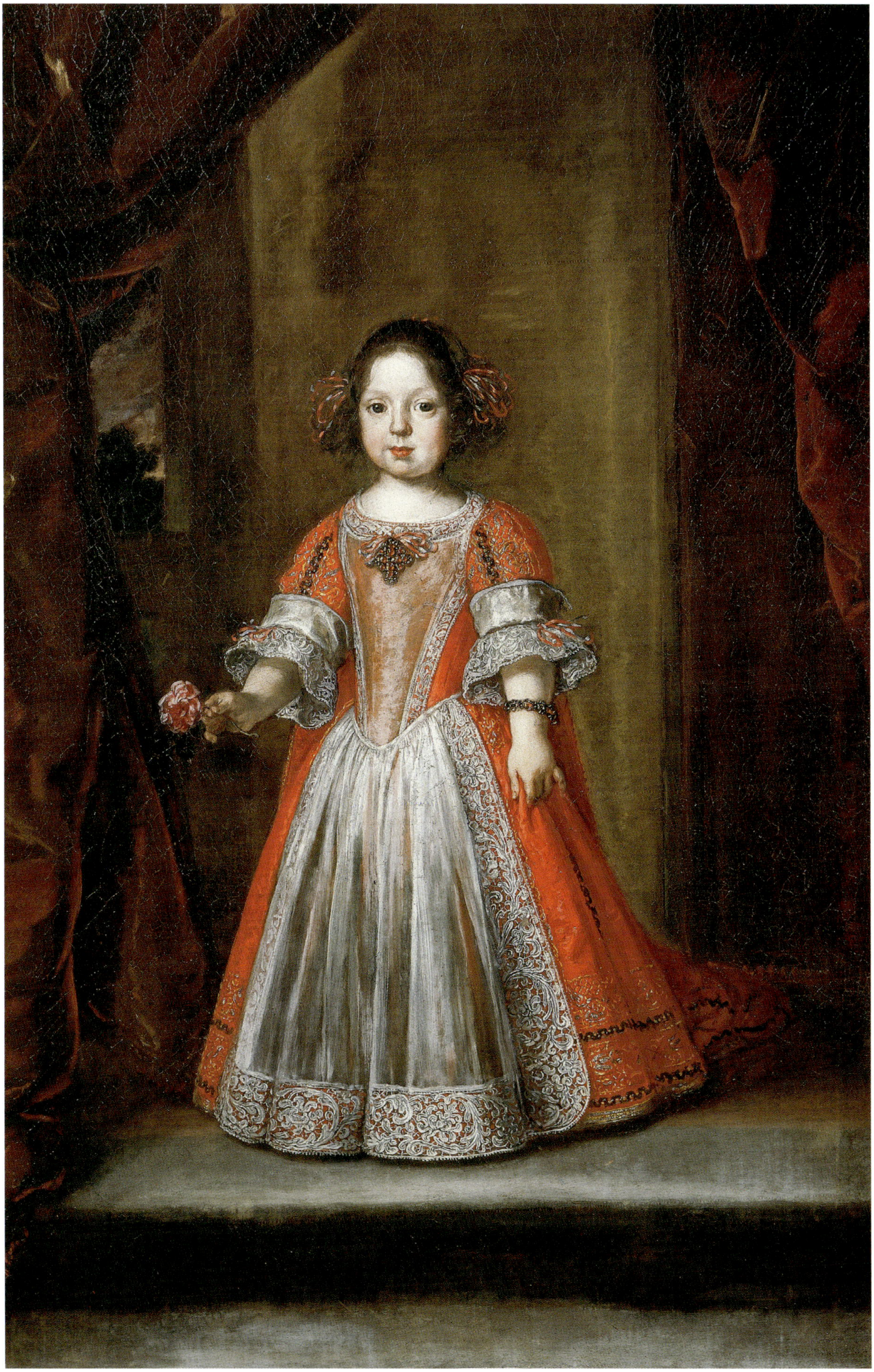

**23** Frans Suttermans (active 1627–1637)
after Antonie van Dyck

*Madonna*

1629 ca.
Florence, Palazzo Pitti, Galleria Palatina, inv. 1912, no. 160
oil on canvas, cm 38 × 24

One of the paintings exhibited in the Suttermans room on the second floor of Palazzo Pitti had a religious subject. The 1688 inventory describes a canvas with the head of a saint, with a purple veil on her head and two fingers of her hand touching her chest:

> Un quadretto in tela alto braccia ⅔ scarso e largo ⅓ buona misura, dipintovi una testa d'una Santa guardante in su con panno paonazzo in capo, e si vede al petto due dita d'una mano, di mano del suddetto, con adornamento intagliato, straforato e dorato      n. 1

Like many of the paintings exhibited at the exhibition in Suttermans' honor, this canvas came from Cardinal Leopoldo de' Medici's collection. As Odoardo Giglioli pointed out, the painting is listed both in the inventory of the cardinal's possessions that was compiled after his death in 1675 and in a Guardaroba journal on 27 February 1677, when they entered the collection of Grand Duke Cosimo III. Another journal documents the official consignment of the canvas to the keeper of Palazzo Pitti on 30 August 1680. The painting also appears in the inventories of the same palace compiled between 1716 and 1723 and in 1761. It was one of the many paintings confiscated by Napoleon Bonaparte's commissaries in 1799 and was only brought back to Florence in 1815.

All the Medici inventories and the lists of works of art removed from Palazzo Pitti and sent to Paris on 1 July 1799 refer to the painting as the head of a saint. It is instead a depiction of the Madonna, copied directly from a *Madonna and Child* painted by Antonie van Dyck during his second Antwerp period (1617–1632). Both SCHAEFFER (1909) and BODART (1977) indicate the *Bridgewater Madonna*, sold at auction by Christie's in 1976, as its prototype (see Christie's sale 2 July 1976, p. 87, no. 83, fig. 83). Since he would not have had the chance to see Van Dyck's original, recent studies all refuse the traditional attribution of this small copy to Giusto Suttermans. LARSEN (1988), for example, attributes this small canvas to Van Dyck's workshop.

The Galleria Palatina *Madonna* does in any case closely resemble several portraits that Suttermans painted with the help of a workshop hand. See, for example, the miniature which portrays *Margherita de' Medici as Saint Margaret*, a work which can be dated between 1628 and 1630 (Florence, Galleria degli Uffizi, inv. 1890, no. 8781, oil on copper, cm 19.6 × 6.9, see L. Goldenberg Stoppato, in *Il Seicento fiorentino* 1986, p. 321, no. 1.165).

This workshop hand may well be Frans Suttermans, who is referred to as his brother's collaborator in Medici documents that date from 1627 to 1629. On 23 January 1626 [ab Incarnatione=1627 modern style] an inventory of the Grand Duke's Guardaroba received a portrait of *Margherita de' Medici* dressed in black from Suttermans, which had been painted by his brother: "Un quadro in tela e telaio di nostro altro braccia 3 ½, largo braccia 2, dentrovi dipinto intero al naturale la Serenissima Principessa Margherita in veste nera tutta guarnita di argento e tavolino e panno da Giusto Surtemanne pittore, fatta di mano del fratello di detto" (Inventario della Guardaroba medicea 1624–1638, ASF, Guardaroba medicea 435, fol. 151s). On 2 February 1627 [modern style], when Giusto wrote to Medici secretary Dimurgo Lambardi from Rome, he added greetings from "signore Francisco" (ASF, Mediceo del Principato 1449, see CRINÒ 1955, pp. 217–218, note 1). In May 1629 Giusto delivered seven Medici portraits to the Guardaroba generale that had been copied by Frans in September 1628: "Sette quadri in tela dentrovi dipinto interi al naturale la Serenissima Arciduchessa e uno il Serenissimo Granduca e uno il principe Giovan Carlo e uno il Signore principe Mattias e uno il principe Francesco e uno il principe Leopoldo e una la principessa Margherita alti braccia 3 ½ da Giusto Surtemanne pittore fatti copiare a Francesco Surtemanne suo fratello sino del mese di settembre prossimo passato". According to this inventory these portraits were sent as gifts to the Duke Albert of Bavaria (see Inventario della Guardaroba medicea 1624–1638, ASF, Guardaroba medicea 435, fol. 207s-d). In the meantime Frans had returned to Antwerp. On 26 January 1628 [ab Incarnatione=1629 modern style] Giusto wrote to secretary Lambardi, mentioning "una lettera di Francesco mio fratello di Fiandra", a letter from my brother Frans from Flanders (ASF, Mediceo del Principato 1449, unpaginated). On 12 April of the same year "Francisco Suttermano" himself wrote to Lambardi from Antwerp in broken Italian. In his letter he spoke with regret of how he missed good Italian wine and informed Lambardi that he was expecting the birth of a child in eight days: "spesse volte me vein gran volio di questo cartutsi et ancor de questo bono vino d'italie in tanto non mancara de bere a la salut Vostra Signoria [. . .]. Fra 8 di spero daver un alter bambino con laiuto di Dio amen" (ASF, Mediceo del Principato 1450, unpaginated).

Filippo Baldinucci mentions that Frans Suttermans worked with Van Dyck after his apprenticeship with Giusto and became an imitator of his style: "[. . .] dopo avere avuta l'arte da Giusto, si pose appresso al Van Dyck, e fu suo grand'imitatore" (1681–1728, ed. 1845–1847, vol. IV, 1846, p. 476). Thus, unlike Giusto, Frans would have certainly had a chance to see the *Madonna* painted by Van

Dyck and could easily have sent this small copy to Florence. Years later, Frans Suttermans settled at the emperor's court in Vienna. In 1637 he was granted a monthly salary of 40 thalers at that court. He died before 31 August 1642, when his widow Anna married the painter Cornelis Meeus in Vienna (see HAJDECKI 1905, pp. 7, 9).

*Archival sources*
Inventario di Leopoldo de' Medici, 1675, ASF, Guardaroba medicea 826, fol. 89, no. 570; Quaderno della Guardaroba generale 1674–1680, 27 February 1676 [ab Incarnatione=1677 modern style], ASF, Guardaroba medicea 799, fol. 208v, no. 570 F. BALDINUCCI n.d. [1678 ca.], BNCF, ms. II.II.110, fol. 350; Quaderno della Guardaroba generale 1679–1685, 30 August 1680, ASF, Guardaroba medicea 870, fol. 75v; Inventario di Palazzo Pitti, 1688, ASF, Guardaroba medicea 932, fol. 132v; Inventario di Palazzo Pitti, 1716–1723, Biblioteca degli Uffizi, ms. 79, fols. 183–184; Inventario di Palazzo Pitti, 1761, ASF, Guardaroba medicea appendice 94, fol. 565v; Nota di quadri spediti a Parigi, 1 luglio 1799, Archivio Storico delle Gallerie fiorentine, shelf no. XL, 1816, no. 48

*Bibliography*
SMITH 1829–1842, III, 1831, p. 47, no. 160; P. Tanzini, in BARDI 1837–1842, III, 1840, unpaginated; CHIAVACCI 1859, pp. 79, 213; VENTURI 1891, III, p. 89, no. 160; SCHAEFFER, 1909, pp. 70, 498; BAUTIER 1912b, p. 46; GIGLIOLI 1912, p. 132, no. 160; JAHN RUSCONI 1937, pp. 285–286, no. 160; TARCHIANI 1939, p. 25; CIPRIANI 1966, p. 244, no. 160; *Rubens e la pittura fiamminga* 1977, pp. 270, 272 (no. 118), 273 (fig.); MASCALCHI 1982, p. 66, note 2, no. e; M. Chiarini, in *Sustermans* 1983, p. 62, sub no. 37; S. Meloni Trkulja, in *Sustermans* 1983, p. 117, no. LXXVI; LARSEN 1988, II, p. 435, no. A 76; L. Borsatti, in F*iamminghi* 1990, p. 38; CHIARINI–PADOVANI 1999, p. 88, no. 27; S. Casciu, in CHIARINI–PADOVANI 2003, I, p. 254, II, pp. 412–413, no. 680; L. Goldenberg Stoppato, in *Il viaggio a Compostela* 2004, pp. 79 (fig.), 85–86, 96 (notes 113–115, 118), 109, no. 30

**24** Workshop of Antonie van Dyck and Giusto Suttermans
*Charles I Stuart (1600–1649) and*
*Henriette Marie de Bourbon (1609–1669)*
1633–1639 ca., retouched in 1675
Florence, Galleria Palatina, inv. 1912, no. 150
oil on canvas, cm 67 × 82.5

One of the paintings mentioned by Filippo Baldinucci in the list of Monsù Giusto's works he compiled while planning the exhibition in 1678 portrayed the king and queen of England: "1 li Re e Regina d'Inghilterra". This double portrait was still in the Suttermans room on the second floor of Palazzzo Pitti when the next inventory of the palace was taken in 1688. The inventory describes the painting in great detail. Both portraits had painted oval frames around them, the king was wearing armor with a turquoise sash and the queen was wearing a dress with a lace collar and a diamond cross pinned on it:

> Un simile alto braccia 1 soldi 2, largo braccia 1 ⅓, dipintovi due ritratti in aovati, che uno del Re d'Inghilterra, padre del regnante, armato con ciarpa turchina, e l'altro della Regina sua moglie con collare di trina e croce di diamanti al petto con perla; et adornamento scorniciato liscio, e tutto dorato n. 1

The portrait is also listed in the inventories of the palace compiled between 1716 and 1723 and in 1761, which bear quite similar descriptions. It is thus rather easy to identify the painting described with a canvas which still can be found in Palazzo Pitti today, in the Galleria Palatina.

The sitters portrayed are Charles I Stuart (1600–1649), who succeeded his father on the English throne in 1625, and his wife Henriette Marie de Bourbon (1609–1669), who was the daughter of Maria de' Medici and King Henri IV of France. Only a few years after he was crowned Charles clashed with his Parliament and the dispute erupted in outright war in August 1642. Charles was defeated in 1646 by the rebel troops commanded by Oliver Cromwell, imprisoned and condemned to death in 1649.

Neither the 1688, nor the 17th-century inventories specify the name of the author of this double portrait. The paternity of this painting has thus been the object of great debate by art historians. Though most of the 19th-century catalogues of the Galleria Palatina consider it a work of Antonie van Dyck (1599–1641), who was portraitist to Charles I from 1632 to 1641, Alfred MICHIELS (1881) attributed it to Giusto Suttermans. Adolfo VENTURI (1891) suggested that it was painted by Cornelis Janssens van Ceulen and Didier BODART (1977) mentioned an attribution to Remigius van Leemput proposed by Godefridus Hoogewerff. Recent studies consider it the work of Van Dyck's workshop.

The double portrait is in fact a pastiche of images copied from a variety of prototypes painted by Van Dyck. As Mary WEBSTER (1971) pointed out, the portrait of the king derives from the portrait of *Charles I on horseback with M. de St-Antoine*, painted by Van Dyck in 1633. In this equestrian portrait Charles is wearing the same lace-trimmed collar, quite similar armor and a blue sash (Royal Collection, oil on canvas, cm 368.4 × 269.9, see M. Rogers, in *Van Dyck* 1999, p. 85, fig. 64). The king's features closely resemble those in the dated portrait of *Charles I in royal robes*, which was painted by Van Dyck in 1636 (Queen's Collection, oil on canvas, cm 253.4 × 153.6, see J. Egerton, in *Van Dyck* 1999, pp. 304–305, no. 90). Other portraits that have been indicated as models for the Galleria Palatina painting are far less convincing: the double portrait in Kromeriz cited by Erik Larsen in 1988 (inv. no. 406, oil on canvas, cm 113.5 × 163, see J. Egerton, in *Van Dyck* 1999, pp. 240–243, no. 65) and the portrait of *Charles I in armor* in an English private collection (see LURIE 1995, fig. on p. 117). The queen's features resemble those in the full-length portrait of *Henriette Marie de Bourbon with her dwarf Jeffrey Hudson*, indicated as a model for the painting in Florence by Webster in 1971 (Washington, National Gallery, Kress Collection, inv. no. 1952.5.39, oil on canvas, cm 219.1 × 134.8, see J. Egerton, in *Van Dyck* 1999, pp. 246–247, no. 67). Her clothing is quite similar to her dress in the double portrait in Kromeriz. In short the double portrait in Florence truly seems to be the work of a close follower of Van Dyck who was familiar with a variety of his master's paintings.

Giusto Suttermans did in any case retouch the portrait of Charles I and Henriette Marie in 1675. The painting is listed in an unpublished bill presented by the painter to the Medici Guardaroba, immediately after a group of portraits that he delivered on the 29 March 1675. The painter asks for four scudi for repainting a ruined canvas with the portraits of the king and queen of England:

[. . .]

E più per aver rifatto un quadro entrovi due ritratti, cioè il Re e la Regina d'Inghilterra, che essendo tutto guasto l'ho avuto a rifar tutto scudi 4 –

In a note penned at the bottom of the bill, keeper Pier Maria Baldi confirms that Suttermans had indeed restored the portrait and specifies that he had repainted the bodies of the sitters since the original painting was ruined:

La undicesima partita, dove dice, che ha rassetto un quadro del Re di Inghilterra, a questo gli ha rifatto il corpo che era guasto. [. . .]

The provenance of the Galleria Palatina's double portrait has yet to be established. Marco Chiarini suggested that Cosimo III de' Medici might have purchased it during his trip to England or afterwards with the help of one of his agents in London. The painting also may have been sent to Florence as a gift from the English court, since Queen Henriette Marie was a relative of the Medici, possibly in exchange for portraits sent from the Medici court. We know in fact that portraits of *Ferdinando II de' Medici* and his wife *Vittoria della Rovere* by Giusto Suttermans were sent to England for King Charles I in 1639. The arrival of the two portraits is mentioned in an unpublished letter from the Medici ambassador in London Amerigo Salvetti to court secretary Andrea Cioli on 15 July 1639: "Al signor Arrigo Robinson è comparso i ritratti del Serenissimo Gran Duca et Gran Duchessa fatti di mano del signor Giusto fino alla cintura. Dice che lui stesso ne parlò à Sua Altezza per haverli, et che gli costano 80 [. . .] et che sono per il cavaliere Mylmey, che li vuole presentare al Re. [. . .]" (ASF, Mediceo del Principato 4200, unpaginated). The portraits had been requested in 1638 by Henry Mildmay, keeper of Charles I's jewels (see the Letter from Amerigo Salvetti to Andrea Cioli, 12 February 1637 [ab Incarnatione=1638 modern style], ASF, Mediceo del Principato 4199, published by CRINÒ 1955, p. 218; CRINÒ 1961, p. 187). Since Salvetti had been excluded from the presentation of these portraits, on 15 July 1639 he requested a second painting with full-length portraits of the grand duke and his wife on the same canvas, which he intended to present to the king. The double portrait he requested still had not been painted at the beginning of 1642 and probably was never sent at all (see the unpublished letter from Amerigo Salvetti to Medici secretary Giovan Battista Gondi, from London, 28 February 1641 [ab Incarnatione=1642 modern style], ASF, Mediceo del Principato 4201, unpaginated; and further correspondence concerning the second portrait published by CRINÒ 1961, pp. 187–190). Crinò suggested that it might be the double portrait of *Ferdinando II de' Medici with Vittoria della Rovere* in the National Gallery in London (inv. no. 89, oil on canvas, cm 161 × 147; see LANGEDIJK 1981–1987, II, 1983, pp. 787–788, no. 38/39). The hypothesis is untenable, since the portrait in London has a French rather than English provenance and was painted twenty-five years later, in 1666.

*Archival sources*
Bill from Giusto Suttermans, 29 March 1675, ASF, Guardaroba medicea 824, no. 1674, fols. 1251, 1252; Inventario di Palazzo Pitti, 1688, ASF, Guardaroba medicea 932, fol. 130r; Inventario di Palazzo Pitti, 1716–1723, Biblioteca degli Uffizi, ms. 79, fol. 87r; Inventario di Palazzo Pitti, 1761, ASF, Guardaroba medicea appendice 94, fol. 531r

*Bibliography*
INGHIRAMI 1828, p. 39; INGHIRAMI 1834, p. 32; P. Thouar, in BARDI 1837–1842, vol. III, 1840, unpaginated; MICHIELS 1881, p. 135, note 1; VENTURI 1891, p. 59; CUST 1900, p. 265, no. 21; SCHAEFFER 1909, pp. 471 (pl.), 535; BAUTIER 1912b, pp. 113–114; JAHN RUSCONI 1937, pp. 122–123; FRANCINI CIARANFI 1964, p. 50, no. 150; CIPRIANI 1966, p. 94, no. 150; *Firenze e l'Inghilterra* 1971, no. 13; *Rubens e la pittura fiamminga* 1977, p. 322, no. XLVIII; LARSEN 1988, vol. II, p. 478, no. A 202/5; *Van Dyck* 1995, pp. 55–58, 113–118, no. 22; M. Chiarini, in CHIARINI–PADOVANI 2003, vol. II, p. 162, no. 256; C. Caneva, in *Maria de' Medici* 2005, p. 353, no. IV.13

# Appendix: Missing Works

**A1** *Portrait of a young princess (Eleonora di Vincenzo I Gonzaga or Eleonora di Carlo Gonzaga-Nevers?)*
oil on canvas, braccia 1, soldi 7 × 1 ⅙=cm 78.3 × 68 ca.

One of the paintings exhibited in the Suttermans room on the second floor of Palazzo Pitti in 1688 was a portrait of a princess wearing a gray dress and a ruff, who was touching her necklace with her right hand:

> Un simile alto braccia 1 soldi 7, largo braccia 1 ⅙, dipintovi di mano de' suddetto il ritratto di Principessa giovane vestita di bigio all'antica con collare a lattughe che con la mano destra si reggie una collana che li pende dal collo, con adornamento di noce intagliato e dorato in parte ___ n. 1

This portrait might well be the portrait of an empress of the Gonzaga family which was mentioned by a journal of the grand ducal Guardaroba on 28 February 1677 [ab Incarnatione=1678 modern style]. On this date it was sent with other five paintings to the keeper of Palazzo Pitti "per metterli nella stanza de' quadri di Giusto Sutterman", to be put in the chamber of paintings by Giusto Suttermans:

> Un quadro in tela alto, anzi dipintovi il ritratto del Imperatrice di casa Gonzagha con adornamento di noce intagliato in parte e dorato, alto braccia 1 ¾ largo braccia 1 ½ in circha, di mano di Giusto___ n. 1

According to the same manuscript this portrait had been sent to the Guardaroba generale by Giovanni Bianchi, the keeper of the Galleria degli Uffizi. The journal of the Galleria degli Uffizi specifies that the portrait of the empress was taken from the room next to the armory on 27 January:

> e A 27 gennaio 1677 [ab incarnatione=1678 modern style]
>
> Un quadro in tela con ornamento di noce intagliato e dorato in parte entrovi dipinto ill ritratto dell'inperatrice regniante di casa Gonzaga alto braccia 1 ¾, largo braccia 1 ½, cavato dalla stanza a lato alla Armeria, consegniato all signor Niccolò Bernardi n.° 1

Two different Gonzaga princesses, both named Eleonora, married Austrian emperors in the 17th century. Eleonora (1598–1655), the daughter of Vincenzo I Gonzaga, married Ferdinand II von Habsburg in 1621. Eleonora (1628–1686), the daughter of Carlo Gonzaga Nevers, was wedded to Ferdinand III von Habsburg in 1651. The Uffizi journal entry from 1678, which indicates that the sitter as the ruling empress, seems to refer to the second Empress Eleonora. The ruff mentioned by the 1688 inventory, a type of collar which went out of style after the 1620's, would make more sense in a portrait of the first Empress Eleonora, who was the sister-in-law of the Grand Duchess of Tuscany Maria Maddalena of Austria.

*Archival sources*
Giornale della Galleria degli Uffizi, 1646–1688, 27 January 1677 [ab Incarnatione=1678 modern style], Biblioteca degli Uffizi, ms. 62, fol. 126; Quaderno della Guardaroba generale 1674–1680, 25, 28 February 1678 modern style, ASF, Guardaroba medicea 799, fols. 271v, 276v; Inventario di Palazzo Pitti, 1688, ASF, Guardaroba medicea 932, fol. 129v; (?)Inventario di Palazzo Pitti, 1761, ASF, Guardaroba medicea appendice 94, fol. 530v

*Bibliography*
L. Goldenberg Stoppato, in *Il viaggio a Compostela* 2004, pp. 74, 75, 102, no. 6

**A2** *Giandomenico Peri (1564–1639), known as Arcidosso*
by 1638
oil on canvas, braccia 1, soldi 2 × ⅝=cm 64.1 × 48.6 ca.

Filippo Baldinucci mentions a portrait of the poet Arcidosso in the list of works by Giusto Suttermans that he compiled while he was planning the 1678 exhibition. The portrait is also described by the 1688 inventory of Palazzo Pitti, hanging with twenty-nine other paintings by Suttermans in a room on the second floor of the palace. According to the inventory, the sitter had his collar hanging from his shirt and a book in his right hand:

> Un simile alto braccia 1 soldi 2, largo ⅝, dipintovi di mano del suddetto il ritratto del poeta Arcidosso, con collare attaccato alla camicia e libro nella mano destra, con adornamento intagliato, e dorato _____ n. 1

Arcidosso is both the name a town on Mount Amiata in southern Tuscany and the nickname of the rustic poet Giandomenico Peri (1564–1639), who wrote comedies and bucolic poetry. The poet was also portrayed by Jacques Callot in an engraving facing the title page of an edition of his *Fiesole distrutta* (see PERI 1621). Peri recited poetry for Cosimo II de' Medici during the grand duke's visit to Arcidosso in 1612 (see SIMONCINI 1995–1996, pp. 77–84). He is also cited in an unpublished list of Grand Duke Ferdinando II sundry expenses for the month of June 1621: "Allo Arcidosso poeta, scudi quindici per mancia" (see Spese della Camera del granduca, 1621, ASF, Camera del Granduca 2b, fol. 14).

Peri's portrait is cited without an attribution in the Palazzo Pitti inventories compiled in 1638 and between 1663 and 1664. It is mentioned as Suttermans' work, not only in the 1688 inventory but also in the 1716–1723 and 1761 inventories. This last inventory describes the poet with gray hair and a gray beard, holding a book in his right hand and wearing a dark yellow, half-open doublet held together with string:

> Uno simile alto braccia, largo braccia ... dipintovi un Ritratto d'un contadino poeta, con barba e spazzola grigia, con un libro nella mano destra, vestito di giubbone giallognolo affibbiato con cordone e mezzo aperto, mano di Giusto Sutterman con adornamento simile n.1, [in the margin:] Ritratto del Poeta Arcidosso

*Archival sources*
Inventario di Palazzo Pitti, 1638, ASF, Guardaroba medicea 525, fol. 38v; Inventario della Guardaroba di Palazzo Pitti, 1638, ASF, Guardaroba medicea 535, fol. 51s; Entrata e Uscita di Palazzo Pitti, 1638–1648, ASF, Guardaroba medicea 530, fol. 136s; Inventario di Palazzo Pitti, 1663–1664, ASF, Guardaroba medicea 725, fol. 54v; BALDINUCCI n.d. [1678 ca.], BNCF, ms. II.II.110, fol. 350; Inventario di Palazzo Pitti, 1688, ASF, Guardaroba medicea 932, fol. 132v; Inventario di Palazzo Pitti, 1716–1723, Biblioteca degli Uffizi, ms. 79, fol. 102; Inventario di Palazzo Pitti, 1761, ASF, Guardaroba medicea appendice 94, fols. 534v–535r

*Bibliography*
L. Goldenberg Stoppato, in *Il viaggio a Compostela* 2004, pp. 75, 108, no. 27

**A3** *Saint Lucy*
by 1638
oil on canvas, braccia 1 × ⅚=cm 58.3 × 48.6 ca.

A painting depicting "Santa Lucia" is cited in the list of works by Suttermans compiled by Filippo Baldinucci while he was planning the exhibition in the painter's honor in 1678. It also is listed among the thirty paintings by the Flemish painter described by the 1688 inventory of Palazzo Pitti in a room on the second floor of the building. According to the inventory, the saint was holding the symbols of her martyrdom, a cup with two eyes on it in her right hand and a palm branch in her left hand:

> Un quadro in tela alto braccia 1 in ca., largo ⅚, dipintovi di mano di Giusto Suttermanni Santa Lucia, che con la mano destra tiene una tazza dove vi sono due occhi e con la sinistra una palma, con adornamento scorniciato liscio n. 1

The same painting is mentioned without an attribution in two inventories of Palazzo Pitti compiled in 1638 and in a journal for objects entering and leaving the same palace for the period between 1638 and 1648. It is listed as a work by Suttermans in all the later inventories of the palace, starting from the one compiled between 1663 and 1664 and up to and including the 1761 inventory. It is also mentioned as a lost work by Suttermans in Pierre Bautier's monograph (1912b).

*Archival sources*
Inventario di Palazzo Pitti, 1638, ASF, Guardaroba medicea 525, fol. 41v; Inventario della Guardaroba di Palazzo Pitti, 1638, ASF, Guardaroba medicea 535, fol. 56s; Entrata e Uscita di Palazzo Pitti, 1638–1648, ASF, Guardaroba medicea 530, fol. 143s; Inventario di Palazzo Pitti, 1663–1664, ASF, Guardaroba medicea 725, fol. 59r; BALDINUCCI n.d. [1678 ca.], BNCF, ms. II.II.110, fol. 350; Inventario di Palazzo Pitti, 1688, ASF, Guardaroba medicea 932, fol. 130v; Inventario di Palazzo Pitti, 1716–1723, Biblioteca degli Uffizi, ms. 79, fol. 100; Inventario di Palazzo Pitti, 1761, ASF, Guardaroba medicea appendice 94, fol. 535r

*Bibliography*
BAUTIER 1912b, pp. 45–46; BAUTIER 1926–1929, p. 321; L. Goldenberg Stoppato, in *Il viaggio a Compostela* 2004, p. 104, no. 14

**A4** *Girolamo Fantini, trumpeter*
1631–1638
oil on canvas, braccia 1 ⅛ × ⅚=cm 65.55 × 48.6 ca.

Filippo Baldinucci mentions this portrait of the "Tromba a Pitti" in the census of works by Giusto Suttermans he compiled while he was planning the exhibition in the painter's honor in 1678, among the paintings entrusted to the keepers "Marmi e Bernardi a Pitti". The same portrait is described in the 1688 inventory of Palazzo Pitti as one of the thirty works by the Fleming hanging in a room on the second floor of the palace. The inventory supplies the sitter's first name and specifies that he was playing his trumpet:

> Un quadro in tela alto braccia 1 ⅛, largo ⅚, dipintovi di mano di Giusto Suttermanni il ritratto di Girolamo trombetta in atto di sonare la tromba, con adornamento intagliato e dorato n. 1

The presence of this portrait in Palazzo Pitti is documented starting from 1638 when it was cited by three different inventories of the palace. None of these inventories, nor the following one compiled between 1663 and 1664, attribute the painting to Suttermans. The painting is however listed as his work in all the 18th-century inventories of Palazzo Pitti. The trumpeter's first name, which is repeated in the 1716–1723 inventory, does not appear in the 1761 inventory.

The trumpeter portrayed was probably Girolamo Fantini from Spoleto, who is mentioned by Warren Kirkendale as the author of a handbook for learning to play the trumpet, *Modo per imparare a sonare di tromba*, which was published in Frankfurt in 1638 (KIRKENDALE 1993, p. 43, note 34). According to Kirkendale, Fantini received a monthly salary of 10 scudi from Ferdinando II de' Medici from 1631 to 1641. The trumpeter is also mentioned in a book of debtors and creditors for objects given by the Medici Guardaroba to court staff and servants. This manuscript lists a silver trumpet and other objects delivered on 11 April 1631 to "Girolamo Fantini da Spuleti, nuovo trombetta di Sua Altezza Serenissima", his highness' new trumpeter (Debitori e creditori della Guardaroba generale, 1628–1633, ASF, Guardaroba medicea 448, fol. 66s). There was also another Medici trumpeter who had the same first name, "Girolamo Porati d'Ancona". However, it is not likely that Porati was the sitter in this portrait painted by 1638, since he was mentioned for the first time as the grand duke's new trumpeter on 12 October 1643 (see Debitori e creditori della Guardaroba generale, 1640–1646, ASF, Guardaroba medicea 563, fol. 113s).

*Archival sources*
Inventario di Palazzo Pitti, 1638, ASF, Guardaroba medicea 525, fol. 38v; Inventario della Guardaroba di Palazzo Pitti, 1638, ASF, Guardaroba medicea 535, fol. 52s; Entrata e Uscita di Palazzo Pitti, 1638–1648, ASF, Guardaroba medicea 530, fol. 136s; Inventario di Palazzo Pitti, 1663–1664, ASF, Guardaroba medicea 725, fol. 54v; BALDINUCCI n.d. [1678 ca.], BNCF, ms. II.II.110, fol. 350; Inventario di Palazzo Pitti, 1688, ASF, Guardaroba medicea 932, fol. 131v; Inventario di Palazzo Pitti, 1716–1723, Biblioteca degli Uffizi, ms. 79, fol. 91; Inventario di Palazzo Pitti, 1761, ASF, Guardaroba medicea appendice 94, fol. 535r

*Bibliography*
L. Goldenberg Stoppato, in *Il viaggio a Compostela* 2004, pp. 75, 105, no. 18

**A5** *Prudenza Carpiani Fiorilli, actress*
oil on canvas, braccia 1 × ¾=cm 58.3 × 43.8 ca.

One of the works by Giusto Suttermans exhibited in the chamber on the second floor of Palazzo Pitti in 1688 was the portrait of an actress named Prudenza. According to the inventory the actress was holding a palette and paintbrushes:

> Un simile alto braccia 1 buona misura, largo ¾ dipintovi di mano del suddetto il ritratto della Prudenza commediante con tavolozza e pennelli nella sinistra, con adornamento simile al suddetto n. 1

The portrait is also listed in the palace inventories compiled between 1716 and 1723 and in 1761. The first of these 18th-century inventories indicates a provenance from the collection of Cardinal Leopoldo de' Medici. The painting is in fact described by the inventory compiled after the death of the cardinal in 1675. Two journals of the Guardaroba medicea document the passage of this portrait from Leopoldo's to Cosimo III's collection on 27 February 1676 [ab Incarnatione=1677 modern style] and its official consignment to the keeper of Palazzo Pitti on 30 August 1680.

The painting might come from the collection of Leopoldo's brother Giovan Carlo de' Medici (1611–1663). The 1647 inventory of Giovan Carlo's residence in Via della Scala describes two half-length female portraits by Giusto. One of the woman portrayed is clearly identified as Prudenza:

> N.° 2 Quadri entrovi due ritratti di mezze figure di due femmine di mano di Giusto, che una è la Prudenza e l'altra N con adornamento intagliato senza dorare, son' nella seconda stanza di sopra su il terrazzino

These two paintings might well be the two portraits of women by Suttermans mentioned in the 1663 inventory of Giovan Carlo's possessions at the Medici villa in Castello: "Due tele senza telai, entrovi ritratti due dame di mano di Giusto, solo la testa". Leopoldo may have acquired the portrait of *Prudenza* when Giovan Carlo's possessions were sold off after his death to cover his debts (see MASCALCHI 1984, pp. 268, 272, notes 1–2).

Though biographies of Prudenza were published by Francesco BARTOLI (1781–1782, ed. 1978, II, pp. 99–101) and Luigi RASI (1897–1905, II, 1905, pp. 313–314), neither author knew her last name. According to Bartoli, Prudenza was the prima donna in the company of actors known as the Affezionati during the Bolognese carnival season in 1634. Rasi mentions a comedy written by Prudenza, *La Pazzia*. Her full name was discovered by Anna Evangelista, who transcribed a letter signed by "Prudenza Carpiani Fiorili comica" and sent, with a small dog, to Giovan Carlo de' Medici from Bologna on 2 April 1635 (see ASF, Mediceo del Principato 5307, fol. 425r; EVANGELISTA 1978–1979, appendix, p. 446):

> [. . .] Bench'io sia stata in fin di morte, non mi sono però mai scordata la benignità et clemenza con la quale Vostra Altezza Serenissima si degnò gratiare la mia debole si, ma divota servitù, et in segno di ciò mando a Vostra Altezza Serenissima questa canina, simbolo di quella fedeltà, con la quale servo et osservo il gloriosissimo nome di Vostra Altezza Serenissima [. . .].

*Archival sources*
Inventario di Giovan Carlo de' Medici (Via della Scala), 1647, ASF, Scrittoio delle Regie Possessioni 4279, fol. 43r; (?)Inventario di Giovan Carlo de' Medici (Villa di Castello), 1663, ASF, Miscellanea medicea 31, insert 10, fol. 135v; Inventario di Leopoldo de' Medici, 1675, ASF, Guardaroba medicea 826, fol. 83r, no. 456; Quaderno della Guardaroba generale, 1674–1680, 27 February 1676 [ab Incarnatione=1677 modern style], ASF, Guardaroba medicea 799, fol. 200v, no. 456; Quaderno della Guardaroba generale 1679–1685, 30 agosto 1680, ASF, Guardaroba medicea 870, fol. 70r; Inventario di Palazzo Pitti, 1688, ASF, Guardaroba medicea 932, fol. 131v; Inventario di Palazzo Pitti, 1716–1723, Firenze, Biblioteca degli Uffizi, ms. 79, fols. 218–219; Inventario di Palazzo Pitti, 1761, ASF, Guardaroba medicea appendice 94, fol. 581r

*Bibliography*
L. Goldenberg Stoppato, in *Il viaggio a Compostela* 2004, pp. 75, 106–107, no. 22


**A6** *Isabella Clara von Habsburg (1629–1685), archduchess of Austria and duchess of Mantua*
1653 or 1656
oil on canvas, braccia 1 ⅛ × ⅝=cm 65.55 × 48.6 ca.

One of the thirty paintings by Suttermans that were exhibited on the second floor of Palazzo Pitti was a portrait of the Archduchess of Mantua. According to the 1688 inventory, she was wearing a gray dress with a black veil, a pearl necklace and earrings:

> Un quadro in tela alto braccia 1 ⅛ largo ⅝ dipintovi il ritratto dell'Arciduchessa di Mantoa, con veste bigia, veletto nero, vezzo, e pendenti di perle grosse, di mano di Giusto Suttermanni, con adornamento intagliato, e dorato   n. 1

The sitter in this lost portrait was mistakenly identified by Pierre Bautier as Caterina de' Medici (1593–1629), the daughter of Grand Duke Ferdinando I and the wife of the Duke of Mantua Ferdinando I Gonzaga. Since the inventory refers to her as an archduchess she must instead be Isabella Clara, the daughter of Archduke Leopold von Habsburg and his wife Claudia de' Medici, who married Duke Carlo III Gonzaga-Nevers in 1649. Documentary sources prove that Suttermans visited Mantua in 1653 and in 1656. He probably painted this portrait of Isabella Clara during one of these visits.

The portrait comes from the collection of Cardinal Leopoldo de' Medici. It is described in 1675 in the inventory of his possessions and on 27 February 1676 [ab Incarnatione=1677 modern style], when the collection was registered in the books of the grand duke's Guardaroba. The painting was consigned to the keeper of Palazzo Pitti on 30 August 1680. The inventory of the palace compiled between 1716 and 1723 describes it in a room on the second floor where the portraits of *Passignano*, *Galileo Galilei* and *Margherita de' Medici as a widow* (cat. nos. 10, 14, 18) were also exhibited at that time. The portrait of the archduchess might also be one of the thirteen paintings by Suttermans listed together by the 1761 inventory of the palace, in the ninth room of the apartment of Grand Prince Ferdinando.

*Archival sources*
Inventario di Leopoldo de' Medici, 1675, ASF, Guardaroba medicea 826, fol. 77r, no. 364; Quaderno della Guardaroba generale 1674–1680, 27 February 1676 [ab Incarnatione=1677 modern style], ASF, Guardaroba medicea 799, fol. 191v, no. 364; Quaderno della Guardaroba generale 1679–1685, 30 August 1680, ASF, Guardaroba medicea 870, fol. 63r; Inventario di Palazzo Pitti, 1688, ASF, Guardaroba medicea 932, fol. 130v; Inventario di Palazzo Pitti, 1716–1723, Biblioteca degli Uffizi, ms. 79, fol. 268; (?)Inventario di Palazzo Pitti, 1761, ASF, Guardaroba medicea appendice 94, fol. 530v

*Bibliography*
BAUTIER 1912b, pp. 71–72; GIANNANTONI 1937, p. 12; L. Goldenberg Stoppato, in *Il viaggio a Compostela* 2004, p. 104, no. 13


**A7** *Lorenzo di Ferdinando I de' Medici (1600–1648)*
1655
oil on canvas, braccia 1, soldi 3 × soldi 18=cm 67 × 52.2 ca.

One of the thirty paintings by Suttermans exhibited in the same room on the second floor of Palazzo Pitti was a portrait of don Lorenzo de' Medici, the youngest brother of Grand Duke Cosimo II. According to the 1688 inventory, he was wearing a black, slashed doublet with a small, lace-trimmed, white collar:

> Un quadro in tela alto braccia 1 soldi 3, largo soldi 18, dipintovi di mano di Giusto Suttermanni il ritratto del serenissimo principe don Lorenzo vestito di nero trinciato con collarino piccolo con trine et adornamento scorniciato liscio e tutto dorato   n. 1

The painting came from the collection of the sitter's brother Cardinal Carlo de' Medici. It is mentioned without the name of the painter both in the inventory of Carlo's collection and in two books of the Guardaroba on 30 June 1667, when it entered the grand ducal collection. It was one of the portraits sent to Palazzo Pitti on 28 February 1678 expressly for the "stanza de' quadri di Giusto Suttermans", for the Suttermans room. It is attributed to him not only in the 1688 inventory of the palace, but also in the one which was compiled between 1716 and 1723. This inventory describes the portrait of don Lorenzo hanging with twelve other paintings by the Fleming in the room known as the "camera della Scarabattola d'oro", in the apartment of the deceased Grand Prince Ferdinando. It thus can be recognized as one of the thirteen paintings listed together in a room of the same apartment in 1761 inventory:

> Tredici Quadri in tela alti braccia 1 soldi 2 larghi braccia 1 ⅝ in ca. per ciascheduno dipintovi dicesi di mano di Monsieur Giusto Suttermans diversi Ritratti di Principi, Principesse, et altri suggetti, che otto di uomini fino a mezo busto, e cinque di donne simili con adornamento scorniciati tutti intagliati, e dorati, segnati n.° 438

The portrait that was exhibited in 1678 may well be the same one mentioned on 10 December 1655 in a book of Cardinal Carlo's debtors and creditors, which was called to my attention by Elena Fumagalli. On that date the painter received a payment of 20 scudi from Carlo for a portrait of deceased Prince Lorenzo: "E addì X detto scudi 20 moneta pagati a Giusto Suttermano pittore per valuta di un ritratto di don Lorenzo, beata memoria [...]". The same painting is mentioned in a letter sent by Averardo Ximenes on 6 October 1658 (see cat. no. 1 for a full transcription).

This portrait of don Lorenzo should not be confused with the bust-length, oval portrait of don Lorenzo dressed in a similar black, slashed doublet that belongs to the Gallerie fiorentine (Palazzo Pitti, storage, inv. 1890, oil on canvas, cm 64 × 49, see LANGEDIJK 1981–1987, II, 1983, p. 1127, no. 70/10). The oval portrait was exhibited in the Galleria degli Uffizi in the 17th century and can be recognized in the Uffizi inventories of that period thanks to the description of its highly ornamented frame which is carved in wood and topped with a crown. Another portrait of don Lorenzo in similar garb belongs to the Stibbert Museum's series of octagonal Medici portraits (Florence, Museo Stibbert, inv. no. 4108, oil on canvas, cm 79 × 64, see LANGEDIJK 1981–1987, II, 1983, p. 1127, no. 70/10b). Unfortunately the painting listed in the 1688 Pitti inventory was slightly smaller than the Stibbert portrait and was not described as an octagonal.

*Archival sources*
Debitori e creditori di Carlo de' Medici, 1651–1663, 10 December 1655, ASF, Scrittoio delle Regie Possessioni 4173, fol. 360s; Letter from Averardo Ximenes to Carlo de' Medici, Florence, 6 October 1658, ASF, Mediceo del Principato 5242, fol. 241, published by PIERACCINI 1924–1925, II, 1925, pp. 405, 409, note 181; Inventario di Carlo de' Medici, 1667, ASF, Guardaroba medicea 758, fol. 3v; Quaderno della Guardaroba generale 1666–1674, I, 30 June 1667, ASF, Guardaroba medicea 750, fol. 58v; Inventario della Guardaroba generale 1666–1680, 30 June 1667 and 28 February 1678, ASF, Guardaroba medicea 741, fols. 357s-d; Quaderno della Guardaroba generale 1674–1680, 28 February 1678 modern style, ASF, Guardaroba medicea 799, fol. 276v; BALDINUCCI n.d. [1678 ca.], BNCF, ms. II.II.110, fol. 350; Inventario di Palazzo Pitti, 1688, ASF, Guardaroba medicea 932, fol. 132v; Inventario di Palazzo Pitti, 1716–1723, Biblioteca degli Uffizi, ms. 79, fol. 88; (?)Inventario di Palazzo Pitti, 1761, ASF, Guardaroba medicea appendice 94, fol. 530v

*Bibliography*
L. Goldenberg Stoppato, in *Il viaggio a Compostela* 2004, pp. 74, 107–108, no. 26

## A8 *Portrait of an Indian with a crown or a wreath around his neck*
1668
oil on canvas, braccia 1 ¼ × 1=cm 71.5 × 58.3 ca.

One of the thirty paintings by Suttermans exhibited together on the second floor of Palazzo Pitti in 1688 was a portrait of an Indian. According to the inventory compiled at that time, he was dressed in red and had a wreath or a crown around his neck:

> Un quadro in tela alto braccia 1 ¼, largo braccia 1 in ca., dipintovi un Indiano vestito di rosso con corona al collo e con la mano destra si reggie o tiene il vestito, di mano di Giusto Suttermanni, con adornamento intagliato e dorato  n. 1

The same painting, referred to as the "Moro Indiano", appears on the list compiled by Filippo Baldinucci while he was planning the exhibition in 1678. He lists it with paintings entrusted to the keepers "Marmi e Bernardi a Pitti". According to two books of the Guardaroba generale, the portrait was sent to Palazzo Pitti on 31 October 1671 and was hung by the palace's keeper Diacinto Maria Marmi in the 'Salone del Trucco', the room where they played trucco, a game somewhat like pool. The portrait of the Indian is cited in all the palace inventories from 1688 to 1761.

Suttermans presented the bill for this portrait to the Guardaroba generale on 18 December 1668. It is listed on the bill immediately after another painting exhibited in 1678, the Crespi portrait of *Mattias de' Medici*:

> Un altro Ritratto fatto dal vivo d'un Indiano moro con panicino rosso intorno in un[o] alto braccia [e] ¼, largo a proporzione, consegniato come sopra [in Camera di Sua Altezza Serenissima] al quaderno 104 scudi 30

Like the portrait of *Mattias*, the *Portrait of an Indian* was registered in the Guardaroba's inventory on 30 June 1670.

*Archival sources*
Bill from Giusto Suttermans, 18 December 1668, ASF, Guardaroba medicea 768, fol. 518; Quaderno della Guardaroba generale, 1666–1674, I, 30 June 1670, 31 October 1671, ASF, Guardaroba medicea 750, fols. 198r, 224r; Inventario della Guardaroba generale 1666–1680, 30 June 1670 and 31 October 1671, ASF, Guardaroba medicea 741, fols. 472s-d; BALDINUCCI n.d. [1678 ca.], BNCF, ms. II.II.110, fol. 350; Inventario di Palazzo Pitti, 1688, ASF, Guardaroba medicea 932, fol. 130r; Inventario di Palazzo Pitti, 1716–1723, Biblioteca degli Uffizi, ms. 79, fol. 86; (?)Inventario di Palazzo Pitti, 1761, ASF, Guardaroba medicea appendice 94, fol. 530v

*Bibliography*
L. Goldenberg Stoppato, in *Il viaggio a Compostela* 2004, p. 102, no. 8

## A9 *Old Man holding a book*
by 1675
oil on canvas, braccia 1 (short measure) × ¾=cm 58 × 43.8 ca.

The 1688 inventory of Palazzo Pitti describes, among the paintings by Suttermans exhibited together on the second floor of the palace, a portrait of an old man with a long white beard who was reading a book:

> Un quadro in tela alto braccia 1, largo ¾, dipintovi di mano di Giusto Suttermanni un Vecchio con libro in mano che legge, con barba canuta lunga, con adornamento simile al suddetto  n. 1

This painting came from the collection of Cardinal Leopoldo de' Medici. It is listed both in the 1675 inventory of his collection and in the Guardaroba's journal on 27 February 1676 [ab Incarnatione=1677 modern style], when Leopoldo's possessions officially entered Grand Duke Cosimo III's collection. According to a second journal, the painting was entrusted to the keeper of Palazzo Pitti on 30 August 1680.

*Archival sources*
Inventario di Leopoldo de' Medici, 1675, ASF, Guardaroba medicea 826, fol. 83v, no. 461; Quaderno della Guardaroba generale 1674–1680, 27 February 1676 [ab Incarnatione=1677 modern style], ASF, Guardaroba medicea 799, fol. 201r, no. 461; Quaderno della Guardaroba generale 1679–1685, 30 August 1680, ASF, Guardaroba medicea 870, fol. 70r; Inventario di Palazzo Pitti, 1688, ASF, Guardaroba medicea 932, fol. 129v

*Bibliography*
L. Goldenberg Stoppato, in *Il viaggio a Compostela* 2004, pp. 75, 102, no. 7

## A10 *La Fornaina*
oil on canvas, braccia 1 ⅛ × ⅝=cm 65.5 × 48.6 ca.

A portrait of a woman called the "Fornaina" is listed in the census of paintings by Monsù Giusto taken by Filippo Baldinucci in 1678, while he was planning the exhibition in the painter's honor. The portrait is described by the 1688 inventory of the palace, hanging with twenty-nine other paintings by Suttermans in a room on the second floor of Palazzo Pitti. According to the inventory the sitter was wearing a black, low-cut dress:

> Un simile alto braccia 1 ⅛, largo ⅚, dipintovi di mano del suddetto il ritratto della Fornaina vestita di nero scollacciata, con adornamento simile al suddetto [intagliato e dorato] ___ n. 1

The same portrait by Suttermans is mentioned in the inventory of the palace compiled between 1716 and 1723. According to this inventory the woman was wearing a rose tucked into her neckline. This inventory lists the portrait of Fornaina with twelve other canvases by the same painter in a room known as the "camera della Scarabattola d'oro", in the apartment of Grand Prince Ferdinando de' Medici. Thus it may well be one of the thirteen "Ritratti di Principi, Principesse et altri suggetti", portraits of princes, princesses and other sitters, listed together in the ninth room of the same apartment in 1761.

*Archival sources*
BALDINUCCI n.d. [1678 ca.], BNCF, ms. II.II.110, fol. 350; Inventario di Palazzo Pitti, 1688, ASF, Guardaroba medicea 932, fol. 131v; Inventario di Palazzo Pitti, 1716–1723, Firenze, Biblioteca degli Uffizi, ms. 79, fol. 87; (?)Inventario di Palazzo Pitti, 1761, ASF, Guardaroba medicea appendice 94, fol. 530v

*Bibliography*
L. Goldenberg Stoppato, in *Il viaggio a Compostela* 2004, pp. 75, 106, no. 20

## A11 *La Fochina*

oil on canvas, braccia 1 soldi 2 × ⅚=cm 64.1 × 48.6 ca.

A portrait of a woman called "Fochina" appears on the list of paintings by Giusto Suttermans compiled by Filippo Baldinucci in 1678, when he was planning the exhibition in the painter's honor. The same portrait is described in detail by the 1688 inventory of Palazzo Pitti, hanging in a room on the second floor of the palace with twenty-nine other paintings by the same painter. According to the inventory, Fochina was wearing a low-necked red dress with a gold shawl and holding a laurel wreath in her right hand and a book under her left arm:

> Un quadro in tela alto braccia 1 soldi 2, largo ⅚, dipintovi di mano di Giusto Suttermanni il ritratto della Fochina vestita di rosso con manto dorè scollacciata, che con la mano destra tiene una corona di lauro e sotto il braccio sinistro tiene un libro, con adornamento intagliato, e dorato_____ n. 1

The painting is mentioned, duly attributed to Suttermans, in the inventories of Palazzo Pitti compiled between 1716 and 1723 and in 1761. A similar portrait of a woman dressed in red with a yellow shawl and a sprig of laurel in her right hand belongs to the Accademia Carrara in Bergamo (oil on canvas, cm 64 × 51, see LANGEDIJK 1981–1987, II, 1983, p. 1509, no. 110/72, fig. 110/72; L. Borsatti, in *Fiamminghi* 1990, pp. 38, 39, fig.). Unfortunately there is a significant difference between the two paintings. While the inventories mention a book tucked under Fochina's left arm, the sitter in Bergamo is holding a roll of paper or parchment.

*Archival sources*
BALDINUCCI n.d. [1678 ca.], BNCF, ms. II.II.110, fol. 350; Inventario di Palazzo Pitti, 1688, ASF, Guardaroba medicea 932, fol. 132r; Inventario di Palazzo Pitti, 1716–1723, Biblioteca degli Uffizi, ms. 79, fol. 88; (?)Inventario di Palazzo Pitti, 1761, ASF, Guardaroba medicea appendice 94, fol. 530v

*Bibliography*
L. Goldenberg Stoppato, in *Il viaggio a Compostela* 2004, pp. 75, 107, no. 24

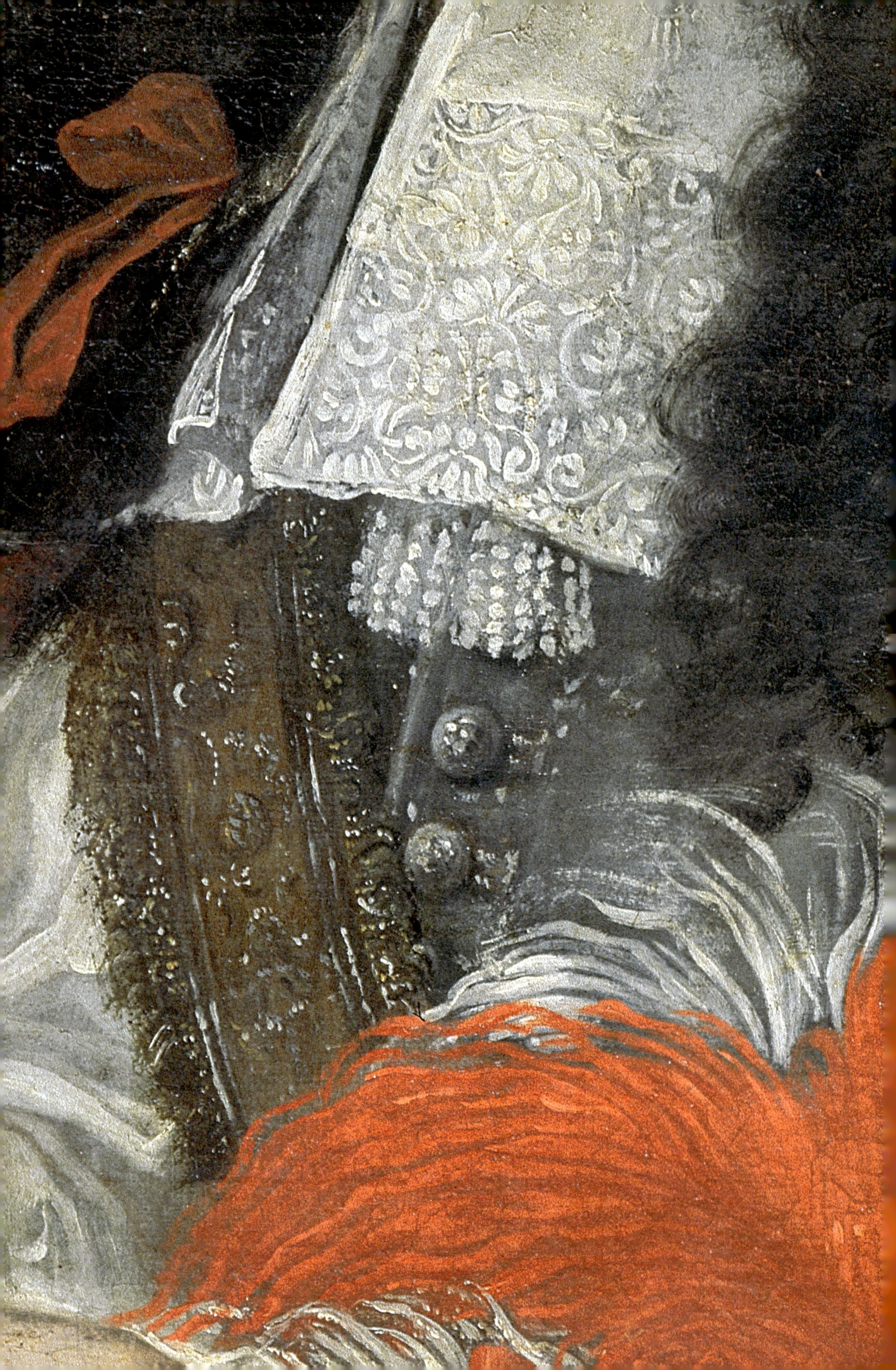

# Bibliography

## Manuscripts*

Registro dei battezzati Maschi 1571–1577
*Registro dei battezzati al fonte di San Giovanni tenuto dal preposto di S. Giovanni, Maschi*, from 1/5/1571 to 30/9/1577, Florence, Archivio dell'Opera di Santa Maria del Fiore, Book 16

Uscite della compagnia dei Santi Barbara e Quirino 1589–1653
*Questo libro a laude di Iddio si sua Madre Santa Vergine Maria e a laude di tutti santi del paradiso serve per Uscita compagnia di fiamminghi di Santa Barbera e di Santo Chorino*, 1589–1653, ASF, Compagnie religiose soppresse 206, fasc. no. 14

Debitori e creditori dell'Arazzeria 1598–1624
*Questo libro si chiama Debitori e creditori dell'Arazzeria del serenissimo Gran Duca di Toscana don Ferdinando de' Medici nostro signore, Dio lo mantengha, segnato A verde, al tempo dell'administratione del molto illustre signor cavaliere Vincento Giugni, guardaroba generale, et cameriere secreto dell prefata Altezza Serenissima [ . . . ] seguito regnante il Gran Duca Cosimo secondo suo figli, e [ . . . ] sotto il Gran duca Ferdinando secondo, che piaccia a Iddio conservarlo lungo tempo*, 1598–1624, ASF, Guardaroba medicea 212

*Ricordi dell'Arazzeria A 1598–1624*
*Questo libro in carta pecora bianca, spranghe verde, segnato A con Arme ducale detto memoriale, attiene all'Arazzeria del serenissimo Gran Duca nostro signore nella administratione del m. illustre signor cavaliere Vincenzo Giugni Guardaroba generale, et cameriere secreto della prefata Altezza Serenissima, sul quale ci sarà notato più e diversi ricordi che occorreranno alla detta Arazzeria, copie di Rescritti, di mandati, di suppliche, di conti, et d'altre Robe che si provederanno per servizio di detta Arazzeria, tenuto per me Tommaso Corbinelli, ministro in detta Arazzeria, A*, 1598–1624, ASF, Guardaroba medicea 213

Debitori e creditori della Guardaroba generale 1618–1638
*Questo libro nominato spoglio segnato A coperto di carta pechora bianca e coreggie bianche, è della guardaroba di Sua Altezza Serenissima in sul quale si descriveranno tutti i debitori e credtori che si troveranno fatti per tempi passati e in avenire a tutti gli stracciafogli, e libri di campagnia di questa guardaroba per ridurre in memoria, e racholti insieme, tutti detti debitori delle robe date fora e nominatamente a chi l'ara aute*, 1618–1638, ASF, Guardaroba medicea 365

Inventario della Guardaroba generale 1618–1624
*Questo libro in carta pecora coregge turchine, intitolato Inventario Generale segnato B, è della Guardaroba generale del Serenissimo Gran Duca Cosimo secondo di Toscana 4⁰ al tempo dell'administrazione del molt'illustre et clarissimo signor cavaliere Vincenzo Giugni guardaroba maggiore, cominciato con il nome di Dio questo dì 3 di settembre 1618*, ASF, Guardaroba medicea 373

Entrata e Uscita dell'Arazzeria 1619–1621
Untitled [Entrata e Uscita dell'Arazzeria], 1619–1621, ASF, Guardaroba medicea 376

Quaderenuccio della compagnia dei Santi Barbara e Quirino 1620–1627
*Quaderenuccio dove si terrà conto di tutti i danari che preverranno a entrata e di quelli che si spenderà, alla giornata per la Compagnia di Santa Barbara et Santo Corino posta nella Chiesa della Nuntiata di Fiorenza per me cavaliere Giovanni Hoppenbronwers*, 1620–1627, ASF, Compagnie religiose soppresse 206, fasc. no. 13

Spese della Camera del Granduca 1621
*Ordini di Sua Altezza Serenissima [Ferdinando II de' Medici] del 1621*, ASF, Camera del Granduca 2b

Recapiti della Depositeria 1621–1622
*Depositeria Generale, Recapiti di Cassa, Anno 1622*, 1621–1622, ASF, Depositeria Generale, Parte Antica 1010

Spese della Camera del Granduca 1622–1623
*Ordini per il Serenissimo Gran Duca, l'Anno 1622*, 1622–1623, ASF, Camera del Granduca 3b

Tinghi 1623–1644
C. Tinghi, *Questo libro nominato diario terzo del Serenissimo Gran Duca Ferdinando secondo Gran Duca di Toscana e per comesione di Sua Altezza sarà tenuto da Ceseri di Bastiano Tinghi citadino fiorentino aiutante di camera di Sua Altezza Serenissima [ . . . ]*, 11 November 1623–13 July 1644, ASF, Miscellanea medicea 11

Inventario della Villa di Poggio Imperiale 1624
*Inventario originale, Debitori e creditori della Villa Imperiale, 1624*, ASF, Guardaroba medicea 479

Inventario della Guardaroba generale 1624–1638
*Questo libro in carta pecora intitolato Inventario Generale, segnato A, è della Guardaroba generale del serenissimo gran duca Ferdinando secondo di Toscana al tempo dell'administrazione del molt'illustrissimo signor balì Niccolò Giugni, guardaroba maggiore, cominciato questo dì primo di aprile 1624*, 1624–1638, ASF, Guardaroba medicea 435

Inventario di Maria Maddalena d'Austria 1625
*Questo libro servirà per Inventario di tutte le robbe che verranno a entrata et a uscita nella Guardarobba del Serenissima Arciduchessa, cioè nel suo stanzino delli armarii, cominciandosi questo dì primo di luglio 1625*, ASF, Guardaroba medicea 423

Morti della Grascia 1626–1669
Untitled [Morti 1626–1669], ASF, Ufficiali poi Magistrato della Grascia 195

Debitori e creditori della Guardaroba generale 1628–1633
*Questo libro segnato B coreggie verde si domanda Debitori, e creditori della Guardaroba Generale di Sua Altezza Serenissima regnante Ferdinando secondo, e Guardaroba Generale l'Illustrissimo et Clarissimo signore Balì Nicholo Giugni, cominciato addì primo d'aprile 1628*, 1628–1633, ASF, Guardaroba medicea 448

Morti della Grascia 1626–1669
Morti 1626–1669, ASF, Ufficiali poi Magistrato della Grascia 195

Conti di Vittoria della Rovere 1632–1638
*Filza di Conti della Serenissima Granduchessa Vittoria, 1632–1638*, ASF, Guardaroba medicea 955

Debitori e creditori della Guardaroba generale 1633–1638
[title page missing, on the cover:] *Debitori e Creditori, C*, 1633–1638, ASF, Guardaroba medicea 476

Debitori e creditori [di oggetti] della Guardaroba generale 1637–1640
*Questo libro si chiama Debitori e Creditori di ministri della Casa Serenissima che averanno in consegna robe dalla Guardaroba Generale di Sua Altezza sotto l'amministratione del Illustrissimo signore Marchese, segnato A coreggie bianche, cominciato addì 19 di dicembre 1637*, 1637–1640, ASF, Guardaroba medicea 515

Giornale della Guardaroba di Palazzo Pitti 1637–1662
*Questo libbro intitolato Giornale della Guardarobba del Palazzo di Pitti, segnato A primo coperto di carta pecora bianca con tre coregge rosse, cominciato questo dì 10 ottobre 1637 sotto il comando dell'Illustrissimo signore Marc[h]ese Francesco Coppoli Guardarobba Generale di Sua Altezza Serenissima e [ . . . ], tenutto per me Biagio di Giovanni Battista Marmi Guardarobba primo*, ASF, Guardaroba medicea 494

Inventario della Guardaroba di Palazzo Pitti 1638
*Inventario Generale della Guardaroba de Pitti*, ASF, Guardaroba medicea 535

Inventario di Palazzo Pitti 1638
*Inventario di tutti e Mobili che sono nel Palazzo de Pitti di Sua Altezza Serenissima in consegna a Biagio Marmi Guardaroba, cominciato questo dì 26 febbraio 1637 [ab Incarnatione=1638 modern style]*, ASF, Guardaroba medicea 525

Spese della Camera del Granduca 1638–1639
*Spese estraordinarie del Serenissimo Gran Duca cominciate il primo settembre 1638 a tutto agosto 1639*, ASF, Camera del Granduca 20b

Entrata e Uscita di Palazzo Pitti 1638–1648
*Entrata e Uscita della Guardaroba del Palazzo de' Pitti di Sua Altezza Serenissima*, 1638–1648, ASF, Guardaroba medicea 530

Copia dell'inventario della Guardaroba generale 1640
*Copia dell'Inventario originale del Guardaroba delle robe fabbricate di Sua Altezza Serenissima in conto all'Illustrissimo signore Marchese Francesco Coppoli*, 1640, ASF, Guardaroba medicea 571

Inventario della Guardaroba generale 1640
*A dì 17 settembre 1640, Inventario originale della Guardaroba Generale di Sua Altezza Serenissima in consegna al signor Zanobi Bartoli guardaroba trattone una copia, messa in conto del signor Marchese Francesco Coppoli*, 17 September–24 November 1640 [with an appendix 1641–1642], ASF, Guardaroba medicea 572

Consegne della Guardaroba generale 1640–1642
Untitled [Consegne della Guardaroba generale], 25 September 1640–5 January 1641 [ab Incarnatione=1642 modern style], ASF, Guardaroba medicea 711, insert 2, fols. 162–167

Debitori e creditori della Guardaroba generale 1640–1646
*Questo libro si chiama debitori e creditori de' ministri della Casa Serenissima che haveranno in consegna robe dalla Guardaroba Generale di Sua Altezza Serenissima sotto l'amministrazione dell'Illustrissimo signore marchese Francesco Coppoli Guardaroba Generale e sopraintendente della Galleria e sotto la custodia del signore Zanobi Bartoli guardaroba, segnato A, coreggie bianche cominciato a dì settembre 1640 per mano di Cristofano di Giovanni Landini computista della Guardaroba delle cose fabbricate di Sua Altezza Serenissima*, 1640–1646, ASF, Guardaroba medicea 563

Inventario della Guardaroba generale 1640–1666
*Questo libro in carta pecora coregge bianche, intitolato Inventario Generale segnato A, è della Guardaroba Generale del Serenissimo Gran Duca Ferdinando secondo, di Toscana 5°, al tempo dell'administrazione del signor Zanobi Bartoli, guardaroba, e soprintendente dell'illustrissimo signor marchese Francesco Coppoli, guardaroba maggiore, tenuto da me Tommaso del Barbigia, cominciato questo dì 17 settembre 1640*, ASF, Guardaroba medicea 585

Entrata e Uscita H dell'Accademia 1641–1650
MDCXXXXI *Entrata dell'Accademia tenuta per me Domenico Pugliani Camarlingo cominciata il dì 1 novembre 1641, Uscita dell'Accademia tenuta per Domenico Pugliani Camarlingo cominciata A dì primo di novembre 1641*, 1641–1650, ASF, Accademia del Disegno 106

Rescritti e mandati della Segreteria 1645–1650
*Libro dove si terrà nota et registro di tutti i rescritti, et mandati che si faranno attenenti alla Segreteria della Serenissima Casa, cominciato questo dì 24 di luglio 1645*, 1645–1650, ASF, Mediceo del Principato 1840

Giornale della Galleria degli Uffizi 1646–1688
*1646, Questo libro servirà a tenere conto di tutte le cose che si caveranno della Galleria di Sua Altezza Serenissima con ordine del Illustrisimo Signore marchese Malespina o de' Serenissimi Padroni*, 1646–1688, Biblioteca degli Uffizi, ms. 62

Inventario di Giovan Carlo de' Medici (Via della Scala) 1647
*Inventario delle Masserizie del Giardino di Via della Scala del Serenissimo Prencipe Cardinale Giovan Carlo sotto la custodia di Lorenzo Cerrini Guardaroba di detto luogo, fatto dal signor Francesco Dati ministro generale alla presenza del medesimo Cerrini e del signor Francesco Conti Guardaroba di Sua Altezza Reverendissima, di Francesco Fei, giovane dello scrittoio quali scrissero il dì primo di gennaio 1646 ab Incarnatione* [=1647 modern style] *et altro simile tiene in mano il medesimo Cerrini*, ASF, Scrittoio delle Regie Possessioni 4279, fols. 39v–70r

Debitori e creditori di Carlo de' Medici 1651–1663
*Questo libro Debitori e Creditori segnato G è del serenissimo principe cardinale don Carlo de' Medici*, 1651–1663, ASF, Scrittoio delle Regie Possessioni 4173

MARMI n.d. [1662–1667]
D. M. Marmi, *Norma per il Guardarobba del Gran Palazzo nella città di Fiorenza dove habita il Serenissimo Gran Duca di Toscana, Per la quale si dimostra da Diacinto Maria Marmi al presente Guardarobba di detto Palazzo il modo più facile, per renderli più spedito, e diligente nel maneggio di ella, Dedicata all'Illustrissimo Signor Marchese Cerbone del Monte Guardarobba Generale, e Primo Gentilhuomo della Camera di Sua Altezza Serenissima*, n.d. [1662–1667], BNCF, ms. II.I. 284

Inventario di Giovan Carlo de' Medici (Villa di Castello) 1663
*Inventario solenne di tutte le robe che si ritrovano nel Palazzo della Villa di Castello attenenti a Sua Altezza Reverendissima sotto la custodia di Giovanni di Giovanni Battista Bucherelli, qual villa Palazzo e beni per la morte di detto signor cardinale sono ritornati al Serenissimo Gran Duca perché di quelli del Cardinale era usufruttuario per durante sua vita*, 9 May 1663, ASF, Miscellanea medicea 31, insert 10, fols. 121r–144v

Inventario di Palazzo Pitti 1663–1664
*Inventario di Tutti i mobili che si trovano nel Palazzo de' Pitti di Sua Altezza Serenissima consegnati a Jacinto Maria Marmi nuovo Guardaroba, entrato per la morte di Biagio Marmi suo zio, il quale Inventario deve far credito a tutti li conti di Biagio suddetto alla Guardaroba Generale e Debito in avvenire al detto Jacinto, fatto questo dì suddetto da me Lorenzo Betti, ministro di detta Guardaroba Generale*, 30 December 1663–30 November 1664, ASF, Guardaroba medicea 725

Inventario di Leopoldo de' Medici n.d. [1663–1671?]
*Inventario Generale de' Quadri del Serenissimo Principe Leopoldo di Toscana, con nomi degli Autori di essi, secondo l'incluso Alfabeto*, n.d. [1663–1671?], Florence, Biblioteca Riccardiana, ms. Riccardi 2443

Quaderno della Guardaroba generale 1666–1674, I
*Questo libro in carta pecora coreggie bianche intitolato Quaderno segnato A primo è della Guardaroba generale del serenissimo gran duca Ferdinando 2do, di Toscana 5°, al tempo del administrazione di me Niccolò Bernardi guardaroba, cominciato questo dì 30 di marzo 1666, che di presente è Guardaroba maggiore l'illustrissimo signor marchese Cerbone dal Monte [ . . . ]*, 1666–1674, ASF, Guardaroba medicea 750

Quaderno della Guardaroba generale 1666–1674, II
*Questo libro in carta pecor a coreggie bianche intitolato Quaderno segnato A 2do è della Guardaroba Generale del Serenissimo Gran Duca Ferdinando 2do di Toscana 5° al tempo del administrazione di me Niccolò Bernardi guardaroba, cominciato questo dì primo di maggio 1666, che di presente è guardaroba maggiore l'illustrissimo signor marchese Cerbone dal Monte, che il signore Dio ci conceda buon principio e ottimo fine*, 1666–1674, ASF, Guardaroba medicea 751

Inventario della Guardaroba generale 1666–1680
*Questo libro in carta pecora coreggie bianche intitolato Inventario Generale segnato A, è della Guardaroba Generale del Serenissimo Gran Duca Ferdinando secondo, di Toscana 5°, al tempo dell'administrazione del signore Niccolò Bernardi guardaroba, e soprantendenza dell'illustrissimo signor marchese Cerbone dal Monte, guardaroba maggiore, cominciato questo dì 30 marzo 1666*, ASF, Guardaroba medicea 741

Rescritti della Segreteria 1666–1688
*Rescritti 1666–1688*, ASF, Mediceo del Principato 1843

Inventario della Compagnia dei Santi Barbara e Quirino 1667
*Inventario delle robe che si sono trovate in essere nella Compagnia di S. Barbera e S. Quirino questo sopradetto giorno et inventariate alla presenza de' capitani di detta compagnia e consegnate a Jona di Tobia scrivente, provveditore di essa come appresso*, 1 May 1667, ASF, Compagnie religiose soppresse 203, insert D, unpaginated

Inventario di Carlo de' Medici, 1667
*Inventario di mobili compié dalla Guardaroba generale di Sua Altezza Serenissima dall'eredità pervenuta al serenissimo principe Cosimo di Toscana per la morte della felice memoria del serenissimo et eminentissimo cardinale Carlo decano in ordine ad un motù proprio del serenissimo gran duca* [Ferdinando II *de' Medici*] *emanato sotto di [ . . . ], messo in filza di giustificazione della Guardaroba del Taglio a numero, E a di 30 giugno 1667 detti mobili si sono messi a entrata in Guardaroba generale delle robe fabbricate sotto detto giorno al quaderno A primo a c. 49 fino a c. 78, dal signor Zanobi Betti guardaroba del Taglio e perché detti mobili parte ne son mandati in Galleria, parte tirati in Guardaroba, parte restati nel Casino di via Larga di San Marco, e parte nel giardino di detto Casino et alcuni affissi, se ne è fatto l'appresso cifere in margine alle particolare acciò si vegga la distribuzione di detto come appresso [ . . . ]*, ASF, Guardaroba medicea 758

Conti della Guardaroba generale 1669–1671
*Conti della Guardaroba, 1669–1671*, ASF, Guardaroba medicea 785ter

Morti della Grascia 1669–1694
*Libro 6° [di Morti] 1669 al 1694*, ASF, Ufficiali poi Magistrato della Grascia 196

Copie di partite insolute del conto di Giusto Suttermans con Vittoria della Rovere 1671
*Copia di partite levate de verbo, ad verbum, dal conto del signor Giusto Sutterman pittore, esistente fra le carte della Guardaroba della Serenissima Gran Duchessa Vittoria di Toscana Padrona*, 4–22 December 1671, in Conti della Guardaroba generale, 1669–1671, ASF, Guardaroba medicea 785ter, fols. 524r–528v

Morti 1671–1690
*Libro di Morti segnato* V, *1671 al 1690*, ASF, Medici e speziali 260

Matrimoni 1671–1720
*Repertorio generale dei Matrimoni della città di Firenze dall'Anno 1671 all'anno 1720, Tomo Terzo*, ASF, Manoscritti 583

Quaderno della Guardaroba generale 1674–1679
*Questo libro in carta pecora coreggie rosse, intitolato Quaderno segnato B primo, è della Guardaroba generale del serenissimo Gran Duca di Toscana Cosimo Terzo al tempo del administrazione di me Niccolò Bernardi guardaroba, cominciato questo dì primo di luglio 1674, che di presente è guardaroba maggiore l'illustrissimo signor marchese Cerbone dal Monte, che il signore Dio ci conceda buon principio e ottimo fine*, 1674–1679, ASF, Guardaroba medicea 801

Quaderno della Guardaroba generale 1674–1680
*Questo libro in carta pecora coreggie rosse, intitolato Quaderno secondo segnato B, è della Guardaroba generale del serenissimo gran duca Cosimo Terzo di Toscana, al tempo del adiminustrazione di me Niccolò Bernardi guardaroba, cominciato questo dì primo agosto 1674, che di presente è guardaroba maggiore l'illustrissimo signor marchese Cerbone dal Monte [ . . . ]*, 1 August 1674–30 June 1680, ASF, Guardaroba medicea 799

Inventario di Leopoldo de' Medici, 1675
*Inventario de Mobili e Masserizie dell'Eredità del Serenissimo e Reverendissimo Signore Principe Cardinale Leopoldo di Toscana, cominciato questo di suddetto* [14 November 1675], *steteci consegnate l'appie descritte robe da Paolo Cennini Guardaroba di detto signor Cardinale*, ASF, Guardaroba medicea 826

BALDINUCCI n.d. [1678 ca.]
F. Baldinucci, *Ritratti in mano al Bernardi, Marmi e Bernardi a Pitti, Ritratti di Monsù Giusto interi, Ritrovati altri simili ritrovati, Guardarobba Generale altri simili*, n.d. [1678 ca.], in MARMI n.d. [by 1731], fols. 350–352

Quaderno della Guardaroba generale 1679–1685
*Questo libro in carta pecora coreggie turchine intitolato Quaderno secondo segnato C è della Guardaroba generale del serenissimo gran duca Cosimo Terzo di Toscana, al tempo del administrazione di me Niccolò Bernardi guardaroba, cominciato questo di primo agosto 1679 che di presente è Guardaroba maggiore l'illustrissimo signor marchese Cerbone dal Monte, [ . . . ]*, 1679–1685, ASF, Guardaroba medicea 870

BALDINUCCI 1681
F. Baldinucci, *Nota di tutti ritratti de' pittori che sono nel muso di Sua Altezza Serenissima questo dì 12 febbraio 1680* [ab Incarnatione=1681 modern style], ASF, Miscellanea medicea 368, fol. 420r

Quadri alla festa di S. Luca 1681
*Quadri alla festa di S. Luca tutti del Palazzo*, 1681, in MARMI n.d. [by 1731], fols. 133–134

Inventario della villa dell'Ambrogiana 1683
*Inventario di tutt'i Mobili che si ritrovano nel Palazzo dell'Ambrogiana, che già erano in debito a Diacinto Bitossi e di poi a Francesco suo fratello e oggi consegnati da me Antonio Citerni d'ordine del illustrissimo signore marchese Cerbon' del Monte guardaroba maggiore a Francesco Peri nuovo guardaroba, come per benigno rescritto di Sua Altezza Serenssima del di 2 di luglio stante*, 1683, ASF, Guardaroba medicea 883bis

Inventario di Palazzo Pitti 1688
*Inventari di tutti li mobili esistenti nel Palazzo de Pitti di Sua Altezza Serenissima consegnati a Giuseppe del Nobolo, aiuto di Diacinto Maria Marmi guardaroba del suddetto Palazzo ch'à ottenuto il riposo, et, dovendo il medesimo inventario far credito al sopranominato Marmi e debito al detto Giuseppe del Nobolo, fatto da me Antonio Citerni, ministro della Guardaroba generale questo anno 1687* [ab Incarnatione=1688 modern style], ASF, Guardaroba medicea 932

Inventario della Villa del Poggio Imperiale 1691
*1691, Inventario di Mobili e Robe diverse della Proprietà di Sua Altezza Serenizzima esistenti nella Villa Imperiale e consegnato il tutto a Francesco Alessandro Maria del Nobolo nuovo guardaroba subentrato in luogo di Lorenzo suo padre ancor vivente*, ASF, Guardaroba medicea 991

Inventario della Villa del Poggio Imperiale 1692 [property of Vittoria della Rovere]
*Inventario ridotto a capi dall'Inventario andante di tutti i Mobili e Robe diverse della proprietà della Serenissima Gran Duchessa Vittoria, esistenti nella Villa Imperiale e consegnato il tutto a Francesco Alessandro Maria del Nobolo, nuovo guardaroba subentrato in luogo di Lorenzo suo padre ancor vivente*, 1692, ASF, Guardaroba 995

Provvisionati del Palazzo 1694
*Sono in cassa del Palazzo questo dì 25 giugno 1694*, ASF, Guardaroba medicea 1084, insert V, fol. 44

Inventario della Compagnia dei Santi Barbara e Quirino, n.d. [late 17th century– early 18th century?]
*Inventario della Compagnia di S. Barbara cioè delle robe trovate dopo la morte di Piero d'Arigho fiammingo, e consegnate al nuovo provveditore [ . . . ]*, n.d. [late 17th century– early 18th century?], ASF, Compagnie religiose soppresse 203, insert D, unpaginated

Cariche della Corte n.d. [18th century]
*Cariche d'onore concesse da' Serenissimi Gran Duchi, tomo secondo, che contiene gl'arrolati della Corte B: arrolati della Corte di Toscana dal 1540 sino al presente estratti da vari libri della Serenissima Casa*, n.d. [18th century], ASF, Manoscritti 321

Inventario dei quadri di Palazzo Pitti n.d. [1702?]
*Quadri del Reale Palazzo Pitti*, n.d. [1702?], ASF, Guardaroba medicea 1185

Inventario degli Uffizi 1704–1714
*Inventario generale di tutto quanto fu consegnato a Giovan Francesco Bianchi custode della Galleria di Sua Altezza Reale dopo la morte del di lui genitore, dal 1704 al 1714*, Biblioteca degli Uffizi, ms. 82

Inventario di Ferdinando di Cosimo III de' Medici 1713
*Inventario dei Mobil, e Masserizie della proprietà del serenissimo signor principe Ferdinando di gloriosa ricordanza, ritrovate doppo la di lui morte nel suo appartamento nel Palazzo de' Pitti, e sono l'appresso, cioè*, 1713, ASF, Guardaroba medicea 1222

Inventario di Palazzo Pitti 1716–1723
*Inventario di Quadri che si ritrovano negl'appartamenti del gran Palazzo de Pitti di Sua Altezza Reale, alcuni dei quali sono dell'eredità del Serenissimo Cardinale Leopoldo, e per qui col proprio numero, come ancora per maggior chiarezza con la presente cifra S:C:L:, altri sono dell'eredità del Serenissimo Gran Principe Ferdinando ambi di gloriata memoria e questi si noteranno col proprio numero e con la presente cifra S:P:F:, altro sono di proprietà del Serenissimo Gran Duca Cosimo Terzo felicemente regnante [ . . . ]*, 1716–1723, Biblioteca degli Uffizi, ms. 79

MARMI n.d. [by 1731]
A. F. Marmi, *Notizie di vite e opere di diversi pittori*, n.d. [by 1731], BNCF, ms. Nazionale, II.II.110

Inventario della Villa Ambrogiana 1732
*Io Bernardo d'Andrea Cantini nuovo guardaroba dell Palazo della Villa dell'Ambrogiana di Sua Altezza Reale confesso con la presente d'avere riceuto in consegnia tutte le robe che sono descritte nel presente inventario*, 10 July–4 September 1732, ASF, Guardaroba medicea 1392

Inventario della Compagnia dei Santi Barbara e Quirino 1745
*Inventario delle suppellettili, che sono al presente nella venerabile Compagnia di Santa Barbera e San Quirino de' Tedeschi e Fiamminghi nella SS. Nunziata di Firenze*, 1745, ASF, Compagnie religiose soppresse 203, insert D, unpaginated

Inventario della Villa di Pratolino 1748
*Inventario dei Mobili, Tappezzerie e robe ritrovate nel real' Palazzo di Pratolino, dopo levati i sigilli riconosciuti senz'alterazione dove erano stati apposti alle porte di ciascuno appartamento, mediante la morte di Giov. Jacopo Melli, già guardaroba, per la consegna a Michele Paoloschi, nuovo guardaroba, in esecuzione di benigno rescritto di Sua Maestà Imperiale emanato sotto dì 10 giugno cadente dal suo regio consigilio di finanze, conguinto all'ordine dell'illustrissimo e clarissimo signore senatore cavaliere marchese Vicenzo Riccardi, guardaroba maggiore, riposto nella filza segnata A dell'amministrazione vegente dell'Illustrissimo signor Gio: Giuseppe Vauthier primo guardaroba sotto n. 265, il tutto descritto e consegnato da me Filippo Neri Canovaio, uno dei ministri della Guardaroba generale della Maestà Sua, coll'intervento, e presenza di Ferdinando Melli figlio del sopradetto defunto, questo dì primo agosto 1748, in Pratolino*, ASF, Guardaroba medicea appendice 84

Registro di Morti 1749–1763
*Questo Libro intitolato di lettera D 2ndo deve servire per notare tutti i fedeli defunti che saranno rimessi mese per mese dai dei Becchini dei Quattro Quartieri che piaccia a Sua Divina Maestà di mandare a godere la Gloriosa Eterna tutte l'anime dei medesimi, scritte da me Adamo di Tommaso Pasquini della Cancelleria di questa Arte de' Medici e Speziali di Firenze, cominciato il dì primo di maggio 1749, al tempo dell'eccellentissimo signore dottore Andrea Rossellini cancelliere di detta Arte*, May 1749–August 1763, ASF, Medici e Speziali, 265

Inventario degli Uffizi 1753
*Inventario generale di tutte le preziose antichità & insigni memorie che si conservano nella Galleria di Sua Maestà Imperiale in Firenze compilato [ . . . ] in virtù del rescritto di Sua Maestà Imperiale in data del 1° dicembre 1753 con quale è stata graziosamente conferita a Giuseppe Bianchi la carica di nuovo custode della suddetta Imperiale Galleria per tenere in consegna in luogo del defunto Francesco Bianchi suo zio*, Biblioteca degli Uffizi, ms. 95

Inventario della Villa Ambrogiana 1758
*Inventario di tutti li mobili esistenti nell'Imperiale Palazzo dell'Ambrogiana, fatto d'ordine dell'illustrissimo signore Bernardino Riccardi, guardaroba maggiore, principiato il dì 6 febbraio 1758 e finito il 24 del detto mese, da me sottoscritto Giuseppe Sani, scrivano della Guardaroba generale*, ASF, Guardaroba medicea appendice 92

Inventario di Palazzo Pitti 1761
*Inventario Generale dei Mobili e di tutt'altro che si ritrova nell'Imperial Palazzo de' Pitti di Firenze, fatto per la consegna data a Carlo Gilles guardaroba del medesimo a tutto il dì 30 maggio 1761 da Carlo Guasconti e Lorenzo Benvenuti in ordine al motuproprio de 14 giugno 1758 dell'Imperial Consiglio di Finanze*, ASF, Guardaroba medicea appendice 94

Inventario della Compagnia dei Santi Barbara e Quirino 1764
*Inventario delle Supellittili che sono al presente nella venerabile Compagnia di Santa Barbera, e San Quirino de' Tedeschi, e Fiamminghi, posta nella chiesa della Santissima Annunziata di Firenze*, 25 July 1764, ASF, Compagnie religiose soppresse 203, insert D, unpaginated

Inventario della Villa del Poggio Imperiale 1768
*Inventario di tutta la mobiglia, effetti e robe che si ritrovano nella Reale Villa del Poggio Imperiale, sotto la custodia di Gaetano Puliti custode della medesima, cominciato il dì 19 maggio e terminato il dì 22 giugno 1768*, ASF, Imperiale e Reale Corte 4855

Inventario degli Uffizi 1769
*Inventario generale di tutte le antichità, pitture, e altre preziose rarità che si conservano nella Real Galleria di Sua Altezza Reale Pietro Leopoldo Io Arciduca d'Austria, Gran Duca di Toscana, copia esatta cavata dall'Inventario originale ed autentico fatto e finito a dì 17 maggio 1769, e d'ordine di Sua Altezza Reale depositato ed esistente nell'Uffizio delle Revisioni e Sindacati*, Biblioteca degli Uffizi, ms. 98

Inventario degli Uffizi 1784
*Inventario Generale della Real Galleria di Firenze compilato nel 1784, Essendo Direttore della Medesima Giuseppe Bencivenni già Pelli N.P.F. colla presenza ed assistenza del signore Pietro Mancini ministro dell'Uffizio delle Revisioni e Sindacati, Vol. I, che contiene i marmi, le pitture, i disegni, e le terre*, Biblioteca degli Uffizi, ms. 113

Inventario del Palazzo di Siena 1798
*Inventario di tutt'i Mobili, Biancheria, e Metalli, Porcellane et altro esistenti come appresso nel Real Palazzo di Siena provenienti dalla consegna di Giuseppe La Tour in conto vecchio, e che restano alla consegna del medesimo in conto nuovo*, 1798, ASF, Imperiale e Reale Corte 5028

Nota di quadri spediti a Parigi 1799
*Nota di Quadri esistenti già nel Quartiere detto di Pietro da Cortona nel R Palazzo dei Pitti, e quindi incassati dai commissari Francesi e spediti al Direttorio di Parigi*, 1 July 1799, Archivio Storico delle Gallerie fiorentine, shelf no. XL, 1816, no. 48

Inventario degli Uffizi 1825
*Catalogo Generale della R. Galleria di Firenze*, 1825, Florence, Biblioteca degli Uffizi, ms. 173

Conto di Fedele Acciai n.d. [1827]
*Spese fatte da me Fedele Acciai pittore restauratore del Imperiale e Reale Galleria*, n.d. [August 1827], Florence, Archivio storico delle Gallerie fiorentine, shelf no. LI/II, 1827, insert 50, fols. 59–60

Inventario degli Uffizi 1881
*Inventario generale dei dipinti posseduti della R. Gallerie di Firenze*, 1881, Florence, Soprintendenza speciale per il Polo Museale Fiorentino, Ufficio Ricerche

## BOOKS

PERI 1621
G. D. Peri, *Fiesole distrutta*, Florence, 1621

BALDINUCCI 1681–1728, ed. 1845–1847
F. Baldinucci, *Notizie dei professori del disegno da Cimabue in qua, per le quali si dimostra come, e per chi le belle arti di pittura, scultura e architettura, lasciata la rozzezza delle maniere greca e gotica, si siano in questi secoli ridotte all'antica loro perfezione*, Florence, 1681–1728, edited by F. Ranalli, Florence, 1845–1847

MOÜCKE 1752–1762
F. Moücke, *Serie di ritratti degli eccellenti pittori dipinti di propria mano che esistono nell'Imperial Galleria di Firenze colle vite in compendio de' medesimi, in Museo Fiorentino che contiene i ritratti de' pittori consacrato alla Sacra Cesarea Maestà dell'Augustissimo Francesco i imperadore de' romani [ . . . ]*, Florence, 1752–1762

MARRINI 1754–1766
O. Marrini, *Serie di ritratti di celebri pittori dipinti di propria mano in seguito a quella già pubblicata nel Museo Fiorentino, esistente appresso l'Abate Antonio Pazzi con brevi notizie intorno a' medesimi compilate dall'Abate Orazio Marrini*, Florence, 1754–1766

BARTOLI 1781–1782, ed. 1978
F. Bartoli, *Notizie istoriche de' comici italiani*, Padova, 1781–1782, offset reprint, Bologna, 1978

BOTTARI–TICOZZI 1822–1825
G. Bottari and S. Ticozzi, *Raccolta di lettere sulla pittura, scultura ed architettura*, Milan, 1822–1825

INGHIRAMI 1828
F. Inghirami, *L'Imp. e Reale Palazzo Pitti*, Fiesole, 1828

SMITH 1829–1842
J. Smith, *Catalogue Raisonné of the Works of the Most Eminent Dutch, Flemish and French Painters*, London, 1829–1842, 9 vols.

INGHIRAMI 1834
F. Inghirami, *La Galleria dei Quadri esistente nell'Imp. e Reale Palazzo Pitti*, Fiesole, 1834

NAGLER 1835–1852
G. K. Nagler, *Neues allgemeines Künstler - Lexicon oder Nachrichten von dem Leben und den Werken der Maler, Bildhauer, etc.*, Munich, 1835–1852, 22 vols.

BARDI 1837–1842
L. Bardi, *L'Imperiale e Reale Galleria Pitti illustrata per cura di Luigi Bardi, regio calcografo, dedicata a S.A.I. e R. Leopoldo Secondo, Granduca di Toscana*, Florence, 1837–1842, 4 vols.

GUALANDI 1844–1856
M. Gualandi, *Nuova Raccolta di lettere sulla pittura, scultura ed architettura, scritte dai più celebri personaggi dei Secoli XV a XIX, con note ed illustrazioni*, Bologna 1844–1856, 3 vols.

BURCKHARDT 1855, ed. 1952
J. Burckhardt, *Der Cicerone*, Basel, 1855, edited by P. Mingazzini and F. Pfister, Florence, 1952

FÉTIS 1857
E. Fétis, *Artistes belges à l'étranger: Juste Sustermans*, Brussels, 1857

CHIAVACCI 1859
E. Chiavacci, *Guida dell'I. e R. Galleria del Palazzo Pitti*, Florence, 1859

WAAGEN 1863–1864
G. F. Waagen, *Manuel de l'histoire de la peinture, Écoles allemande, flamande et hollandaise*, translation Hymans-Pétit,

Brussels-Leipzig-Gand-Paris, 1863–1864, 3 vols.

MICHIELS 1865–1878
A. Michiels, *Histoire de la Peinture Flamande*, Paris, 1865–1878, 11 vols.

SIRET 1866
A. Siret, *Dictionnaire historique des peintres . . .*, Brussels-Livorno-Leipzig, 1866

*National Exhibition Leeds* 1868
*National Exhibition of Works of Art at Leeds*, 4th ed., Leeds, 1868

ROMBOUTS–VAN LERIUS 1872
P. Rombouts and T. Van Lerius, *Les Liggeren et autres Archives Historiques de la Gilde Anversoise de Saint Luc*, Antwerp, 1872

SEUBERT 1878–1879
A. Seubert, *Allgemeines Künstlerlexicon der Leben un Werke der berühmtesten Bildenden*, Stuttgart, 1878–1879, 3 vols.

MICHIELS 1881
A. Michiels, *Van Dyck et ses élèves*, Paris, 1881

MICHIELS 1882
A. Michiels, "Un ami de Van Dyck", in *Revue britannique*, January 1882, pp. 185–200

VENTURI 1882
A. Venturi, *La R. Galleria Estense in Modena*, Modena, 1882

WAUTERS n.d. [1883?]
A. J. Wauters, *La Peinture Flamande*, Paris, n.d. [1883?]

BERTOLOTTI 1885
A. Bertolotti, *Artisti in relazione coi Gonzaga Signori di Mantova. Ricerche e studi negli archivi mantovani*, Modena, 1885

PIGORINI 1887
L. Pigorini, *Catalogo della Regia Pinacoteca di Parma*, Parma, 1887

ROSSI 1889
U. Rossi, "Francesco Pourbus il giovane a Parigi", in *Archivio storico dell'arte*, II, 1889, pp. 404–408

VENTURI 1891
A. Venturi, *La Regia Galleria Pitti in Firenze*, Dornach-Paris, 1891

KENNER 1893
F. Kenner, "Die Portratsammlung des Erzherzogs Ferdinand von Tirol", in *Jahrbuch der Kunsthistorischen Sammlungen des Allerhöchsten Kaiserhauses*, XIV, 1893, pp. 37–186

MÜLLER–SINGER 1894–1901
H. A. Müller and H. W. Singer, *Allgemeines Künstler - Lexicon ...*, Frankfurt, 1894–1901, 5 vols.

BECKETT 1895
F. Beckett, "Tre Portraeter af Danske", in *Illustreret Tidende*, XXXVI, no. 52, 1895, pp. 737–738

LAFENESTRE–RICHTENBERGER n.d. [1895?]
G. Lafenestre and E. Richtenberger, *La Peinture en Europe, Florence*, Paris, n.d. [1895?]

RICCI 1896
C. Ricci, *La R. Galleria di Parma*, Parma, 1896

RIDOLFI 1896
E. Ridolfi, *Le RR. Gallerie e il Museo Nazionale di Firenze*, in *Le Gallerie Nazionali Italiane*, II, 1896, pp. 3–18

RASI 1897–1905
L. Rasi, *I Comici italiani: Biografia, Bibliografia, Iconografia*, Florence, 1897–1905

CUST 1900
L. Cust, *Anthony van Dyck. A Historical Study of his Life and Works*, London, 1900

VENTURI 1900
A. Venturi, *La Galleria Crespi in Milano. Note e raffronti*, Milan, 1900

CROWE 1904
J. A. Crowe, *The German, Flemish and Dutch Schools of Painting*, VII Impression, III edition, London 1904, 2 vols.

*Bryan's Dictionary* 1904–1905
*Bryan's Dictionary of Painters and Engravers*, new edition revised and enlarged by G. C. Williamson, London, 1904–1905, 5 vols.

HAJDECKI 1905
A. Hajdecki, "Die Niederländer in Wien", in *Oud-Holland*, XXIII, 1905, pp. 1–26

JOURDAIN 1905
M. Jourdain, "Venetian Needlepoint", in *The Connoisseur*, XII, no. 48, August 1905, part II, pp. 241–247

SCHMERBER 1906
H. Schmerber, *Betrachtungen über die Italienische Malerei im 17. Jahrhundert*, Strassburg, 1906

WURZBACH 1906–1910
A. von Wurzbach, *Niederländisches Künstler - Lexikon*, Vienna-Leipzig, 1906–1910, 3 vols.

THIEME–BECKER 1907–1950
U. Thieme and F. Becker, *Allgemeines Lexikon der Bildenden Kunstler*, Leipzig, 1907–1950, 37 vols.

GIGLIOLI 1909
O. H. Giglioli, "Notiziario: R. Galleria Pitti", in *Rivista d'arte*, VI, 1909, pp. 147–155

SCHAEFFER 1909
E. Schaeffer, *Van Dyck. Des Meisters Gemälde*, Stuttgart-Leipzig, 1909

PIERACCINI 1910
E. Pieraccini, *Catalogue de la Galerie Royale des Uffizi à Florence*, Prato, 1910

WAUTERS 1910
A. J. Wauters, "Le Siècle de Rubens et l'Exposition d'Art Ancien", in *Revue de Belgique*, CXXV, 1910, pp. 312–326

BAUTIER 1911a
P. Bautier, "On a Lost Portrait by Justus Suttermans", in *The Burlington Magazine*, XIX, July 1911, pp. 234–239

BAUTIER 1911b
P. Bautier, "Un portrait attribué a Suttermans (Exposition de l'Art belge au XVIIe siècle, Bruxelles 1910)", in *Bulletin des Musées Royaux des arts décoratifs et industriels . . . a Bruxelles*, X, 1911, pp. 89–91

*Mostra del Ritratto* 1911
*Mostra del Ritratto italiano dalla fine del sec. XVIe all'anno 1861*, exhibition catalogue (Florence, Palazzo Vecchio, March–July 1911), 2nd ed., Florence, 1911

BAUTIER 1912a
P. Bautier, "Trois Études sur Juste Suttermans, portraitiste (1597–1681)", in *Annales de la Société royale d'Archéologie de Bruxelles*, XXVI, 1912, pp. 189–200 (extract pp. 5–16)

BAUTIER 1912b
P. Bautier, *Juste Suttermans Peintre des Médicis*, Brussels-Paris, 1912

BAUTIER 1912c
P. Bautier, "Contribution à l'Étude du peintre Suttermans", in *Monatshefte für Kunstwissenschaft*, V, 1912, pp. 377–378

BAUTIER 1912d
P. Bautier, "Deux portraits allégoriques de princesses de Médicis par Suttermans", in *L'Art flamand et hollandaise*, January 1912, pp. 4–7

BAUTIER 1912e
P. Bautier, "Twee Allegorische Portretten van Vorstinnen uit het Huis van Medicis, door Suttermans", in *Onze Kunst*, 1912, pp. 153–156

GIGLIOLI 1912
O. H. Giglioli, "Notiziario: R. Galleria Palatina", in *Rivista d'arte*, VIII, 1912, pp. 131–136

NUGENT 1912
M. Nugent, *All'Esposizione del ritratto. Note e impressioni*, Florence, 1912

TARCHIANI 1912
N. Tarchiani, "Il pittore dei Medici Giusto Sustermans", in *Il Marzocco*, 18 February 1912, p. 2

ZIMMERMANN 1912
H. Zimmermann, "Besprechung von Pierre Bautier, Juste Suttermans, peintre des Médicis, Bruxelles-Paris", 1912, in *Kunstgeschichtliche Anzeigen*, 1912, pp. 58–61

FAVARO 1913
A. Favaro, "Studi e ricerche per una iconografia galileiana", in *Atti del Reale Istituto Veneto di Scienze, Lettere ed Arti*, LXXII, II, 1913, pp. 995–1051

FIERENS GEVAERT 1913
P. Fierens Gevaert, *La Peinture au Musée Ancien de Bruxelles*, Brussels-Paris, 1913

SIMAR 1913
T. Simar, book review, "P. Bautier, Jules Suttermans, peintre des Médicis, Bruxelles, Van Oest, 1912", in *Bulletin Bibliographique et Pédagogique du Musée Belge*, XVII, nos. 3–4, 15 May–15 April 1913, pp. 135–136

VENTURI 1913
A. Venturi, "Di alcune opere d'arte della Collezione Messinger", in *L'Arte*, XVI, 1913, pp. 141–153

GRAVES 1913–1915
A. Graves, *A Century of Loan Exhibitions, 1813–1912*, London, 1913–1915, 5 vols.

BAUTIER 1914
P. Bautier, "Das Porträt eines Medici von Suttermans in der Sammlung Oppenheim in Köln", in *Der Cicerone*, 1914, pp. 613–616

HOOGEWERFF 1915
G. J. Hoogewerff, "Enkele Portretten en een Brief van Justus Suttermans", in *Onze Kunst*, XIV, 1915, pp. 33–50 (extract pp. 1–18)

GIGLIOLI 1917
O. H. Giglioli, "Una pittura inedita di Giusto Suttermans erroneamente attribuita a Giovanni da San Giovanni", in *L'Arte*, XX, 1917, pp. 52–53

FRIZZONI 1919
G. Frizzoni, "Il Ritratto di Vittoria della Rovere legato alla Galleria dell'Accademia in Bergamo", in *Bollettino d'Arte*, XIII, 1919, pp. 1–8

GRÜNZWEIG 1919–1932
A. Grünzweig, "Weshalb Justus Suttermans nicht in den Maltesorden Eintrat", in *Mitteilungen des Kunsthistorisches Institutes in Florenz*, III, 1919–1932, pp. 533–536

*Christie's sale 22 February 1924*
*Catalogue of Old Pictures, The Property of the Right Hon. Lady Haversham, Removed from 9 Grosvenor Square . . . which Will be Sold by Auction by Messrs. Christie, Manson & Woods, London, on Friday, 22 February 1924*, London, 1924

PIERACCINI 1924–1925
G. Pieraccini, *La Stirpe de' Medici di Cafaggiolo*, Florence, 1924–1925, 3 vols.

BAUTIER 1926–1929
P. Bautier, *Suttermans (Corneille), Suttermans (Jean) et Suttermans (Juste ou Josse)*, in *Biograhie nationale publiée par l'Academie royale des Sciences des lettres et des beaux-arts de Belgique*, Brussels, 1866–1938, XXIV, 1926–1929, pp. 312–328

GAMBA 1927
C. Gamba, *Il Ritratto fiorentino* in *Il Ritratto italiano dal Caravaggio al Tiepolo alla Mostra di Palazzo Vecchio nel MCMXI*, Comune di Firenze, Bergamo, 1927, pp. 63–99

GÖZ 1928
M. Göz, *Just Sustermans ein flämischer Bildnismaler im Italien des 17. Jahrhunderts*, Günzberg, 1928

BATTISTINI 1930
M. Battistini, "Juste Suttermans, Notes d'Archives", in *De gulden Passer*, 1930, pp. 189–210.

CORNETTE 1930
A. H. Cornette, *La Peinture à l'Exposition d'Art flamande ancien à Anvers – 1930 – Guide illustré de 40 planches hors texte*, Brussels-Paris, 1930

*Exposition Internationale* 1930
*Exposition Internationale, Coloniale, Maritime et D'Art Flamand, Sections D'Art Flamand Ancien, I, Peintures-Dessins-Tapisseries. Catalogue*, exhibition catalogue, Antwerp, June–September 1930), Brussels, 1930

HENDY 1931
P. Hendy, *The Isabella Stewart Gardner Museum. Catalogue of the Exhibited Paintings and Drawings*, Boston, 1931

*Rubens et son temps* 1936
*Rubens et son temps*, exhibition catalogue (Paris, Musée de l'Orangerie, 1936), Paris, 1936

GIANNANTONI 1937
N. Giannantoni, "Noterelle d'iconografia Gonzaghesca", in *Mantus*, I, 1937, pp. 8–13

JAHN RUSCONI 1937
A. Jahn Rusconi, *La R. Galleria Pitti in Firenze*, Rome, 1937

*Mostra Iconografica Gonzaghesca* 1937
*Mostra Iconografica Gonzaghesca. Catalogo della opere*, exhibition catalogue (Mantova, Palazzo Ducale, 16 May–19 September 1937), Mantova, 1937

SINGER 1937–1938
H. W. Singer, *Neuer Bildniskatalog*, Leipzig, 1937–1938, 5 vols.

KÜHN STEINHAUSEN 1939
H. Kühn Steinhausen, "Die Bildnisse de Kurfürstin Johann Wilhelm und seiner Gemahlin Anna Maria Luisa Medici", in *Düsseldorfer Jahrbuch*, XLI, 1939, pp. 125–199

*Mostra Medicea* 1939
*Mostra medicea*, exhibition catalogue (Florence, Palazzo Medici-Riccardi, 1939), edited by U. Ojetti, Florence, 1939

QUINTAVALLE 1939
A. O. Quintavalle, *La Regia Galleria di Parma*, Rome, 1939

TARCHIANI 1939
R. Tarchiani, *La R. Galleria Pitti in Firenze*, Rome, 1939

BAUTIER 1940
P. Bautier, "Les Portraits de Vittoria della Rovere Grande-Duchesse de Toscane par Suttermans", in *Revue Belge d'Archéologie et d'Histoire de l'Art*, X, 1940, no. 1, pp. 35–39

QUINTAVALLE 1948
A. O. Quintavalle, *Catalogo della mostra parmense di dipinti noti ed ignoti dal XIV al XVIII Secolo*, Parma, 1948

MARANGONI 1951
M. Marangoni, *La Galleria Pitti a Firenze*, Milan, 1951

DREI 1954
G. Drei, *I Farnese. Grandezza e decadenza di una dinastia italiana*, Rome, 1954

CRINÒ 1955
A. M. Crinò, "Contributo allo studio dell'attività di Giusto Sutterman", in *Rivista d'Arte*, XXX, 1955, pp. 217–228

FRANCINI CIARANFI 1955
A. M. Francini Ciaranfi, *Pitti. Galleria Palatina*, Novara, 1955

*Kunsthaus Zürich* 1958
*Kunsthaus Zürich. Sammlung, Inventarkatalog der Gemälde und Skulpteren*, Zürich, 1958

*Dizionario Biografico degli Italiani* 1960– [...]
*Dizionario Biografico degli Italiani*, Rome, 1960– [...]

CRINÒ 1961
A. M. Crinò, "Inediti su alcuni contatti tosco-britannici nel Seicento", in *English Miscellany*, CII, 1961, pp. 147–209

GAMULIN 1961
G. Gamulin, "Contributo ai Toscani", in *Radovi odsjeka za povijest umjetnosti*, 3, 1961, pp. 20–26

GAMULIN 1961–1964
G. Gamulin, *Stari Majstori u Jugoslaviji*, Zagreb, 1961–1964, 2 vols.

CAPPI BENTIVEGNA 1962–1964, vol. II, 1964
F. Cappi Bentivegna, *Abbigliamento e costume nella pittura italiana*, Rome, 1962–1964, 2 vols.

HEINZ 1963
G. Heinz, "Studien zur Porträtmalerei an den Höfen österreichischen Erblande", in *Jahrbuch der Kunsthistorischen Sammlungen in Wien*, 59, XXIII, 1963, pp. 99–224

WINNER 1963
M. Winner, "Volterranos Fresken in der Villa della Petraia. Ein Beitrag zu gemalten Zyken der Medici geschichte", in *Mitteilungen des Kunsthistorischen Institutes in Florenz*, X, 1961–1963, fasc. IV, February 1963, pp. 219–252

DENTLER 1964
C. L. Dentler, *Famous Foreigners in Florence 1400–1900*, Florence 1964

FRANCINI CIARANFI 1964
A. M. Francini Ciaranfi, *La Galleria Palatina (Pitti). Guida per il visitatore e Catalogo delle opere esposte*, Florence, 1964

LEVI PISETZKY 1964–1966
R. Levi Pisetzky, *Storia del Costume in Italia*, Milan, 1964–1966, 5 vols.

GUARNIERI 1965
G. Guarnieri, *L'ordine di Santo Stefano nei suoi aspetti organizzativi e tecnico-navali sotto il gran magistero medico*, Pisa, 1965

CIPRIANI 1966
N. Cipriani, *La Galleria Palatina nel Palazzo Pitti a Firenze. Repertorio illustrato di tutti i dipinti, le sculture, gli affreschi e gli arredi*, Florence, 1966

KOCH 1967
G. F. Koch, *Die Kunstaustellung. Ihre Geschichte von den Anfängen bis zum Ausgang des 18. Jahrhunderts*, Berlin, 1967

KÜHN STEINHAUSEN 1967
H. Kühn Steinhausen, *Anna Maria Luisa de' Medici Elettrice Palatina*, Florence, 1967

CAMERANI 1968
S. Camerani, *La Moglie di Cosimo II: Margherita Luisa D'Orléans*, in *Donne di casa Medici* 1968, pp. 139–155

*Donne di casa Medici* 1968
*Donne di casa Medici*, Firenze, 1968

ROSSI NISSIM 1968
L. Rossi Nissim, *Vittoria della Rovere*, in *Donne di casa Medici* 1968, pp. 115–137

*Artisti alla Corte Granducale* 1969
*Artisti alla Corte Granducale*, exhibition catalogue (Palazzo Pitti, Appartamenti reali, May–July 1969), edited by M. Chiarini, Florence, 1969

BODART 1970
D. Bodart, *Les Peintres des Pays-Bas méridionaux et de la principauté de Liege à Rome au XVIIème Siècle*, Brussels-Rome, 1970

LAVIN 1970
I. Lavin, "Dusquesnoy's Nano di Créqui and Two Busts by Francesco Mochi", in *The Art Bulletin*, III, 1970, pp. 132–149

BUSIRI VICI 1971
A. Busiri Vici, *I Poniatowski e Roma*, Florence, 1971

*Firenze e l'Inghilterra* 1971
*Firenze e l'Inghilterra. Rapporti artistici e culturali dal XVI al XX secolo*, exhibition catalogue (Florence, Palazzo Pitti, Appartamenti monumentali, July–September 1971), edited by M. Webster, Florence, 1971

PRINZ 1971
W. Prinz, *Die Sammlung der Selbstbildnisse in den Uffizien*, I, *Geschichte der Sammlung mit Regesten zur Tätigkeit der Agenten und Dokumentenanhang*, Berlin, 1971

*Mostra di Opere restaurate* 1972
*Mostra di Opere restaurate dalla Soprintendenza alle Gallerie... Firenze Restaura, il laboratorio nel suo quarantennio*, exhibition catalogue (Florence, Fortezza da Basso, 18 March–4 June 1972), edited by U. Baldini and P. Dal Poggetto, Florence, 1972

RUDOLPH 1973
S. Rudolph, "Mecenati a Firenze tra Sei e Settecento II: Aspetti dello stile Cosimo III", in *Arte Illustrata*, 1973, no. 54, pp. 213–228.

BORRONI SALVADORI 1974
F. Borroni Salvadori, "Le esposizioni d'arte a Firenze 1674–1767", in *Mitteilungen des Kunsthistorischen Institutes in Florenz*, XVIII, 1974, fasc. 1, pp. 1–166

*Gli Ultimi Medici* 1974
*Gli Ultimi Medici. Il tardo barocco a Firenze, 1670–1743*, exhibition catalogue (Detroit, The Detroit Institute of Arts, 27 March–2 June; Florence, Palazzo Pitti, 28 June–30 September, 1974), Florence, 1974

BORRONI SALVADORI 1975
F. Borroni Salvadori, "L'esposizione del 1705 a Firenze", in *Mitteilungen des Kunsthistorischen Institutes in Florenz*, XIX, 1975, fasc. 3, pp. 393–402

CHIARINI 1975
M. Chiarini, "I Quadri della collezione del principe Ferdinando di Toscana", in *Paragone / Arte*, XXVI, 1975, no. 301, pp. 57–98, no. 303, pp. 75–108, no. 305, pp. 53–88

CHIARINI 1976
M. Chiarini, *Antonio Domenico Gabbiani e i Medici*, in *Kunst des Barock in der Toskana*, Munich, 1976, pp. 335–342

HEINZ–SCHÜTZ 1976
G. Heinz and K. Schütz, *Katalog der Gemäldegalerie, Porträtgalerie zur Geschichte Österreichs von 1400 bis 1800*, Vienna, 1976

MELONI TRKULJA 1976
S. Meloni Trkulja, *I due primi cataloghi di mostre fiorentine*, in *Scritti di storia dell'arte in onore di Ugo Procacci*, Venezia, 1976, II, pp. 579–585

STROCCHI 1976
M. L. Strocchi, "Il Gabinetto d'opere in piccolo del Gran principe Ferdinando a Poggio a Caiano. II", in *Paragone / Arte*, XXVII, no. 311, January 1976, pp. 83–116

CHIARINI 1977a
M. Chiarini, "An Unusual Subject by Justus Sustermans", in *The Burlington Magazine*, CXIX, January 1977, pp. 38 (fig.), 40–41

CHIARINI 1977b
M. Chiarini, "The Formation of the Galleria Palatina", in *Apollo*, September 1977, pp. 208–219

KULTZEN 1977
R. Kultzen, "Justus Sustermans as an Animal Painter", in *The Burlington Magazine*, CXIX, January 1977, pp. 37–40

*La Quadreria di don Lorenzo* 1977
*La Quadreria di don Lorenzo de' Medici*, exhibition catalogue, (Villa Medicea di Poggio a Caiano, 18 June–31 July, 1 September–16 October 1977), edited by E. Borea, Florence, 1977

MATTIOLI 1977
D. Mattioli (edited by), *Fiamminghi a Mantova tra Cinque e Seicento* in *Rubens a Mantova*, exhibition catalogue (Mantova, Palazzo Ducale, 25 September–20 November 1977), Milan, 1977, pp. 68–72

PINTO 1977
S. Pinto, "The Royal Palace from the Lorraine Period to the present day", in *Apollo*, September 1977, pp. 220–231

*Pittura Francese* 1977
*Pittura francese nelle collezioni pubbliche fiorentine*, exhibition catalogue (Florence, Palazzo Pitti, 24 April–30 June 1977), Florence, 1977

*Rubens e la pittura fiamminga* 1977
*Rubens e la pittura fiamminga del Seicento nelle collezioni pubbliche fiorentine*, exhibition catalogue (Florence, Palazzo Pitti, 22 September–9 December 1977), edited by D. Bodart, Florence, 1977

MELONI TRKULJA 1978
S. Meloni Trkulja, "La Collezione Pazzi (autoritratti per gli Uffizi): un'operazione sospetta, un documento malevolo", in *Paragone / Arte*, 1978, no. 343, pp. 79–123

EVANGELISTA 1978–1979
A. Evangelista, *Il teatro della Dogana detto di Baldracca. Contributo per la storia della Commedia dell'arte a Firenze*, Doctoral dissertation, Università degli Studi di Firenze, advisor Ludovico Zorzi, Academic year 1978–1979

RIGHI 1979
L. Righi, "Note su Jan van Ghelder, pittore fiammingo alla corte estense", in *Atti e Memorie della Deputazione di Storia Patria per le Antiche Provincie Modenesi*, series XI, I, pp. 141–158, 1979

*Gli Uffizi* 1979, ed. 1980
*Gli Uffizi. Catalogo generale*, Florence, 1979, ed. 1980

*Al servizio del granduca* 1980
*Al servizio del granduca. Ricognizione*

*di cento immagini della gente di corte*, exhibition catalogue (Florence, Palazzo Pitti, Sala Bianca, 24 July–21 September 1980), edited by S. Meloni Trkulja, Florence, 1980

Langedijk 1981–1987
K. Langedijk, *The Portraits of the Medici. 15th–18th Centuries*, Florence, 1981–1987, 3 vols.

*La Galleria Palatina* 1982
*La Galleria Palatina. Storia della quadreria granducale di Palazzo Pitti*, exhibition catalogue (Florence, Palazzo Pitti, Sala della Nicchie, 23 September 1982–31 January 1983), Florence, 1982

Mascalchi 1982
S. Mascalchi, *Anticipazioni su Mecenatismo del Cardinale Giovan Carlo de' Medici e suo contributo alle collezioni degli Uffizi*, in *Gli Uffizi: quattro secoli di una Galleria, Convegno internazionale di studi. Fonti e Documenti*, Florence, 1982, pp. 41–82

Chiarini 1983
M. Chiarini, *Sustermans e Rubens* in *Rubens a Firenze*, edited by M. Gregori, Florence, 1983, pp. 267–272

Meijer 1983
B. Meijer, "Florence, Justus Sustermans at Palazzo Pitti", in *The Burlington Magazine*, CXXV, no. 969, December 1983, pp. 785–786

Mosco 1983
M. Mosco, "Ritratti medicei del Sustermans in mostra a Palazzo Pitti (23 July–30 October 1983)", in *Arte Cristiana*, no. 699, Novembre–December 1983, pp. 367–370

*Sustermans* 1983
*Sustermans. Sessant'anni alla corte dei Medici*, exhibition catalogue (Florence, Palazzo Pitti, Sala delle Nicchie, July–October 1983), edited by M. Chiarini and C. Pizzorusso, Florence, 1983

Mascalchi 1984
S. Mascalchi, "Giovan Carlo de' Medici: An Outstanding but Neglected Collector in Seventeenth Century Florence", in *Apollo*, CXX, no. 4, 1984, pp. 268–272

*Baroque Portraiture* 1984–1985
*Baroque Portraiture in Italy: Works from North American Collections*, exhibition catalogue (Sarasota, Ringling Museum 1984–1985 / Hartford, Wadsworth Atheneum 1985), edited by J. Spike, Sarasota, 1984

*I principi bambini* 1985
*I principi bambini. Abbigliamento e infanzia nel Seicento*, exhibition catalogue (Florence, Palazzo Pitti, Galleria del Costume, 19 January–21 April 1985), Florence, 1985

*Natura viva* 1985
*Natura viva in Casa Medici. Dipinti di animali dai depositi di Palazzo Pitti con esemplari del Museo Zoologico 'La Specola'*, exhibition catalogue (Florence, Palazzo Pitti, Andito degli Angiolini, 14 December 1985–April 1986), edited by M. Mosco, Florence, 1985

*Il Seicento fiorentino* 1986
*Il Seicento fiorentino. Arte a Firenze da Ferdinando I a Cosimo III*, exhibition catalogue (Florence, Palazzo Strozzi, 21 December 1986–4 May 1987), Florence, 1986

*La Maddalena tra sacro e profano* 1986
*La Maddalena tra sacro e profano*, exhibition catalogue (Florence, Palazzo Pitti, May–September 1986), edited by M. Mosco, Milan-Florence, 1986

Bertini 1987
G. Bertini, *La Galleria del Duca di Parma. Storia di una collezione*, Bologna, 1987

Padoa Rizzo 1987
A. Padoa Rizzo, "La Cappella della compagnia di Santa Barbara dei tedeschi e fiamminghi alla Santissima Annunziata di Firenze. Opere d'arte e di arredo sec. XVI–XVIII", in *Antichità viva*, XXVI, no. 4, November–December 1987, pp. 10–20

*Pitture fiorentine del Seicento* 1987
*Pitture fiorentine del Seicento*, exhibition catalogue (Florence, Palazzo Ridolfi, 28 April–31 May 1987), Turin, 1987

*Christian IV and Europe* 1988
*Christian IV and Europe*, exhibition catalogue (Copenhagen, March–September1988), edited by S. Heiberg, Herning, 1988

*La pittura in Italia. Il Seicento* 1988, ed. 1989
*La pittura in Italia. Il Seicento*, edited by M. Gregori and E. Schleier, Milan, 1988, ed. 1989

Larsen 1988
E. Larsen, *The Paintings of Anthony Van Dyck*, Freren, 1988, 2 vols.

*Palazzo Pitti* 1988
*Palazzo Pitti. Guida alle collezioni e catalogo completo della Galleria Palatina*, edited by M. Chiarini, Florence, 1988

Damian 1990
V. Damian, *Collections du Musées de Chambéry. Peintures florentines*, Chambéry, 1990

Danesi Squarzina 1990
S. Danesi Squarzina, *Un inedito di Giusto Suttermans* in *Studi sul Seicento fiammingo e olandese*, Rome, 1990

*Fiamminghi* 1990
*Fiamminghi. Arte fiamminga e olandese del Seicento nella Repubblica Veneta*, exhibition catalogue (Padova, Palazzo della Ragione, 15 June–1 October 1990), Milan, 1990

*Il Palazzo della Provincia a Siena* 1990
*Il Palazzo della Provincia a Siena*, edited by F. Bisogni, Rome, 1990

Goldenberg Stoppato 1990–1991
L. Goldenberg Stoppato, *Al servizio della Serenissima Arciduchessa. Giusto Suttermans, 1621–1631*, Doctoral Dissertation, Università degli Studi di Firenze, Facoltà di Lettere e Filosofia, Indirizzo storico-artistico, Advisor Guglielmina Gregori, Academic Year 1990–1991

Langedijk 1992
K. Langedijk, *Die Selbstbildnisse der Holländischen und Flämischen Künstler in der Galleria degli Autoritratti der Uffizien in Florenz*, Florence, 1992

Borella–Giusti Maccari 1993
G. Borella and P. Giusti Maccari, *Palazzo Mansi di Lucca*, Lucca, 1993

*Fifty Paintings* 1993
*Fifty Paintings 1535–1825*, exhibition catalogue (London, Matthiesen Fine Art / New York, Stair Sainty Matthiesen), New York, 1993

Fratellini 1993
B. M. Fratellini, *Da Marcolfo a Bertoldo: raffigurazioni e ritratti di nani e buffoni dal XIV al XVIII secolo* in *Il Ritratto e la memoria. Materiali 3*, Rome, 1993, pp. 123–160

*Gli Appartamenti Reali* 1993
*Gli Appartamenti Reali di Palazzo Pitti. Una reggia per tre dinastie: Medici, Lorena e Savoia tra Granducato e Regno d'Italia*, edited by M. Chiarini and S. Padovani, Florence, 1993

Kirkendale 1993
W. Kirkendale, *The Court Musicians in Florence during the Principate of the Medici, With a Reconstruction of the Artistic Establishment*, LXI, in the series *Historiae Musicae Cultores*, Florence, 1993

De Maere–Wabbes 1994
J. De Maere and M. Wabbes, *Illustrated Dictionary of the 17th Century Flemish Painters*, edited by J. A. Martin, Brussels, 1994

Giusto 1994
M. Giusto, *Il ritratto pubblico e privato nel Seicento a Parma e a Piacenza* in *La pittura in Emilia e in Romagna. Il Seicento*, edited by J. Bentini and L. Fornari Schianchi, Milan, 1994, II, pp. 182–193

Godi–Mingardi 1994
G. Godi and C. Mingardi, *Le Collezioni d'Arte della Cassa di Risparmio di Parma e Piacenza*, Parma, 1994

Matteoli 1994
A. Matteoli, "Ritrattistica del Cigoli: un ritratto di Don Antonio De' Medici e altri (autografi e no)", in *Bollettino della Accademia degli Euteleti*, 61, 1994, pp. 105–130

Danesi Squarzina 1995
S. Danesi Squarzina, *Cultura degli emblemi in un ritratto del primo Seicento* in, '*Fiamenghi che vanno e vengono non li si puol dar regola'. Paesi Bassi e Italia fra Cinquecento e Seicento: pittura, storia e cultura degli emblemi*, edited by I. Baldriga, Rome, 1995, pp. 13–26

Christie's sale, 7 April 1995
*Important and Fine Old Master Paintings, The properties of the Argenti Family, the late Mrs. Helen Landford - Brooke, The Marquise of Lansdowne removed from Meikleour House*, sale catalogue, *Friday, 7 April 1995, Christie's*, London, 1995

*Van Dyck* 1995
*Van Dyck and his Age*, exhibition catalogue (Tel Aviv Museum of Art, 29 October 1995–28 January 1996), edited by D. J. Lurie, Tel Aviv, 1995

Simoncini 1995–1996
F. Simoncini, *I festeggiamenti per le visite granducali in Toscana tra la fine del XVI e l'inizio del XVII secolo*, Doctoral Dissertation, Università degli Studi di Firenze, Storia dello Spettacolo, advisor Siro Ferrone, Academic Year 1995–1996

Capitelli 1996
G. Capitelli, *Una testimonianza documentaria per il primo nucleo della raccolta del principe Camillo Pamphilj*, in *Capolavori della collezione Doria Pamphilj da Tiziano a Velásquez*, exhibition catalogue (Fondazione Arte e Civiltà, Viale Sabotino 22, Milan, 28 September–8 December 1996), Milan, 1996, pp. 57–69

Turner 1996
J. Turner (edited by), *The Dictionary of Art*, London, 1996, 34 vols.

Gobbo 1997
B. Gobbo, *L'eredità estense: dipinti e pittori neerlandesi a Modena* in Limentani Virdis 1997, pp. 235–265

Goldenberg Stoppato 1997
L. Goldenberg Stoppato, "Van Dyck. Grande pittura e collezionismo a Genova", in *Antichità Viva*, Year XXVI, no. 1, January–February 1997, pp. 60–61

Limentani Virdis 1997
C. Limentani Virdis (edited by), *La pittura fiamminga nel Veneto e nell'Emilia*, Verona, 1997

*Opere d'arte della famiglia Medici* 1997
*Opere d'arte della famiglia Medici*, exhibition catalogue (Pechino–Shangai 1997) edited by C. Acidini Luchinat and M. Scalini, Cinisello Balsamo 1997

Pietrogiovanna 1997
M. Pietrogiovanna, *La splendida corte. La produzione artistica del Nord a Parma e nel Reggiano*, in Limentani Virdis 1997, pp. 267–323

*Le virtù e i piaceri in Villa* 1998
*Le virtù e i piaceri in Villa. Per il nuovo museo comunale della Villa Doria Pamphilj*, exhibition catalogue (Rome, Villa Vecchia, 2 October–6 December 1998), edited by C. Benocci, Milan, 1998

*Repertory Liguria* 1998
*Repertory of Dutch and Flemish Paintings in Italian Public Collections*, vol. I, *Liguria*, edited by M. Fontana Amoretti and M. Plomp, Florence, 1998

Chiarini–Padovani 1999
M. Chiarini and S. Padovani, *Palazzo Pitti, Galleria Palatina e Appartamenti Reali. Firenze*, Rome, 1999

*Crafting the Medici* 1999
*Crafting the Medici. Patrons and Artisans in Florence, 1536–1737*, exhibition catalogue (Providence, Brown University, David Winton Bell Gallery, 18 September–24 October 1999), Providence, 1999

*Die Pracht der Medici* 1999
*Die Pracht der Medici. Florenz und Europa*, exhibition catalogue (Munich, 4 December 1998–21 February 1999 / Vienna, Kunsthistorisches Museum, Palais Harrach, 8 March–6 June 1999 / Blois, Château de Blois, 26 June–17 October 1999 / Florence, 19 June–3 October 1999), edited by C. Acidini Luchinat and M. Scalini, Munich-London-New York, 1999

Fornari Schianchi 1999
L. Fornari Schianchi (edited by), *Galleria Nazionale di Parma. Catalogo delle opere. Il Seicento*, Milan, 1999

*Van Dyck* 1999
*Van Dyck 1599–1641*, exhibition catalogue (Antwerp, Koninklijk Museum voor

Schone Kunsten, 15 May–15 August 1999 / London, Royal Academy of Arts, 11 September–10 December 1999), edited by C. Brown and H. Vlieghe, Italian edition, Milan, 1999

HASKELL 2000
F. Haskell, *The Ephemeral Museum. Old Master Paintings and the Rise of the Art Museum*, New Haven & London, 2000

HASKELL 2001
F. Haskell, *Antichi maestri in tournée: le esposizioni d'arte e il loro significato*, in the series "Lezioni Comparettiane", edited by T. Montanari, Pisa, 2001

PANESSA 2001
G. Panessa, *Figure femminili nelle comunità straniere*, in O. Vaccari, *Donne Livornesi*, Livorno, 2001, pp. 49–58

*Power & Glory* 2001
*Power & Glory. Medici Portraits from the Uffizi Gallery*, exhibition catalogue (Philadelphia, The Pennsylvania Academy of Fine Arts, 15 September–9 December 2001), edited by C. Caneva, Philadelphia, 2001

*Scienziati a Corte* 2001
*Scienziati a Corte. L'arte della sperimentazione nell'Accademia Galileiana del Cimento (1657–1667)*, exhibition catalogue (Galleria degli Uffizi, 18 March–18 June 2001), edited by P. Galluzzi, Livorno, 2001

*Velázquez* 2001
*Velázquez*, exhibition catalogue (Rome, Fondazione Memmo, Palazzo Ruspoli, 30 March–30 June 2001), Milan, 2001

CANEVA–VERVAT 2002
C. Caneva and M. Vervat (edited by), *Il Giuramento del Senato fiorentino a Ferdinando II de' Medici. Una grande opera del Suttermans restaurata*, Florence, 2002

*Fiamminghi e Olandesi* 2002
*Fiamminghi e Olandesi. Dipinti dalle collezioni lombarde*, exhibition catalogue (Milan, Palazzo Reale e Pinacoteca Ambrosiana, 23 May–18 August 2002), edited by B. Meijer, Cinisello Balsamo, 2002

*I Volti del Potere* 2002
*I Volti del Potere. La ritrattistica di corte nella Firenze Granducale*, exhibition catalogue (Sala delle Reali Poste, Piazzale degli Uffizi, 30 May–28 July 2002), edited by C. Caneva, Florence, 2002

CHIARINI–PADOVANI 2003
M. Chiarini and S. Padovani (edited by), *La Galleria Palatina e gli Appartamenti Reali di Palazzo Pitti. Catalogo dei dipinti*, Florence, 2003

*I gioielli dei Medici* 2003
*I gioielli dei Medici dal vero e in ritratto*, exhibition catalogue (Florence, Palazzo Pitti, Museo degli Argenti, 12 September 2003–February 2004), edited by M. Sframeli, Livorno, 2003

GOLDENBERG STOPPATO 2003
L. Goldenberg Stoppato, "Suttermans, Painter and Courtier of the Medici", in *Italian History and Culture. Villa Le Balze, Georgetown University*, 9, 2003, pp. 31–42

ACIDINI LUCHINAT 2004
C. Acidini Luchinat, *Le arti a Firenze, regnante Cosimo III*, in *Il viaggio a Compostela* 2004, pp. 57–69

*Galileo e Pisa* 2004
*Galileo e Pisa*, exhibition catalogue (Geneva, Musée d'Histoire des Sciences, 19 October 2004–15 February 2005), edited by R. Vergara Caffarelli, Ospedaletto (Pisa), 2004

GOLDENBERG STOPPATO 2004a
L. Goldenberg Stoppato, *Giusto Suttermans, ritrattista di casa Medici, e la mostra allestita in suo onore al granduca Cosimo III*, in *Il viaggio a Compostela* 2004, pp. 71–113

GOLDENBERG STOPPATO 2004b
L. Goldenberg Stoppato, "Per Domenico e Valore Casini, ritrattisti fiorentini", in *Mitteilungen des Kunsthistorisches Institutes in Florenz*, XLVIII, 2004, fasc. 1–2, pp. 165–210

*I Della Rovere* 2004
*I Della Rovere: Piero della Francesca, Raffaello, Tiziano*, exhibition catalogue (Senigallia, Palazzo del Duca / Urbino, Palazzo Ducale / Pesaro, Palazzo Ducale / Urbania, Palazzo Ducale, 4 April 2004–3 October 2004), edited by P. Dal Poggetto, Milan, 2004

*Il viaggio a Compostela* 2004
*Il viaggio a Compostela di Cosimo III de' Medici*, exhibition catalogue (Santiago de Compostela, Museo Diocesano, 15 October 2004–17 January 2003), edited by X. A. Neira Cruz, Santiago de Compostela, 2004

PAOLUCCI–LAPI BALLERINI 2004
A. Paolucci and I. Lapi Ballerini (edited by), *Palazzo degli Alberti. Le collezioni d'arte della Cariprato*, Milan, 2004

BAROCCHI–GAETA BERTELÀ 2005
P. Barocchi and G. Gaeta Bertelà, *Collezionismo mediceo e storia artistica*, II, *Il cardinale Carlo, Maria Maddalena, don Lorenzo, Ferdinando II, Vittoria della Rovere 1621–1666*, Florence, 2005

GOLDENBERG STOPPATO 2005
L. Goldenberg Stoppato, "Cosimo III come benefattore di Livorno in un inedito ritratto del Volterrano conservato a Varsavia", in *Nuovi studi livornesi*, XII, 2005, pp. 153–159

*Luce e Ombra* 2005
*Luce e Ombra, caravaggismo e naturalismo nella pittura toscana del Seicento*, exhibition catalogue (Pontedera, Centro per l'arte Otello Cirri e Museo Piaggio "Giovanni Alberto Agnelli", 18 March–12 June 2005), edited by P. Carofano, Pisa, 2005

*Maria de' Medici* 2005
*Maria de' Medici (1573–1642), una principessa fiorentina sul trono di Francia*, exhibition catalogue (Florence, Palazzo Pitti, Museo degli Argenti, 19 March–4 September 2005), edited by C. Caneva and F. Solinas, Livorno, 2005

## * MANUSCRIPT TITLES

The abbreviations for the titles of the manuscripts are in Italian, out of respect for the language they were written in. For the sake of comprehension, we include the following list of the most commonly used terms translated into English:

Arazzeria = Tapestry works
Battezzati = Baptisms
Camera = Chamber
Cariche = Appointments
Compagnia = Confraternity
Consegne = Consignments
Conto = Bill
Creditori = Creditors
Debitori = Debtors
Entrata = Credit
Giornale = Journal
Guardaroba = Wardrobe department
Inventario = Inventory
Mandati di pagamento = Payment orders
Matrimoni = Marriages
Morti = The Deceased
Provvisionati = Salaried staff
Quaderno = Ledger
Recapiti di cassa = Cashier's payments
Registro = Book
Rescritti = Rescripts
Ricordi = Memorial
Spese = Expenditures
Uscita = Debit

printed in June 2006
by Genesi, Città di Castello
for s i l l a b e